A rich and bold demonstration tha
pretive lenses to the biblical texts r
that the Confucian touchstones of

for historical critical scholarship. No one is more qualified to build this bridge
where West meets East than Jerry Hwang.

Joshua Berman, PhD
Associate Professor of Hebrew Bible,
Bar-Ilan University, Israel

Doing contextual theology in Asia is profoundly biblical because it does what
the Bible, and particularly the Old Testament, does: dialogue with the context.
This is the argument of Jerry Hwang in this careful, wide-ranging, and learned
book, and I could not agree with his argument more. Paraphrasing Tertullian,
he asks what does contextualization have to do with the Old Testament and
his answer is "nearly everything."

Stephen Bevans, PhD
Louis J. Luzbetak, SVD Professor of Mission and Culture, Emeritus,
Catholic Theological Union, Illinois, USA

For most of us, the Bible was written *for* us but it was not written directly *to* us,
and that raises the issue of contextualization. How do we understand properly
what the text actually meant in its original context so we can appropriately
interpret and apply it within our contexts? Jerry Hwang's *Contextualization and
the Old Testament* provides helpful insights as he attempts to help us engage
the text more accurately and honestly.

Bryan Beyer, PhD
Bible Professor Emeritus,
Columbia International University, South Carolina, USA

The global church is becoming increasingly aware of the need for high quality
research and writing in the field of contextualization. There is an especially
acute need for works which address the Old Testament and which consider
specific contemporary contexts. This book does both of those things and more,
making it an important and precious one. Hwang brings together his expertise
in Old Testament studies and missiology, and his profound insights into Asian

and Western cultural perspectives, to produce a thought-provoking work that will equip the church to develop theologies that are both deeply biblical and authentically local.

Derek Brotherson, PhD
Principal, Lecturer in Missions and Preaching,
Sydney Missionary & Bible College, Australia

This is an expansive book by a mature scholar. Hwang argues that the Old Testament's interaction with the ancient world offers models of how Christian faith can engage culture today. On the one hand, these engagements illumine how to theologize better in Asia's diverse contexts. On the other hand, Asian reflections on Bible translation and other topics can sharpen – even correct – current missiological perspectives and accepted givens in Old Testament scholarship. An important contribution!

M. Daniel Carroll R. (Rodas), PhD
Scripture Press Ministries Professor of Biblical Studies and Pedagogy,
Wheaton College, Illinois, USA

Dr. Hwang provides an important contribution to missiology and hermeneutics bringing clarity to the "contextualization debate." His emphasis upon, in, and with the Old Testament draws the reader into recognizing the ways the Old Testament interacts within its own ancient Near Eastern cultural milieu, by both drawing from it and serving as a polemic within it. While delivering profound insights into Asian and Western contextualizing of Scripture and the gospel, his approach is applicable across all cross-cultural settings.

Ingrid Faro, PhD
Dean of Theology,
Scandinavian School of Theology, Sweden

I have long sensed a need for an in-depth exploration of contextualization from an Old Testament perspective. Jerry Hwang's book masterfully fills that gap. With exceptional nuance and insight, Hwang explores how Old Testament writers critically engaged their ancient Near Eastern contexts. At the same time, he shows how the Old Testament offers a rich resource for Christians in Asia and elsewhere, as we engage our complex settings today. This book just might change your understanding of both contextualization and the Old Testament!

Dean Flemming, PhD
Professor of New Testament,
MidAmerica Nazarene University, Kansas, USA

In *Contextualization and the Old Testament*, Hwang helpfully extends the discussions on contextualization and syncretism. Usually, this subject is discussed in missiology, but here, Hwang weaves together biblical exegesis, missiology, and anthropology to show that Israel in the Old Testament was also constantly holding the tension between being in, but not being of, the surrounding culture. A timely and necessary book, especially for Asian Christians in the quest for a maturing, theologizing Christian community.

Kwa Kiem-Kiok, PhD
Lecturer in Missiology and Interdisciplinary Studies,
Biblical Graduate School of Theology, Singapore

This is a major scholarly achievement. Jerry Hwang illuminatingly interprets the Hebrew scriptures in the light of Chinese, Thai, Indonesian, Korean, Filipino, Japanese, and other Asian contexts. Anyone studying biblical interpretation, theology, contextualization, missiology, or Asian Christianity will learn from it – and delight in it. *Contextualization and the Old Testament* deserves to become a classic.

Timothy Larsen, PhD
McManis Professor of Christian Thought, Wheaton College, Illinois, USA
Honorary Fellow, School of Divinity, University of Edinburgh, UK

Only a handful of scholars could have written this book and I'm glad Dr Hwang has! He is sensitive to the historical and cultural nuances of both the Old Testament and Asia today and his unique multicultural competence shines through on every page. This book is essential reading for anyone who wants to gain a truer and fuller understanding of the Old Testament from an Asian perspective.

Peter H. W. Lau, PhD
Adjunct Lecturer in Old Testament and Biblical Theology,
Seminari Theoloji Malaysia

Contextualization and the Old Testament is a detailed and nuanced work that enlightens readers on the biblical context and also shows how the principles found in the Old Testament address contextualization issues in the twenty-first century, through illuminating examples from the Asian context. The breadth and depth of Hwang's work raises a host of questions for readers to tackle and wrestle with, in order to provide pathways that will enable churches to faithfully incarnate the gospel to every culture, tribe, and people while remaining true to the Bible. Hwang's book is destined to be a seminal work that future scholars and practitioners in contextualization must learn from, dialogue with, and build upon.

Samuel K. Law, PhD
Vice Principal for Academic Affairs and Associate Professor of Intercultural Studies,
Singapore Bible College

Contextualization and the Old Testament by Dr. Jerry Hwang is simply a brilliant book written by a brilliant scholar. Dr. Hwang is deeply versed in biblical, particularly Old Testament, studies, as well as missiology and related disciplines. He masters wide-ranging literature in both Western and Asian theology. He rightly believes that the Old Testament is an ideal supplier of source material for building conceptual bridges between the ancient Near East and the modern Far East. I was totally fascinated by every page of this book, which every biblical scholar, missionary, seminary student, and pastor ought to read.

Tremper Longman III, PhD
Distinguished Scholar and Professor Emeritus of Biblical Studies,
Westmont College, California, USA

This book is a revelation! Finally we have an Old Testament scholar immersed in Western and Asian cultures bringing his insights to the study of Scripture and to ancient and contemporary contextualization. Hwang's Asian context enables him to challenge numerous commonplaces of classical Old Testament scholarship while illuminating how the biblical authors interacted meaningfully with their ancient Near Eastern context. His insights into the complexity of Asian cultures and the misguided attempts at contextualization, both historical and contemporary, are eye-opening. This is a brilliant book, useful for biblical scholars, theologians, missiologists, and students of Asian cultures.

J. Richard Middleton, PhD
Professor of Biblical Worldview and Exegesis,
Northeastern Seminary at Roberts Wesleyan College, New York, USA

Jerry Hwang has produced an innovative and a comprehensive book on contextualization and the Old Testament between Asian and Western perspectives. Hwang's book furnishes fresh, original insights into the theme of contextualization; it allows the diversity of interpretative voices to be represented, yet his own position is not blurred by them. This book will become a significant guide to how biblical theology is done in a way that exalts the ontological priority of Scripture and its power of contemporaneity in various cultures. It places readers in and with the biblical texts, and under them, that is, under the grip of the effectual nature of Holy Scripture. Keen-minded readers will reap from it how the gospel can be communicated and lived out in Asia and abroad. Hwang is to be praised for such a worthy undertaking to which readers will be indebted.

Dennis Ngien, PhD
Alister E. McGrath Chair of Christian Thought & Spirituality,
Tyndale University, Canada

At last, a comprehensive, well-researched, and nuanced treatment of contextualization in the Old Testament! Professor Hwang offers a fascinating examination of the complex interface of local culture and religion with the faith of ancient Israel. He then compellingly draws implications for today from a decidedly Asian perspective, yielding insights from which all readers will benefit.

Craig Ott, PhD
Professor of Mission and Intercultural Studies,
Trinity Evangelical Divinity School, Illinois, USA

Jerry Hwang in *Contextualization and the Old Testament* has produced nothing less than a landmark *tour de force* in scholarship that will shape how contextualization is understood for the next generation of missiologists. Hwang follows all the key concepts of the Old Testament from sin, to God, to covenant, to law, and to kingship, at every point demonstrating the way contextualization has operated within the biblical witness itself. No longer can contextualization be seen as some negotiated tension between a "changeless text" and "ever-changing cultures." Rather Hwang demonstrates how contextualization is deeply embedded within the text itself. The author's keen knowledge of Asia and the multi-religious context of global Christianity has provided an invaluable resource that promises to become a standard reference for years to come.

Timothy C. Tennent, PhD
President and Professor of World Christianity,
Asbury Theological Seminary, Kentucky, USA

What has contextualization to do with the Old Testament? Jerry Hwang reflects on this question with brilliance and breadth in *Contextualization and the Old Testament*. It is the fruit of his vast cross-cultural experience combined with the discernment of a seasoned biblical scholar. He explores an array of overlooked ways that the Old Testament bolsters the work of contextualization across diverse global settings. This book is both provocative and practical. Even if readers don't agree with Hwang on some points, they'll benefit from his groundbreaking contribution to a long overdue conversation.

Jackson Wu, PhD
Theologian-in-Residence,
Mission ONE, Arizona, USA

In these pages Hwang navigates much, much more than between the Asian and Western perspectives highlighted in the book's subtitle, traversing also between theology and missiology; between the ancient Near Eastern and Israelite world on the one horizon and contemporary late modern global dynamics characterizing the 2020s on the other; between Hebrew Bible scholarship that is predominantly of Euro-American derivation on the one hand and popular piety and ecclesial practice cultivated through South, East, and Southeast

Asia religio-cultural sensibilities on the other. The result is the Old Testament speaking afresh to the universality of the biblical message in ways that depends on *both* the cultural particularities of the *evangel*'s medium *and* the contextual specificities of any receptor audience's perspective. Welcome to a Pacific Rim theological voice that will resound with transnational relevance.

Amos Yong, PhD
Dean of the School of Mission and Theology, Professor of Theology and Mission,
Fuller Theological Seminary, California, USA

LOGIA
Series

Contextualization and the Old Testament

ASIA THEOLOGICAL ASSOCIATION

Langham
GLOBAL LIBRARY

LOGIA
Series

Contextualization and the Old Testament

Between Asian and Western Perspectives

Jerry Hwang

Published 2022 by Langham Global Library
An imprint of Langham Publishing
www.langhampublishing.org

Langham Publishing and its imprints are a ministry of Langham Partnership

Langham Partnership
PO Box 296, Carlisle, Cumbria, CA3 9WZ, UK
www.langham.org

ISBNs:
978-1-83973-413-7 Print
978-1-83973-724-4 ePub
978-1-83973-725-1 Mobi
978-1-83973-726-8 PDF

British Library Cataloguing-in-Publication Data
A catalogue record for this book is available from the British Library

ISBN: 978-1-83973-413-7

Cover & Book Design: projectluz.com
Cover photograph by Spencer Chow on Unsplash

For the students and alumni of Singapore Bible College,
who serve Christ faithfully in Asia and beyond

CONTENTS

FOREWORD

Dr. Jerry Hwang's new work responds to a series of nagging questions in contextual theology:

- Is there any way to contextualize biblical faith without having a certain degree of syncretism?
- How can the Hellenistic-Western worldview be mitigated as the subtext (or even pretext in its defective forms) in an Asian contextual theology?
- What does the Old Testament have to do with contextualizing God's truth in Asian contexts?

As an American-born Chinese, an Old Testament scholar, and a missionary serving in both the West and Asia over decades, Dr. Hwang demonstrates in these pages his excellent research skills and rich experiences of living in both Asian and Western cultures.

This book engages the multifaceted religious and social realities of Asia with keen cultural sensitivity and theological insight. Dr. Hwang guides us to think through the challenging disparities between different worlds: biblical and extra biblical, the Near East and Far East, and Western and Asian, all while paying attention to their distinctive nuances. With competency in biblical, Western, and Asian languages, he tackles numerous controversies in translation and contextualization which bear on the Old Testament, such as the biblical idea of sin and its Chinese translation as *zui*, recent debates about the name of God and its relationship to "Allah," the misuse of divine blessings in contemporary prosperity theology, the inadequacy of the Western patron-client model, and the necessity of Asian understandings of kinship to interpret covenant and law in a familial relational setting.

In doing contextual theology for Asia, perhaps the greatest obstacle of all is the accusation that Christian mission is associated with Western imperialism. With commendable clarity, both through the biblical accounts (again, of the Old Testament!) and a theological articulation of the relationship of creation to history, Dr. Hwang offers convincing rebuttals to the objection that Christian mission equates to colonialism in the history of Asia.

This book is an essential textbook which is historically informed, exegetically faithful, theologically robust, practical, visionary, and filled with unswerving evangelical conviction. It should be studied carefully by seminarians, pastors, missionaries, and lay Christians who want to understand how God's truth and the gospel can be contextualized in everyday life.

Again, my congratulations to Dr. Hwang for an outstanding contribution to contextual theology that stems from his superb Old Testament scholarship and life experiences in the mission field as a missionary teacher!

Clement Mook-Soo Chia, PhD
Principal, Singapore Bible College
June 2022

ACKNOWLEDGMENTS

A wealth of religious and cultural traditions lies within walking distance of Singapore Bible College, where I live and work. Turning left from the College gates takes me past a Oneness Pentecostal church, an Assemblies of God church, and a Presbyterian church. Turning right takes me past a temple to Guanyin (a traditional Chinese deity) and a Japanese new religious movement's building. Going across the street, I encounter a "hawker centre" (Singaporean outdoor food court) with Hindu altar shelves at Indian food stalls, prayer spaces set aside for observant Muslim migrant workers from South Asia during Ramadan, and metal barrels that the government has laid out for ethnic Chinese to burn paper money or make offerings to ancestors during the Hungry Ghost Festival. Behind the hawker centre are two more Christian churches of rather different kinds. As the most religiously diverse country in the world, Singapore and its particular mandate for pluralism have afforded researchers like myself a special opportunity to learn and do intercultural comparisons of a kind that would not be possible elsewhere.

The rich world within the gates of the College has also been my teacher during the last twelve years when I have served as a faculty member. During this time, the campus has been a place of instruction for me: students from over twenty Asian nations have shared with me how the Old Testament, as the word of God originally from and for Asia, empowers them to overcome the misconception that Christianity is a Western religion. It is to these students and alumni of the College's School of Theology (English) that this book is warmly dedicated. I have written with them constantly in mind, with the prayer that they will go further than I have in doing contextual theology that is deeply biblical, fully evangelical, and authentically Asian.

I am also grateful to Drs. Andrew Spurgeon and Steve Pardue of ATA Publications for believing in this project. They not only gave it a push when things stalled briefly, but they also offered constructive criticism of the manuscript and extended the invitation to serve as general editor of Logia, the new monograph series for which this is the first volume. The editorial and marketing team at Langham Publishing, co-sponsor of the series, has also provided invaluable help in the process. Many other OT scholarly friends in Asia have lent their expertise through the years in ways too numerous to mention. I owe a great debt to Rowena Oriente, an alumna of Singapore Bible College from the Philippines, who provided invaluable help with the indexes for this book. My thanks are due as well to various journals for permission to modify my previously published articles for use in the present work. Full citations of the relevant articles are given in the first footnotes of chapters 2, 3, and 4 in this book.

To God be the glory!

Jerry Hwang
Easter Sunday, April 2022
Singapore

ABBREVIATIONS

ANE	Ancient Near East, ancient Near Eastern
COS	*The Context of Scripture.* Edited by W. W. Hallo. 3 vols. Leiden: Brill, 1997–
DDD	*Dictionary of Deities and Demons in the Bible.* Edited by K. van der Toorn, B. Becking, and P. W. van der Horst. Leiden: Brill, 1995
KJV	King James Version
KTU	*Die keilalphabetischen Texte aus Ugarit.* Edited by M. Dietrich, O. Loretz, and J. Sanmartín. AOAT 24/1. Neukirchen-Vluyn, 1976. 2d enlarged ed. of *KTU: The Cuneiform Alphabetic Texts from Ugarit, Ras Ibn Hani, and Other Places.* Edited by M. Dietrich, O. Loretz, and J. Sanmartín. Münster, 1995
L&N	*Greek-English Lexicon of the New Testament: Based on Semantic Domains.* Edited by J. P. Louw and E. A. Nida. 2nd ed. New York: United Bible Societies, 1989
NASB	New American Standard Bible
NIDNTTE	*New International Dictionary of New Testament Theology and Exegesis.* Edited by Moisés Silva. 5 vols. Grand Rapids, MI: 2014
NIV	New International Version of the Bible
NLT	New Living Translation of the Bible
NRSV	New Revised Standard Version of the Bible

CHAPTER 1

INTRODUCTION

"Contextualized theology is not just desirable; it is the only way theology can be done." – Dean Flemming[1]

"Contextualization produces infinite variety in biblical interpretation." – Robert Thomas[2]

The above two quotes by Dean Flemming and Robert Thomas offer starkly different views of *contextualization*, the mandate of the missionary to present the gospel in culturally meaningful ways. For Flemming, contextualization is an essential part of the New Testament and its plurality of methods to communicate the gospel. The cultural environment of the NT becomes a crucial ally in testifying to the truth of Jesus Christ. But for Thomas, contextualization is a threat that mingles the unchanging gospel with the changing norms of culture. All efforts at contextualization are a slippery slope that leads to *syncretism*, the mixing of truth with untruth. Both Flemming and Thomas, interestingly, are evangelical scholars of the New Testament who share a commitment to the primacy of Scripture. Working from the same foundational conviction, they nonetheless arrive at contradictory conclusions as to how God's word speaks across the ages and crosses cultures.

Is contextualization desirable or dangerous? What is the proper relationship between the gospel and culture? How is the Bible both God's timeless revelation as well as his time-bound word for particular times and places? These challenges are not limited to missiology and its usual focus on contextualizing the gospel for other cultures. There are also fundamental issues of hermeneutics which require understanding how one's *own* culture has received the gospel (and perhaps altered it) during the process of our emerging self-understanding as the people of God. The main obstacles in contextualizing the gospel, in

---

1. Dean E. Flemming, *Contextualization in the New Testament: Patterns for Theology and Mission* (Downers Grove, IL: IVP Academic, 2005), 298.
2. Robert L. Thomas, *Evangelical Hermeneutics: The New versus the Old* (Grand Rapids, MI: Kregel, 2002), 410.

other words, have not usually been in repackaging the gospel intelligibly for *them*.[3] For Bible-believing Christians to assume that the task mainly involves translating the essence of Christian truth into local expressions – as in the usual dichotomies between Scripture's message and culture's methods[4] – risks becoming the sort of imperialism that assumes that *we* have faith and truth, while *they* have interpretation and culture.

There is uncomfortable truth in the half-joke among missionaries that "it's contextualization when I do it, syncretism when you do it."[5] Indeed, the reality that missiology's vast literature on contextualization is produced most-ly "from the West to the rest" raises at least two important questions about ethnocentrism.[6] First, is contextualization a well-meaning imposition from Western missiology which neglects to involve non-Western Christians in the process of developing an indigenous theology? Second, has the paternalism of Western colonialism been unknowingly reproduced by Western missiology in dictating to non-Western Christians the "contextual" forms their theology ought to take? An increasing number of both Western and non-Western theologians are saying yes, suggesting that both the theory and the application of contextualization as traditionally understood need a deeper look.[7]

---

3. The late Paul Hiebert, perhaps the leading evangelical authority on contextualization, lament-ed that the crucial step of self-critique in his method tends to go missing in the hands of Western missionaries. For further discussion of Hiebert and the inconsistent application of his steps in "critical contextualization," see R. Daniel Shaw et al., "Contextualization, Conceptualization, and Communication: The Development of Contextualization at Fuller's Graduate School of World Mission/Intercultural Studies," *Missiology: An International Review* 44 (2016): 100–103.
4. Cf. Gailyn Van Rheenen, "Syncretism and Contextualization: The Church on a Journey Defining Itself," in *Contextualization and Syncretism: Navigating Cultural Currents*, ed. Gailyn Van Rheenen, Evangelical Missiological Society Series 13 (Pasadena, CA: William Carey Library, 2006), 4–5.
5. As related by Gary Corwin, "A Second Look: Telling the Difference," *Evangelical Missions Quarterly* 40 (2004): 282.
6. Jonathan C. Ingleby, *Beyond Empire: Postcolonialism and Mission in a Global Context* (Central Milton Keynes: AuthorHouse, 2010), 45.
7. A prominent example is furnished by recent disagreements over Insider Movements (IMs) among those of Muslim, Hindu, and Buddhist cultural backgrounds. The question at hand is whether Christian converts from such backgrounds can retain aspects of their previous affiliations since it is difficult to distinguish clearly between "religion" and "culture." Even a scholar who broadly advocates IMs like William A. Dyrness finds that "the language of contextualization carries a heavy and perhaps inescapable colonial baggage and mostly presumes that someone might know better than the people themselves how to contextualize the gospel" (*Insider Jesus: Theological Reflections on New Christian Movements* [Downers Grove, IL: IVP Academic, 2016], 23). Notably, the same point is made by a non-Western opponent of IMs such as Ayman S. Ibrahim ("Understanding Insider Movements," The Gospel Coalition, 18 December 2015, https://www.thegospelcoalition.org/reviews/understanding-insider-movements/).

Introduction

[handwritten: Xnity as agent of Western Imperialism]

The charge that Christianity has been an unwitting agent of Western imperialism is particularly resonant in Southeast Asia, the context in which I live and serve. With the sole exception of Thailand, every country in this region has come under the rule of a nominally Christian empire from the West sometime during the last two hundred years.[8] The resulting mix of "Christianity, commerce, and civilization" (in missionary-explorer David Livingstone's famous words) has often led Asian peoples to make instinctive connections between Christianity and imperialism (whether cultural, military, economic, or religious) long after their nations gained independence. Among the many forms that imperialism has taken in Asia, the most distressing by far is the West's appropriation of the Old Testament's conquest narratives. The book of *[handwritten: O.T conquest narratives]* Joshua often functioned for the empires of Christendom as a pseudo-biblical imperative to subdue the "pagans" and enlighten the "heathen." This history of colonialist interpretation has been as painfully true of Asia as of Africa and the Americas. The synergy between the Old Testament and imperial domination is memorably summarized by Susan Juster and Linda Gregerson:

> The Bible was the foremost travel guide in modern European history. With its tales of the rise and fall of great empires devoted to rival gods, of religious seekers driven from their homes in search of elusive Promised Lands, of the marvelous and monstrous wonders lying just beyond the borders of the known world, the Old Testament provided a vivid template for the explorations

---

Debates over IMs in Muslim contexts have been especially common since the early 1980s among Western missiologists (following the publication of Phil Parshall, *New Paths in Muslim Evangelism: Evangelical Approaches to Contextualization* [Grand Rapids, MI: Baker, 1980]). Unfortunately, it was decades before the voices of Muslim-background believers (MBBs) began to be heard through the systematic fieldwork published by Jan Hendrik Prenger, *Muslim Insider Christ Followers: Their Theological and Missional Frames* (Pasadena, CA: William Carey Library, 2017). The time lapse of nearly forty years between hearing the voices of Western outsiders and those of non-Western insiders underscores the problem.

8. Besides what is now Thailand (formerly Siam), the rest of Southeast Asia's present-day nations and their lands have all been colonized at one time or another by France (Cambodia, Indonesia, Laos, Vietnam), Great Britain (Brunei, Indonesia, Malaysia, Myanmar, Singapore), the Netherlands (Indonesia), Portugal (East Timor, Malaysia), Spain (the Philippines), or the United States (the Philippines). Besides these Western empires, Asian empires have also occupied parts of other Asian lands (e.g. Japan's occupation of most of Southeast Asia during World War II).

Evangelical studies of how the Protestant missionary movement in Asia became entangled with Western imperialism are still at an early stage. For a good place to begin, see Brian Stanley, *The Bible and the Flag: Protestant Missions and British Imperialism in the Nineteenth and Twentieth Centuries* (Leicester: Apollos, 1990).

and conquests of the great European Age of Discovery. . . . Exhortations to conquer new peoples and lands in the name of God were the lingua franca of western imperialism.[9]

It would be mistaken, of course, to say that Western empires were uniformly predatory in Asia or that no good ever resulted from colonialism (whether intentional or inadvertent).[10] However, the reality that Western powers in Asia often drew theological support from the Old Testament for their endeavors has always posed a challenge to Asian Christians who embrace the authority of all Scripture for faith, practice, and mission. For even as Western imperialism has mostly run its course in Asia, echoes of Christendom and conquest remain when cross-cultural missionary work from Asians to Asians persists in using martial language for its outreach efforts – missions is going to the *front lines* for the sake of *advancing* the gospel, the task of sending missionaries is *mobilization* or *deployment*, while the people and structures that support missionaries are the *sending base*.[11] Asian Christians have become accustomed to conceiving the non-Christian "other" as hostile and dangerous (though their cultures were once the ones labeled in this way). But to Asians outside the Christian fold, such language still feels condescending at best and violent at worst.[12] This is not to say that *spiritual* warfare is inappropriate in missions, only that military terminology which primarily envisions a *physical* battle is far more common in missions literature with Western roots than in the Old Testament itself (despite the misinformed stereotype about a genocidal God within its pages).[13]

---

9. Linda Gregerson and Susan Juster, eds., "Introduction," in *Empires of God: Religious Encounters in the Early Modern Atlantic* (Philadelphia: University of Pennsylvania Press, 2010), 1.

10. For a nuanced overview of how European colonialism was both supported and undermined by the Bible, see Mark G. Brett, *Decolonizing God: The Bible in the Tides of Empire* (Sheffield: Sheffield Phoenix Press, 2009), 7–31.

11. English terms for missions are often modified by Asian Christians into functional equivalents that lack martial connotations. For example, the English term "mobilization" is typically rendered into Chinese as *dongyuan* ("to marshal troops for battle"). However, Chinese Christians in missions circles often prefer the neutral term *tuidong* ("to push forward, organize") to portray the task of recruiting and sending missionaries.

12. Years ago, precisely this backlash happened when a campus fellowship at a Singaporean university recruited participants for its upcoming short-term missions trips by emphasizing the joylessness and hostility toward the gospel of the target countries.

13. The overuse of military metaphors in Western evangelicalism's approach toward the "other" is the key insight of Harvie M. Conn, *Eternal Word and Changing Worlds: Theology, Anthropology, and Mission in Trialogue* (Grand Rapids, MI: Zondervan, 1984).

At first glance, the place of the OT in a distinctively Asian understanding of mission seems to encounter both historical and theological problems. The connection explored particularly in this book between contextualization and the OT might seem weak and unwise, for what missional good could derive from this part of the Bible which apparently commands Yahweh's people both to bless the nations and to destroy them? These are some of the reasons that Asian evangelicals have generally shied away from contextual application of the OT. In this regard they differ from African evangelicals who have enthusiastically undertaken such readings of the OT due to its natural connections with their cultures.[14] Before returning to address doubts on the OT's relevance for Asia, it is necessary to explore the related issue of how the OT has always had a marginal status in Western missiology. This was particularly the case in what became known as the "contextualization debate."

THE "CONTEXTUALIZATION DEBATE" IN WESTERN MISSIOLOGY

Discussions about contextualization have been ongoing during the last fifty years. The term was first applied to missiology in 1972 by Shoki Coe, a Taiwanese theologian. He used it to expand the boundaries of what the Catholic Church traditionally called *inculturation* or *indigenization* – the process of helping the gospel take root in the Majority World. For Coe, *contextualization* captured the additional dimension of self-theologizing that allows emerging societies to cultivate their own Christian identity. This has been the ecumenical stance of the World Council of Churches (which sponsored Coe's work) in advocating culture as the starting point for doing theology rather than Scripture.

Evangelicals from both the Western and the non-Western worlds such as John Stott, Byang Kato, and René Padilla responded by emphasizing the authoritative role of Scripture in contextualization. This was especially the case in the papers presented at the International Congress on World Evangelization

---

14. As observed by Knut Holter, a South African OT scholar: "Just as the OT has proved to be an African book, to do OT scholarship has likewise proved to be an African enterprise. Therefore, wherever African OT scholarship will be heading, with regard to institutional context and thematic orientation, it deserves attention" ("The Current State of Old Testament Scholarship in Africa: Where Are We at the Turn of the Century?," in *Interpreting the Old Testament in Africa: Papers from the International Symposium on Africa and the Old Testament in Nairobi, October 1999*, eds. Knut Holter, Mary N. Getui, and Victor Zinkuratire [Nairobi: Acton, 2002], 25). Cited in Aloo O. Mojola, "The Old Testament or Hebrew Bible in Africa: Challenges and Prospects for Interpretation and Translation," *Verbum et Ecclesia* 35 (2014): 7.

(ICWE) in Lausanne (1974) as well as the Willowbank Consultation on the Gospel and Culture in Bermuda (1978). But what lay unresolved in the aftermath of Lausanne and Willowbank (as the two meetings were later called) was the degree to which evangelical understandings of contextualization require an either-or choice between the gospel and culture.[15] The dominant stance in evangelical missiology in the West has usually been a combination of the *translation* and *countercultural* models in regarding contextualization as the production of conceptual maps between an unchanging word and a changing world.[16]

During the process of reorienting contextualization with the Bible at the center, the waters of the "contextualization debate" muddied further when the term was extended beyond missiology. It was used for every form of applying the Bible to the modern setting[17] or even "everything the church is and does" in the world.[18] Evangelical scholars have also employed contextualization in a more limited sense to describe the Bible's way of doing theology by quoting itself in new contexts (as when Deuteronomy cites earlier passages from the Pentateuch).[19] Despite the confusion generated by these conflicting definitions for contextualization, what evangelicals of various kinds (whether academics or practitioners, as well as missiologists and other scholars) held in common was a mostly adversarial relationship between the Bible and culture. This was natural given the polarized terms of engagement that arose during the "contextualization debate" (alongside the "Bible wars" which also occurred during the 1970s).

However, two related problems arose in evangelical missiology's preference for a translational model which tends toward only two poles. The first was that the "contextualization debate" assumed that the pole of "eternal/unchanging

---

15. Kwame Bediako, "The Willowbank Consultation Jan 1978: A Personal Reflection," *Themelios* 5 (Jan. 1980): 25.
16. A. Scott Moreau, *Contextualization in World Missions: Mapping and Assessing Evangelical Models* (Grand Rapids, MI: Kregel Academic, 2012), 13. The translation and cultural models represent only two of the six models for contextual theology as influentially catalogued by Stephen B. Bevans, *Models of Contextual Theology*, rev. and expanded ed., Faith and Cultures Series (Maryknoll, NY: Orbis, 2002). It should also be noted that Moreau's book goes on to argue that Bevans's translation model tends to group together evangelical approaches to contextualization in potentially reductionistic ways.
17. E.g. Grant R. Osborne, *The Hermeneutical Spiral: A Comprehensive Introduction to Biblical Interpretation*, rev. and expanded ed. (Downers Grove, IL: IVP Academic, 2006), 410–33.
18. E.g. A. Scott Moreau, *Contextualizing the Faith: A Holistic Approach* (Grand Rapids, MI: Baker Academic, 2018), vii.
19. E.g. Peter T. Vogt, *Interpreting the Pentateuch: An Exegetical Handbook*, Handbooks for Old Testament Exegesis (Grand Rapids, MI: Kregel Academic, 2009), 137.

word" was already securely in Western hands, leaving only the "changing world" to study.[20] In response, Lesslie Newbigin pointedly observed that

> this whole mass of missiological writing . . . while it has sought to explore the problems of contextualization in all the cultures of humankind from China to Peru . . . has largely ignored the culture that is the most widespread, powerful, and persuasive among all contemporary cultures – namely, what I have called modern Western culture.[21]

Newbigin's strong critique needs contextualizing of its own since generalizations about "modern Western culture" are problematic in a globalized world. But his warning for the 1980s aptly exposes the assumption, still current in many circles, that the gospel as Western missionaries understand and translate it for others is basically identical to the biblical gospel. The unintended consequence in Asia, among other places, is that Christianity is still often viewed as "the white man's religion."

Second, the "contextualization debate" tended to overlook the diverse processes of theologizing the gospel within cultures that are found in the Bible itself. The assumption of a fixed and static gospel is evident in how the standard missiology textbook by David Hesselgrave and Edward Rommen favors the category of "apostolic contextualization," thereby making the finished revelation of the NT the starting point for acts of cultural translation. This relegates contextualization to a postbiblical set of methods which involve communicating the apostolically revealed message of the Bible in new situations. In doing so, though, the "gospel" to be contextualized is assumed as self-evident rather than being demonstrated from the Bible itself.

A major shift occurred in evangelical circles with the 2005 publication of Dean Flemming's award-winning book, *Contextualization in the New Testament*. As hinted at the start of this chapter, perhaps the main breakthrough of his work was the recognition that an evangelical doctrine of Scripture does not require a monolithic gospel since the NT itself does not contain such a theological position. As Flemming showed in detail, the NT's references to "the gospel" (in the singular) are nevertheless "too pregnant with meaning to be confined to a single set of terms or images, or to one way of telling the

---

20. This wording is indebted to Conn, *Eternal Word*. His book's proposal for a "trialogue" among theology, anthropology, and mission actually moves beyond two poles in the conversation.
21. Lesslie Newbigin, *Foolishness to the Greeks: The Gospel and Western Culture* (Grand Rapids, MI: Eerdmans, 1986), 2–3.

story. . . . The New Testament writers articulate the good news in distinctive ways, with their own styles, literary genres, vocabularies, perspectives and persuasive strategies."[22] The diversity of NT contextualizations lies not only in its variety of communicative methods, but also in how the singular gospel is deeply rooted in its Jewish and Greco-Roman setting: "The gospel cannot exist apart from a concrete historical and cultural home."[23] Flemming was thus the first to show that the supracultural dimensions of the gospel go hand in hand with the NT's affirmation that the gospel is also a coherent story that testifies to Jesus Christ in real time and space.

While Flemming broke new ground in overcoming the forced choice between the gospel and culture, there has remained a legacy of the "contextualization debate" that his work is unable to overcome. This is the difficulty of drawing precise boundaries between contextualization and syncretism. Flemming's discussion of the "Colossian heresy" does offer some guidelines on syncretism, but his concluding chapter acknowledges that the NT contains a paradox: "Throughout the New Testament, the authenticity of the gospel is of highest priority, and it should be for us as well. In general, however, the New Testament writers do not seem to be interested in precisely defining the boundaries of what is genuine theology and what is not."[24] He does go on to reflect on the "range of acceptable contextualizations," yet it is clear that the NT's lack of explicit teaching on syncretism is ultimately the void that has invited competing sides in the "contextualization debate" to plug in their own solutions. Simply put, syncretism was a relatively minor concern for the NT writers during the era that the Christian gospel was entering human cultures for the first time. The NT writings span only fifty to sixty years and are directed to audiences that shared a broadly Greco-Roman frame of reference (with varying amounts of Jewish and local influences as well).

Precisely because of the NT's limited cultural and historical scope, Flemming also observes that a comprehensive biblical treatment of contextualization and syncretism will require study of the OT as well.[25] The present book seeks to provide such an OT complement to Flemming's groundbreaking work on the NT, while also addressing the problem of the OT's glaring absence

---

22. Flemming, *Contextualization in the New Testament*, 297.
23. Flemming, 31.
24. Flemming, 303.
25. Flemming, 13, n. 3.

from the "contextualization debate" in Western missiology.[26] The roots of this omission are the greater complexities of the OT as a much longer corpus than the NT which was written over a millennium rather than a few decades.

However, the OT is especially suited for the "contextualization debate" since it narrates the frequent contacts of Israel with many other nations through their lengthy shared history in the ancient Near East. Syncretism is thus a major concern in the OT. Its plethora of cross-cultural encounters are uniquely able, in fact, to offer biblical source material on both contextualization and syncretism. This explains why OT scholarship of the last 150 years in the West has continually grappled with topics that anticipate missiology's "contextualization debate" of the last fifty years. The following overview of these debates, particularly the fraught relationship between Israelite faith and ancient Near Eastern cultures, will be instructive for charting next steps in studying biblical contextualization.

WESTERN OT SCHOLARSHIP'S PRECURSORS TO THE "CONTEXTUALIZATION DEBATE"

The Old Testament contains numerous iterations of its own "contextualization debate" as the shape of Israelite faith unfolded over the course of a millennium. In other words, the theology of the canonical OT was neither an all-at-once nor a once-for-all revelation. It instead developed under Yahweh's sovereignty as a series of responses to the historical and cultural circumstances in which Israel found itself. This is a major reason that the individualized religion of the patriarchal age is not identical to the structured Yahwism of the newly

26. Though no full-length treatment of contextualization in the OT exists, shorter studies can be found in Gleason L. Archer, Jr., "Contextualization: Some Implications from Life and Witness in the Old Testament," in *New Horizons in World Mission: Evangelicals and the Christian Mission in the 1980s – Papers and Responses Prepared for the Consultation on Theology and Mission, Trinity Evangelical Divinity School, School of World Mission and Evangelism, March 19–22, 1979*, ed. David J. Hesselgrave (Grand Rapids, MI: Baker, 1979), 199–216; Saphir Athyal, "The Old Testament Contextualisations," *World Evangelization Magazine*, October 1997, 8–9; Arthur F. Glasser, "Old Testament Contextualization: Revelation and Its Environment," in *The Word among Us: Contextualizing Theology for Mission Today*, ed. Dean S. Gilliland (Eugene, OR: Wipf and Stock, 2002); Millard C. Lind, "Refocusing Theological Education to Mission: The Old Testament and Contextualization," *Missiology: An International Review* 10 (Apr. 1982): 141–60; D. Premnan Niles, "Example of Contextualization in the Old Testament," *The South East Asia Journal of Theology* 21 (1980): 19–33; Brian K. Petersen, "A Brief Investigation of Old Testament Precursors to the Pauline Missiological Model of Cultural Adaptation," *International Journal of Frontier Missiology* 23 (Fall 2007): 117–29. Some of the present book's ideas received a preview in Jerry Hwang, "Contextualization in the Old Testament," *Mission Round Table: The Occasional Bulletin of OMF International Mission Research* 13 (May 2018): 4–9.

liberated nation of Israel.[27] Abraham and Jacob were among those who built altars to Yahweh and offered their own sacrifices in a manner that the later laws of the Pentateuch would frown upon as the Levitical priesthood took on these responsibilities instead. The progressive nature of God's revelation in the OT means that the patriarchs in Genesis did not have the full understanding of monotheism, holiness, and the threat of foreign nations which the rest of the Pentateuch would provide through the ministry of Moses.[28] And besides diverging from each other, patriarchal religion and Mosaic Yahwism in the second millennium BC also differed in significant ways from the Judaism that would emerge after Israel's return from exile in the first millennium BC. The catastrophe of losing its land and seeing its temple destroyed was the God-given occasion for Israel to correct old misunderstandings and receive new revelation about divine presence, to cite some of the theological breakthroughs that the exile made possible.

Theological continuity can certainly be found across all these historical streams of Israelite faith. But the sheer length and breadth of the Old Testament canon is clearly the outcome of a lengthy and sometimes contentious process of forging Israel's unique identity in a running dialogue with its ancient Near Eastern setting. In summary, it was only a deep and sustained interaction with surrounding cultures that allowed miniscule Israel to maintain the confession in the face of stronger empires that its deity was "the LORD Most High [who] is awesome, the great King over all the earth" (Ps 47:2). The following chapters of this book will explore this *contextual* and *contextualizing* posture of the OT within its world as models for our methods of contextualization.

In turn, the diversity in the OT's cultural engagement has spawned many further contextualizations of the OT in Western scholarship. In viewing the OT as authoritative Scripture, Christianity has always been interested in both the subjective element of how to *apply* OT texts as well as the objective element of understanding what they *say*. Questions about the relationship between faith and culture have received special attention. In the precritical era of the early Reformation, for instance, kingship in the OT supplied a mirror for Protestant monarchies to regard their own kings as divinely appointed men.

---

27. This observation is not the *evolutionary* approach to Israelite religion which characterizes Julius Wellhausen's JEDP "documentary hypothesis." Instead, the *theological* point being made is that God himself superintends the process of progressive revelation at each point of Israel's history.

28. R. W. L. Moberly, *The Old Testament of the Old Testament*, Overtures to Biblical Theology (Minneapolis, MN: Fortress, 1992), 87–104.

The boy-king Edward VI of England (1537–1553) was celebrated by influential supporters (e.g. Thomas Cranmer, author of the Thirty-Nine Articles of Anglicanism) as a "new Josiah" whom God had selected to consolidate the gains of the English Reformation.[29] Besides using the OT as a theological warrant for monarchy, Christian Europe also managed to find biblical support for republicanism in the separation of powers envisioned in the Mosaic law.[30] But as post-Reformation Europe was consumed by political and military conflicts that often were based on competing religious claims, it became clear that the survival of Christendom depended on the ability to distinguish between that which is historically or culturally *descriptive* in the Bible and that which is theologically *prescriptive*.

The problem of Christian sectarianism was foremost in the mind of Johann Philip Gabler, a German Protestant theologian, when he delivered a famous lecture in 1787 on upholding "the neglected distinction between religion and theology."[31] By "religion" Gabler meant tracing the diversity in the Bible with its many combinations of authors, genres, and ideas. "Theology" was his term for the more challenging task of adapting the Bible's ideas for a new context with the help of philosophy and cultural analysis. From Gabler came the insight that applying Scripture requires a proper appreciation of cultural and historical distance. The various kinds of distance between "then and now" are an issue both for Scripture's constituent parts which originated in different eras, as well as for the even larger gaps that stand between ancient Scripture and modern reader.

Despite Gabler's warnings, the monocultural assumptions of Christendom continued to operate during the heyday of European colonialism as explorers and missionaries came into extensive contact with non-Western cultures for the first time during the nineteenth century. As texts and artifacts from the ancient Near East were unearthed in places such as Iraq and Palestine, the world around the Bible came to life in vivid color, at times unnerving the Christian public in Europe and North America due to its echoes of the OT. Uneasiness came particularly from the discovery of ancient Near Eastern texts such as *Enuma*

---

29. For the definitive treatment, see Diarmaid MacCulloch, *Thomas Cranmer: A Life*, rev. ed. (New Haven, CT: Yale University Press, 2016).
30. Eric Nelson, *The Hebrew Republic: Jewish Sources and the Transformation of European Political Thought* (Cambridge, MA: Harvard University Press, 2011).
31. Johann P. Gabler, "An Oration on the Proper Distinction between Biblical and Dogmatic Theology and the Specific Objectives of Each," in *Old Testament Theology: Flowering and Future*, ed. Ben C. Ollenburger, trans. John Sandys-Wunsch and Laurence Eldredge, rev. ed., Sources for Biblical and Theological Study 1 (Winona Lake, IN: Eisenbrauns, 2004), 500.

Elish, the Gilgamesh Epic, and the Eridu Genesis. These documents from Mesopotamia spoke of a worldwide deluge that destroyed humanity, while also being dated on linguistic grounds before the time of traditional Mosaic authorship for Genesis.

Along with Charles Darwin's *On the Origin of Species* (1859) and Julius Wellhausen's *Prolegomena to the History of Israel* (1874), the publication of Mesopotamian flood myths in the latter nineteenth century had the effect of placing the OT's creation account on public trial, with archaeologists and comparative studies leading the cross-examination. The growing recognition of non-Western civilizations posed a challenge to more than just the Bible. It was nothing short of the West's self-understanding of its cultural uniqueness as heir to biblical Israel that was at stake.

OT scholarship received another seismic shock at the outset of the twentieth century with the high-profile discovery of the Code of Hammurabi in 1901. This was a Babylonian legal document that contained echoes of the Pentateuch such as "an eye for an eye, a tooth for a tooth" (cf. Exod 21:23–27) while also predating its OT counterpart. Over the next three years, international controversy over "pan-Babylonianism" peaked in a series of public lectures by the German critical scholar Friedrich Delitzsch on "Babel und Bibel" (later translated and published in English as *Babel and Bible*). He ignited an international furor for asserting that the OT was an act of plagiarism from the earlier intellectual and literary forms of ancient Babylon. As the anti-Christian son of the evangelical OT scholar Franz Delitzsch, the younger Delitzsch understood conservative Christians well enough to capitalize on their fear that the OT might be a pious forgery.

In retrospect, it became apparent that pan-Babylonianism's assertions were overstated – hypotheses about literary borrowing in Genesis and Exodus tended to emphasize the similarities of these OT books with Babylonian literature at the expense of their many differences. But it is no exaggeration to say that the "parallelomania"[32] of assuming that similarities are proof of borrowing was dominant in OT scholarship of the late nineteenth and early twentieth centuries, causing major worry for Bible-believing people who regarded the OT purely as divine revelation that had been given more or less directly to their

---

32. The term was made famous by Samuel Sandmel, a scholar of Judaism ("Parallelomania," *Journal of Biblical Literature* 81 [1962]: 1–13). He rightly showed that assuming that all similarities are proof of literary dependence overlooks other, equally plausible explanations. For example, what of parallels that derive from a common source or tradition instead of direct dependence on each other?

culture. Or in missiological terms, one could summarize that the monocultural West's anxiety about syncretism in the OT led to a refusal to acknowledge the possibility of contextualization in the OT.

Another major front in OT comparative studies opened with the 1929 discovery of Canaanite texts and artifacts at Ras Shamra, an archaeological site in modern-day Syria. The texts dated to the thirteenth century BC and were written in Ugaritic, a Semitic language that is closely related to Hebrew while also being chronologically earlier than most of the Hebrew texts found in the OT. Among the thousands of cuneiform tablets unearthed, the most prominent was a series known as the Baal Cycle. This was an Ugaritic mythic text that narrates the combat of the warrior god Baal, the son of the high god El, in his battles with Yam, the god of the sea, as well as Mot, the god of death, before descending to the underworld. Yet Baal rises again to rule over both the realms of the sea and death. The annual death and resurrection of Baal reflects his dual status as warrior deity and fertility deity, with his journey mirrored in the annual rhythms of the natural world.

The availability of the Ugaritic texts did more than illuminate the OT's references to Canaanite deities such as El, Baal, Mot, and Asherah which had previously been obscure. With their description of Canaanite fertility religion and an unruly sea which had chaos monsters in it, they also escalated the debate over whether the OT borrows myths or mythic themes from other ancient Near Eastern cultures. It is undeniable that numerous OT poetic passages presume their audience's awareness of Canaanite mythology about fertility (e.g. Hos 2:8) and the sea as an adversary (e.g. Ps 29:10) which sometimes contains mythic creatures (e.g. Isa 27:1). Thus, it was natural for "pan-Ugaritism" to join forces with "pan-Babylonianism" as the newest form of *parallelomania*. A minority of scholars even asserted that numerous Canaanite terms and motifs had been adopted wholesale by OT writers, most notably the theme of watery chaos which found expression in several OT passages (e.g. Exod 15; Ps 77).[33]

Over time, mainstream OT scholarship offered a more nuanced response to parallelomania (though this was also flawed, for reasons to be explored shortly). Against the hypothesis of uncritical borrowing, scholars began to regard echoes of Babylonian and Canaanite myths as an intentional polemic, all while maintaining Christendom's unspoken assumption that the Scriptures could not possibly contain pagan elements. Central to this strategy was the

---

33. This extreme position was associated with the "Dahood school," following the work of Mitchell J. Dahood, the Catholic scholar of Ugarit.

argument that the OT is unique in its cultural environment for regarding Yahweh as a deity who is transcendent and acts within a linear history, while other ancient Near Eastern deities are immanent and restricted to the cyclical rhythms of creation.[34]

The foremost advocate for the distinctiveness of so-called "salvation history" (*Heilsgeschichte*) was the German OT scholar Gerhard von Rad. In his two-volume *Old Testament Theology*, for example, he famously maintained that the OT prophets' frequent depiction of covenant as marriage was the clever reworking of a Canaanite fertility motif.[35] It was thus commonplace to say that the OT's preeminence in its cultural setting lay in Yahweh's demythologization of ancient Near Eastern motifs in the service of salvation history. Again using the categories of missiology, we might say that the pendulum swung in OT scholarship from syncretism to contextualization, but the latter only of the *countercultural* type. Indeed, a vocal number of conservative evangelicals continue to view satire and mockery as the primary means of the OT's cultural engagement with ancient Near Eastern myth.[36] For them, the suggestion that the OT might contain mythic elements tends to elicit strident reassertions of the Bible's distinctiveness and total absence of "pagan" elements.[37]

Already fifty years ago, mainstream OT studies (including a good number of confessional scholars) moved toward a more balanced understanding of history and myth that no longer forced a strict choice between them.[38] The publication in 1967 of Bertil Albrektson's *History and the Gods* was seminal in this regard. His book showed conclusively that Western OT scholarship's standard dichotomy between history and creation set up an artificial contrast

---

34. Leo G. Perdue, *The Collapse of History: Reconstructing Old Testament Theology* (Minneapolis, MN: Augsburg Fortress, 1994), 113–50.
35. Gerhard von Rad, *Old Testament Theology*, trans. D. M. G. Stalker, 2 vols., Old Testament Library (Louisville, KY: Westminster John Knox, 2001), 2:141: "The idea of marriage between a deity and an earthly partner had long been familiar to him and his contemporaries through the rites of the Canaanite nature religion (the marriage of Baal to the earth is an example). It was, to all appearances, an extremely bold move to transfer this idea that belonged to a religious ideology absolutely incompatible with Jahwism [sic] as Hosea understood it, to the covenant relationship with Jahweh [sic]. Yet, the very fact that the partner to whom this relationship was now applied was conceived altogether in historical terms eliminated the mythological element from this range of concepts."
36. E.g. John D. Currid, *Against the Gods: The Polemical Theology of the Old Testament* (Wheaton, IL: Crossway, 2013).
37. E.g. the subtitle of John N. Oswalt's book *The Bible among the Myths: Unique Revelation or Just Ancient Literature?* (Grand Rapids, MI: Zondervan, 2009).
38. The best history of research remains John W. Rogerson, *Myth in Old Testament Interpretation*, Beihefte zur Zeitschrift für die alttestamentliche Wissenschaft 134 (Berlin: de Gruyter, 1974).

between "demythologized" Yahwism and pagan "myths." The former was supposedly characterized by linear time, the latter by cyclical time (this false dichotomy will be addressed in chapter 8). Instead, Albrektson overcame this either-or proposition by showing that ancient Near Eastern deities, including Yahweh, were commonly understood to act in both creation as well as history. In OT books such as Jeremiah, Hosea, and Job (to cite just a few), Yahweh is portrayed as acting in both realms for the sake of dethroning the prevailing powers in all the realms that they were thought to rule. This comprehensive depiction of monotheism in the OT provides an outstanding example of a contextual and contextualizing dynamic within its ancient Near Eastern setting. The uniqueness of Yahweh among the gods is not in question (as chapter 4 explores in detail), only the way in which Israel's particular form of monotheism was traditionally conceived in Western philosophy as a reflection of Christendom's understanding of its own monotheism.

In sum, comparative methods in OT studies have matured greatly in the last 150 years. They are now at the point of offering a useful toolbox for missiology in understanding how contextualization and syncretism relate to one another. The process of understanding Israelite faith's ability to be distinctive but also firmly grounded in its ancient Near Eastern context is parallel to missiology's task of understanding how to do contextualization using cultural themes and features that are native to Asia. However, where is *Asia*, and what counts as Asian *contextual* theology in a globalized world? These are the important issues to be considered in the next section.

THE SCOPE OF "ASIA" AND "ASIAN CONTEXTUAL THEOLOGY"

The thesis of this book is that the OT's acts of contextualization within its ancient Near Eastern context train modern Christians to live faithfully in their various Far Eastern contexts. But in tracing such connections between different "Eastern" or "Asian" environments, we encounter several questions about the methodology of comparing and moving between cultures. First, what is the scope of Asia as the largest continent in the world? Second, how meaningful is it to generalize about *Asia* with its manifold diversity which encompasses 60 percent of the global population? Third, who possesses the proper qualifications to do Asian *contextual* theology? These questions lack simple answers but are important since Western missiologists and theologians alike have tended to speak imprecisely of a uniform "Asia" that lies on the outskirts of civilization in the "East."[39]

The first question about the scope of "Asia" concerns more than geography. In *The Myth of Continents*, Martin Lewis and Kären Wigen observe that the West's tendency to use Europe and Asia as designations for *us* and *them* started with the ancient Greeks. They coined these terms with the Aegean Sea as a boundary between "Europe" to the north and west of the Sea, "Asia" to the east, and "Libya" denoting Africa to the south.[40] The Greco-Roman period also saw a more limited use of "Asia" for the western part of Anatolia (modern-day Turkey), as in the New Testament's references to "Asia [Minor]"[41] (e.g. Acts 16:6; Rom 16:5; 1 Pet 1:1; Rev 1:4). Especially during the fifteenth century AD, the growth of Christianity in Europe and the withdrawal of Christians from Asia Minor meant that "the boundaries of Christendom increasingly (although never perfectly) coincided with those of the Greeks' Europe. . . . These centuries saw Europe begin to displace Christendom as the primary referent for Western society."[42]

In sum, the boundary between Europe and Asia has always been contested. "Asia" in the modern Western mind has often denoted the faraway peoples of East and Southeast Asia (and sometimes South Asia),[43] thereby bracketing out West Asia and North Asia.[44] By contrast, the terms "Near/Middle East" and "Far East" are still in common use today.[45] This book will grant this Eurocentric view of the "East" for the sake of discussion since "ancient Near East" remains a standard designation for the world around and including biblical Israel. While

---

39. This phenomenon is known variously as "Orientalism" or the "hegemony postulate." Even among those who have worked cross-culturally in particular Asian contexts, there can be a tendency to speak of a universal and undifferentiated "Asia."

40. Martin W. Lewis and Kären Wigen, *The Myth of Continents: A Critique of Metageography* (Berkeley, CA: University of California Press, 1997), 21–22. The authors note that this rough division by continents was never exact, as when the Nile River was typically considered to be the dividing line between Africa and Asia. In addition, ancient Greece cut across the boundary between Europe and Asia.

41. "Asia Minor" was the Roman designation for Anatolia, and has been retained in modern times to distinguish it from the continent of "Asia."

42. Lewis and Wigen, *Myth of Continents*, 25.

43. It has not been until very recently, for example, that cultural discourse in the United States started to view those from South Asian backgrounds (e.g. Indians, Pakistanis, Bangladeshis) as "*Asian* Americans." By contrast, "Asian" in the British Isles has tended to denote cultural roots in South Asia more than East Asia.

44. Lewis and Wigen, *Myth of Continents*, 38–40.

45. The labels "occidental" and "oriental," on the other hand, are generally considered outdated since "oriental" has strong connotations of Orientalism (see n. 39). They derive from the Latin directional terms for east (*oriens*) and west (*occidens*).

I recognize that continental "Asia" should include the parts of West Asia that are in the Middle East,[46] limitations of space mean that this book will use "Asia" following the imperfect convention of referring mainly to South Asia, East Asia, and Southeast Asia.

The difficulty of defining "Asia" with geographical consistency has a close parallel in the second question of what counts as culturally "Asian." The challenge of tracing the scope of Asia in this regard becomes evident when attempting to speak of "*Asian* food." From my own experience in various Western countries, any restaurant with signage saying "Asian food" is an unintentional signal to steer clear – the food served is likely a hodgepodge of East Asian ingredients (e.g. noodles, soy sauce, sesame seeds).[47] The combinations offered will typically be for Western palates (e.g. chop suey, egg foo young) and served alongside Asian foods from different countries (e.g. Chinese chow mein with Mongolian barbeque and Thai prawn crackers) or "Asian" foods invented in the West (e.g. fortune cookies, crab rangoon, California rolls). Most perplexing is when a restaurant supplements "Asian food" with Western staples (e.g. French fries, pasta) to lessen the unfamiliarity of the meal.

But all is not lost in an Asian culinary desert. The impossibility of finding an authentic "*Asian* restaurant" in such a place stands in contrast to the frequent presence of an "Asian *supermarket.*" The latter is a common sight even in non-Asian countries since authentic ingredients from various Asian suppliers can be imported for a broad customer base without mixing or modifying the ingredients from their original state. And even when no such supermarket is available, authentic Asian food can still be made by cultural insiders using whatever is available in a foreign land. For example, when Americanized Chinese restaurants are owned by ethnic Chinese (which is not always the case, as in the P. F. Chang's restaurant chain in North America), all it takes to get genuine Chinese food is to chat with the owners in Chinese and ask for their best attempt at contextualizing Chinese cuisine. This can happen even in the absence of a Chinese-language menu since they simply offer what they would cook and eat on their own. Indeed, the familiarity of Chinese *jiachangcai* (lit. "home-regular-dishes") for insiders is precisely what makes such home cooking inaccessible to outsiders unless they can ask what is "off the menu."

---

46. The spread of Islam across West Asia and Africa has created an Islamic cultural bloc with distinct features which social scientists increasingly designate as "MENA" (Middle East/North Africa).
47. Similarly, South Asian cuisine is often designated as "Indian food" even when such a restaurant's menu also includes items from Pakistan, Bangladesh, Nepal, Sri Lanka, or elsewhere.

For these reasons, this book will seek to do Asian contextual theology with Asian ingredients in all their cultural particularity as insiders would typically use them, rather than synthesizing them into something pan-Asian for the sake of outsiders. Asian contextual theology that is undertaken with non-native categories, languages, and interests in mind always runs the risk of staying "on the menu" by working with foreign ingredients and techniques for foreign palates, even when those doing the theology are culturally Asian.[48] It need not be the case, though, that outsiders are unable to become competent in making or recognizing a genuinely Asian offering (whether of cuisine or theology) once they have enough firsthand experience of its original context. Though they still must defer to cultural insiders, the realities of regional differences and evolving palates in Asia make it impossible even for insiders to distill "authenticity" into a set of supposedly nonnegotiable features. But in the final analysis, Asian insiders who know nothing of cooking or theology can still determine authenticity by tasting the final product and/or deliberating with other insiders to arrive at a consensus.[49]

These observations enable us to address the third question of who has the proper credentials to do Asian contextual theology in a globalized world. For our purposes, the word *contextual* will denote "the processes, the means, the limits, and the criteria necessary for Christian leaders from diverse cultures to construct local evangelical theologies."[50] The necessity of theologies being both "local" and "evangelical" underscores the main issue of how any kind of theology can make claims to authority without modifiers such as "Asian" and "Western." The difficulty of recognizing one's own cultural situatedness comes to the fore in a humorous anecdote by Robert McAfee Brown, a mainline Presbyterian theologian in the United States:

> In 1975, I attended a conference of North and South Americans
> at which there were a number of theologians. After three or four
> days, one of the Latin-American theologians said to us, "Why
> is it that when you talk about *our* position you always describe

---

48. For a similar idea but using a contrast between the ivory tower and the grassroots, see Simon Chan, *Grassroots Asian Theology: Thinking the Faith from the Ground Up* (Downers Grove, IL: InterVarsity Press, 2014).

49. Natee Tanchanpongs, "Developing a Palate for Authentic Theology," in *Local Theology for the Global Church: Principles for an Evangelical Approach to Contextualization*, eds. Matthew Cook et al. (Pasadena, CA: William Carey Library, 2010), 113–14.

50. Matthew Cook, "Foreword," in *Local Theology for the Global Church*, vii.

it as 'Latin-American theology,' but when you talk about *your* position you always describe it as 'theology'?"

A salutary question. For although we would have all denied it, we were in fact assuming that *our* position was normative ("pure" theology untainted by geographical or class biases), whereas *their* position was derivative (theology conditioned by the fact that it was being done in Latin America), a variant on the true theological position, namely ours.

It was true, of course, that their theology was conditioned by the fact that it was being done in Latin America, in situations of oppression, in culturally Catholic settings, chiefly by men who were incorporating Marxist analysis into their theological formulations. We saw all those limiting factors very clearly. What we failed to see (until our friendly questioner forced us to see it) was that our theology was just as culturally conditioned as theirs: it was being done in North America, in situations of affluence, in culturally pluralistic settings, chiefly by men (though now and again by women), who were importing capitalist assumptions into their theological formulations. . . . What we *brought to* our thinking massively influenced what we *took from* it. The fact that we were unaware of this only underlines how deep our ideological captivity was.[51]

Theology from the West evidently has a distinctive shape which fits less well elsewhere.[52] Given this reality, one might wonder if the proper method for Asian contextual theology consists of soundly rejecting the methods and conclusions of Western theology.[53] If this is the case (and so-called "Western

---

51. Robert McAfee Brown, *Theology in a New Key: Responding to Liberation Themes*, 1st ed. (Philadelphia: Westminster Press, 1978), 77–78, italics original. This is not a solely ecumenical observation since evangelical theologians have expressed the same idea, though less memorably than Brown (e.g. Stanley N. Gundry, "Evangelical Theology: Where Should We Be Going?," *Journal of the Evangelical Theological Society* 22, no. 1 [March 1979]: 11–12).
52. At the same time, the "Hellenization thesis" that the Greek/Western theological forms of the NT are at odds with Hebrew/non-Western ones of the OT (as held in different ways by Tertullian, Adolf von Harnack, Jürgen Moltmann, for example) is considerably overstated. For a balanced perspective, see Kevin J. Vanhoozer, "'One Rule to Rule Them All?' Theological Method in an Era of World Christianity," in *Globalizing Theology: Belief and Practice in an Era of World Christianity*, eds. Craig Ott and Harold A. Netland (Grand Rapids, MI: Baker Academic, 2006), 85–126.
53. As suggested by Hwa Yung, *Mangoes or Bananas? The Quest for an Authentic Asian Christian Theology* (Oxford: Regnum, 1997).

theology" is a meaningful abstraction), will not any attempt to be intentionally "Asian" still yield a non-Western form of "ideological captivity" that prioritizes the local dimensions of anthropology and hermeneutics at the expense of universal theology and truth? Or to restate the stakes more positively and in culinary terms, how can Asian insiders do their contextual cooking in a manner that both insiders and outsiders can enjoy, outsiders can learn without claiming to know better than insiders, even as all parties work together for the dissemination of what is authentically Asian?

This book will explore such questions by drawing on how social scientists have theorized the relationship between insiders and outsiders in Asian contexts.[54] This is particularly so in the symbiosis between subjectivity and objectivity that is necessary when moving between cultures in the manner entailed by contextualization and syncretism. The old ideal of cultural *purity* which undergirded the "contextualization debate" is giving way to the paradigm of cultural *hybridity* since "the world is flat."[55] At the same time, it is still necessary for insiders to have the final say in establishing boundaries between good and bad forms of cultural *appropriation* by outsiders.

Thus, we will foreground the voices of Asian insiders about their cultures, but without ignoring how the voices of non-Asian outsiders can lend balance in the cooperative task of doing contextual theology that is deeply biblical, fully evangelical, and authentically Asian. And reversing the direction of scrutiny, the disciplines of OT scholarship, missiology, and theology each have their own history in the West which need to be assessed and enriched from the non-Western perspective that Asians can provide. With an iterative and dialogical method of this kind, Asian and Western lenses can serve as each other's subjects and objects of examination. The mutual understanding that results from this process of oscillating between cultures, with the Bible

---

54. For summary and application to biblical studies, see Márta Cserháti, "The Insider/Outsider Debate and the Study of the Bible," *Communio Viatorum* 50 (2008): 313–22.

55. To quote the influential description of globalization by Thomas L. Friedman, *The World Is Flat: A Brief History of the Twenty-First Century*, updated and expanded ed. (New York: Farrar, Strauss, and Giroux, 2007). At the same time, the term "hybrid" needs qualification. Unlike the animal kingdom in which the hybrid that results from intentional crossing of two specimens is typically sterile, the hybrids that result when cultures meet are unintentional, pluriform, and creative in nature (Ted C. Lewellen, *The Anthropology of Globalization: Cultural Anthropology Enters the 21st Century* [Westport, CT: Bergin & Garvey, 2002], 99).

remaining the linchpin in the center, will provide a series of case studies in *intercultural theology*.[56]

TITLE AND STRUCTURE OF THE BOOK

The attentive reader will notice that this book's title is *Contextualization* and *the Old Testament*, in contrast to the preposition "in" for Dean Flemming's *Contextualization* in *the New Testament*. My use of the conjunction "and" is intended to reflect the multifaceted relationship between contextualization and the Old Testament. The latter provides both a set of models *with* which contextualization beyond the Bible's explicit horizons may occur, as well as being the biblical corpus *in* which contextualization is present. In short, contextualization is a useful concept both for exploring the OT's posture toward its original cultural milieu as well as supplying the theological method for engaging similar non-Western contexts. Flemming's use of the preposition *in* reflects a slightly different methodology which focuses on the NT as the main locus and boundary of contextualization methods.

For our purposes, to restrict the discussion to contextualization "in" the Old Testament would be less than ideal for two reasons. First, the nature of progressive revelation means that the Old Testament does not reveal the fullness of the biblical gospel in the manner that the New Testament does. The OT's lack of a narrative or theological core to contextualize, by contrast with summaries of "*the* gospel" in the NT (e.g. Rom 1:16; 1 Cor 15:3–8),[57] means that the OT's contribution to the "contextualization debate" comes more in the forms of its cultural and theological engagement. Otherwise, the missiologist's quest to be thoroughly biblical will lead to the questionable practice of reading OT narratives prescriptively in search of principles for cross-cultural ministry.[58] Second and related to this, contextualization *with* the Old Testament follows its lead in erecting biblically shaped bridges beyond the ancient Near East in order to produce analogous contextualizations for God's people in the modern Far East. These Eastern regions often have more culturally in common with

56. Henning Wrogemann, *Intercultural Theology*, trans. Karl E. Böhmer (Downers Grove, IL: IVP Academic, 2016).
57. Keeping in mind, however, that presentations of the gospel in the NT vary among themselves and draw heavily on the OT instead of being reducible to a formula (Darrell L. Bock, *Recovering the Real Lost Gospel: Reclaiming the Gospel as Good News* [Nashville: B&H Academic, 2010]; Scot McKnight, *The King Jesus Gospel: The Original Good News Revisited* [Grand Rapids, MI: Zondervan, 2011]).
58. E.g. Marvin J. Newell, *Crossing Cultures in Scripture: Biblical Principles for Mission Practice* (Downers Grove, IL: InterVarsity Press, 2016), 22–166.

each other than both do with the modern West, so a work such as this one *from* the Asian context will naturally differ from Flemming's which was published and marketed by a Western publisher. Contextualization in and with the OT is not merely *for* the Asian context, of course, so this book also has a subtitle of *Between Asian and Western Perspectives*.

We can now embark on the exciting journey of spiraling between Asian and Western cultures in search of contextualization in and with the OT. The subsequent chapters address some of the themes that appear in standard theologies of the OT, such as God-language (chs. 2–3), monotheism (ch. 4), covenant (chs. 5–6), and the relationship between religious icons and divine presence (ch. 7).[59] However, each chapter also reexamines how these themes have traditionally been studied in the West by OT scholars, theologians, and missiologists using conventional methodologies. These perspectives have often been uncritically adopted as *neutral* or even defended as *normative* by Asian Christians and their instinctive respect for tradition, in a case of what we might facetiously call "Western orthodoxy safeguarded by Eastern hierarchy." Theological categories from the non-Western contexts of the OT and Asia which also bear on these topics are usually left aside, such as the contextual nature of Bible translation (ch. 2), the "Term Question" for how to refer to deity using indigenous names (ch. 3), the character of religious pluralism and polytheism (ch. 4), patronage (ch. 5), honor/shame (ch. 6), the West's predilection for abstract and nonvisual icons (ch. 7), and pantheism's relation to creation theology (ch. 8). The definitions of contextualization and syncretism which emerge inductively from these Asian-themed case studies in and with the OT will be summarized in our conclusion (ch. 9).

CONCLUSION

As we retrace this history of Western scholarship and chart a new path with the OT's contextualization models in engagement with Asian cultural realities, it will become evident that the OT has always stood on its own merits as a specimen of Asian contextual theology, albeit originating in the ancient Near East rather than the modern Far East. The following case studies will show that reclaiming this biblical heritage in our missional methods goes a long way in Asia toward rehabilitating the image of Christianity as a Western religion.

---

59. E.g. Robin Routledge, *Old Testament Theology: A Thematic Approach* (Downers Grove, IL: IVP Academic, 2012); Walther Zimmerli, *Old Testament Theology in Outline* (Edinburgh: T&T Clark, 2000).

CHAPTER 2

LANGUAGE, BIBLE TRANSLATION, AND CONTEXTUAL THEOLOGY

Translating the Bible is always the first act of doing contextual theology.[1] For when the word of God passes from the hands of Bible translators into those of its readers, nothing less than an act of theological creation is taking place in the target language. Vernacular terminology used in rendering the Bible itself becomes biblical terminology. A theological vocabulary has come into existence which supplies the raw material to articulate Christian experiences as well as to build broader bridges with non-Christian culture using their shared linguistic heritage. The speech of the people is hereby endowed with the unique dignity of bearing the very words of God.

Several linguistic factors come successively into play as a pioneering Bible translation takes root in Christian communities. In *lexicalization*, the fresh expressions used in the Bible are on their way to becoming conventional, though no turn of phrase can yet be considered idiomatic at this stage. As what is linguistically awkward then becomes linguistically normal and finally theologically normative, the resulting *sacralization* of "Biblish" tends to dampen how the Bible translation originally sounded before terminology that once lacked sacred connotations was repurposed for Christian uses. Living metaphors and figures of speech in Scripture gradually fade in newness under the weight of repetition, convention, and familiarity. This leads to the need for *defamiliarization* in reopening basic questions about what biblical formulations truly mean rather than what they ostensibly say. Only then can the Bible translation's engagement with its linguistic and cultural contexts be heard again from a time before the weight of Christian tradition had dampened its echoes of pre-Christian language, metaphors, and myths.

---

1. Lamin O. Sanneh, *Translating the Message: The Missionary Impact on Culture*, 2nd ed., American Society of Missiology Series 42 (Maryknoll, NY: Orbis, 2009). An earlier version of the present chapter appeared as Jerry Hwang, "Bible Translation as Contextual Theology: The Case of the Chinese Union Version Bible of 1919," *International Journal of Asian Christianity* 5 (2022): 89–114.

The history of the King James Version (KJV) and subsequent English Bibles provides a useful illustration of these phenomena at work. By rehearsing the linguistic issues in the last four hundred years of English Bible translations, we will be poised to identify similar dynamics in an Asian language such as Chinese during the last hundred and fifty years. This applies particularly to the Chinese Union Version (CUV) of 1919, a venerated translation that is simply "the Bible" for Chinese Christians worldwide. Precisely because of the CUV's influence, though, comes the irony that a century of Christian usage has muted the groundbreaking contextual theology that it provided for the Chinese culture of its time (and still can today). The results of this study of the CUV are applicable to any Asian language in which an early translation of the Bible is authoritative to the point that Christians are resistant to revising it or considering other translations. Esteem for the timelessness of such a Bible or its traditional formulations can sometimes come at the expense of grasping its contextual dimensions, whether in Asia or elsewhere.[2]

THE KING JAMES VERSION AS CONTEXTUAL PRODUCTION

The KJV Bible's status as ageless classic tends to obscure how it was also an act of contextual theology from the late sixteenth and early seventeenth centuries. In his magisterial study, Alister McGrath explains that the KJV was the outcome of a long historical process in post-Reformation England which is typically lost on modern readers.[3] With help from McGrath, we will identify the three linguistic phenomena of *lexicalization*, *sacralization*, and *defamiliarization* which are evident in the circumstances of the KJV's publication and its aftermath. The KJV inaugurated theological trajectories that endure in the English-speaking world to the present day.[4]

First, the literary style of the KJV represented a series of choices that favored the *lexicalization* of southern dialects of English.[5] Not only were all the translators from the southeast of England, they were also scholars in the original languages of the Bible whose English renderings were constrained as much

---

2. Eugene A. Nida, "Translating a Text with a Long and Sensitive Tradition," in *Translating Sensitive Texts: Linguistic Aspects*, ed. Karl Simms, Approaches to Translation Studies 14 (Amsterdam: Rodopi, 1997), 189–96.
3. Alister E. McGrath, *In the Beginning: The Story of the King James Bible and How It Changed a Nation, a Language, and a Culture* (New York: Doubleday, 2001).
4. To name just one, the KJV's rendering of Greek *hilastērion* as "propitiation" (e.g. 1 John 2:2) represented a certain understanding of Christ's atonement. Some theologians later proposed a rendering of "expiation" (e.g. RSV, NAB) instead.
5. McGrath, *In the Beginning*, 257.

by the grammar of Hebrew, Aramaic, and Greek as by English grammar (which was itself a moving target). The fact that William Shakespeare was from the south as well meant that his writings and the KJV together shaped the norms of British English to mostly exclude northern English idioms. The southern and literary English of the late sixteenth and early seventeenth centuries would become the vernacular of the Anglophone world for centuries to come.

Second, the KJV included English constructions that were already outdated for its time. The result was the *sacralization* of archaic forms as "biblical" language. Contrary to popular belief, the second-person pronouns "thee," "thou," "thy," and "thine" are neither exalted forms of address, nor were they current in the time of the KJV. These forms had once been singular pronouns (as opposed to plural "ye," "you," "your," and "yours"). But they had fallen out of use in the late sixteenth century and in some quarters were even employed by a superior to talk down to an inferior. However, they were retained since King James I of England directed his translation teams to follow the early sixteenth-century English translations that preceded the KJV. These included Tyndale's New Testament, Coverdale's revision of the Matthew Bible, and the Great Bible of 1539.[6] Alister McGrath notes that in doing so, the publication of the KJV "led directly – yet unintentionally – to the retention of older English ways of speaking in religious contexts, creating the impression that religious language was somehow *necessarily* archaic."[7] In modern English, the persistence of this association between religious terminology and archaisms is evident in the original 1971 version of the New American Standard Bible (NASB). This version of the NASB is undoubtedly the most literal of modern English translations, yet it selectively follows the KJV by using "Thee," "Thou," "Thy," and "Thine" for references to deity but modern pronouns everywhere else.[8] Some may argue that these specialized uses or capitalized divine pronouns reflect the use of honorifics for royalty or deity (as in Asian languages such as Thai, Japanese, and Korean). In reality, the "biblical" language that results is a linguistic hybrid that is intelligible only to seasoned Christians and is the living language of no one.

Third, the literalness with which the KJV translators rendered OT idioms was amusing to its first readers but soon became conventional English.

---

6. McGrath, 266–67.
7. McGrath, 269, italics original.
8. The 1995 and 2020 updates of the NASB no longer use archaic pronouns but continue to capitalize pronouns for deity.

Chief among these is Biblical Hebrew's penchant for using the *construct chain* (the functional equivalent to English "of" constructions) for description since nouns are more common in Hebrew than adjectives. In Psalm 23, for example, the KJV's familiar renderings of Hebrew construct chains, "paths of righteousness" (v. 3) and "valley of the shadow of death" (v. 4), made for awkward English until they underwent lexicalization and sacralization. Repeated use has made these Hebrew idioms familiar, but their foreignness to English is evident if the remaining Hebrew construct chains in Psalm 23 are also translated literally. *Defamiliarization* would happen to the reader of Psalm 23 if the phrases "pastures of green" (v. 2a) and "waters of quietness" (v. 2b) were to appear alongside "paths of righteousness" and "valley of the shadow of death."[9] Newer English translations of Psalm 23's first verse are similarly jarring when they render "I have all that I need" (NLT) or "I lack nothing" (2011 NIV). For modern readers unfamiliar with the Bible, the KJV's well-loved but quaint "I shall not want" sounds like a declaration about lacking desire altogether rather than, more accurately, a confession that all the psalmist's desires have been met.

Developments in biblical studies also play a significant role in defamiliarization. During the twentieth century, for example, OT scholarship identified two misunderstandings of Psalm 23 which depart from the venerable KJV but have not yet been adjusted in most English translations. The first is that "the valley of the shadow of death" (v. 4) is not a case of two Hebrew nouns joined in construct as the KJV translators originally thought. Instead it is cognate to a single Ugaritic superlative term that means "darkest valley" (as reflected only in the NLT and 2011 NIV). The second is that the closing statement, "I will *dwell* in the house of the LORD *for ever*" (v. 6), is more accurately rendered "I will *return* to the house of the LORD *for length of days*." These two corrections make Psalm 23 less suited as a standard text for Christian funerals than as a this-worldly expression of dependence and penitence toward God.[10] Modern English translations have not caught up with this consensus in OT scholarship which, incidentally, has existed for several decades. So the Judeo-Christian cultural myth that associates Psalm 23 with a nearly universal promise of eternal life after death will understandably continue.[11]

---

9. The 1611 KJV does note in the margin that the Hebrew literally reads, "pastures of tender grasse" and "waters of quietness."

10. Knut M. Heim, "Psalm 23 in the Age of the Wolf," *Christianity Today*, February 2016, 60–63.

11. In American civic religion, for example, it is common to read Psalm 23 at commemorative occasions for the dead, even for those who had no outward profession of faith in (any) God.

In summary, the linguistic processes of lexicalization and sacralization have been at work for several centuries in the Anglophone world. The idioms of the King James Bible have become conventional enough that English speakers typically do not recognize their origin. And particularly for English-speaking Christians, the influence of the KJV's archaisms leads to the paradox that "there are always many people whose *faith* is based as much on the *wording* of ancient documents as on their content."[12] The canonical status that the KJV has attained in some circles (as in KJV-Only movements) means that defamiliarization, by contrast, is an ongoing necessity in the English Bible tradition which will remain controversial. When language shifts and the contributions of biblical scholarship necessitate the release of new Bible versions and the updating of old Bible versions, these changes introduce wording and formulations that deviate from English Bible traditions. Another round of the "Bible wars" is never far behind as a result.[13]

THE CHINESE UNION VERSION AS CONTEXTUAL PRODUCTION

The factors just described for the KJV have close parallels to the translation of the Chinese Bible. Anglophone translators from Britain and America who were deeply immersed in the KJV tradition formed the majority among missionary-translators in China during the nineteenth and early twentieth centuries. What is more, the English Revised Version (ERV) of 1885, which usually follows the KJV, served as the base text for the translation committees that produced the Chinese Union Version (CUV) of 1919. The traditions and methods stemming from the KJV Bible have thus exercised a significant but largely unseen influence in Chinese Bible translations.

A full discussion of Chinese Bible translations and their non-Chinese precursors lies beyond the present scope.[14] For our purposes, it is noteworthy how closely the process of translating the CUV was linked to *lexicalization* and *sacralization* in the English Bible tradition. However, the linguistic phenomenon of *defamiliarization* has worked somewhat differently in the Chinese

---

12. Nida, "Translating a Text," 189, italics added.
13. The New International Version, for instance, has been a target from various quarters since its first version of the NT was released in 1978.
14. For a comprehensive history of Chinese Bibles in the Catholic, Protestant, and Orthodox traditions, see Jingtu Tsai, *Sheng jing zai zhong guo: fu zhong wen sheng jin li shi mu lu* [The Bible in China: With a Historical Catalogue of the Chinese Bible] (Hong Kong: Logos and Pneuma Press, 2018). All Chinese in this book is romanized according to China's *pinyin* system.

Bible tradition since the Chinese language never had a Judeo-Christian era in which biblical terminology became fully integrated with the vernacular. The reach of the Chinese Bible's idioms is instead limited to the minority of ethnic Chinese who are Protestant Christians and trace their theological heritage to the Mandarin CUV, a century-old translation that was already showing signs of age at the time of its publication.

The label of "Chinese *Union* Version" suggests that the CUV translators were always of one mind about producing a single Chinese Bible. In reality, the CUV was originally conceived at the 1890 Shanghai Missionary Conference as "one Bible in three versions" – the High *Wenli* CUV (*shen wenli heheyiben*) for the literati, the Easy *Wenli* CUV (*qian wenli heheyiben*) for those with some formal education, and the Mandarin CUV (*guanhua heheyiben*) that the masses could understand. This decision at the Conference was a compromise that sought to accommodate competing views on translating the Bible into Chinese which Western missionaries set forth during the latter nineteenth century.

Nevertheless, the relative status of the three Union versions was unequal from the beginning. An invitation to participate in one of the two *Wenli* translation committees was regarded as more prestigious due to esteem for literary Chinese among the missionary-translators. It was more difficult to recruit members for the translation committee of the Mandarin CUV, because of both Mandarin's lower prestige and the fact that those proficient in the vernacular tended to be busier with grassroots ministry.[15] Adding to these difficulties was that "Mandarin" was a hodgepodge of northern Chinese localisms and dialects which lacked the stabilizing literary history of *Wenli*.[16] These obstacles led the committee members for the Mandarin CUV to lack confidence in Mandarin's ability and suitability for translating the Bible.[17]

The situation in China changed dramatically between the Shanghai Missionary Conference of 1890 and the publication of the CUV in 1919. During these three decades, the fading importance of *Wenli* as well as philosophical differences among *Wenli* committee members eventually led to a decision in 1907 to merge the *Wenli* translations. The advent of republican

---

15. Jost Oliver Zetzsche, *The Bible in China: The History of the Union Version or the Culmination of Protestant Missionary Bible Translation in China*, Monumenta Serica Monograph Series 45 (Sankt Augustin: Monumenta Serica Institute, 1999), 222.

16. George Kam Wah Mak, *Protestant Bible Translation and Mandarin as the National Language of China*, Sinica Leidensia 131 (Leiden: Brill, 2017), 13–14, n. 52, explains that *Wenli* was not a term used by Chinese themselves, but the idiosyncratic name that the missionary-translators gave to *wenyanwen* (i.e. classical/literary Chinese).

17. Marshall Broomhall, *The Bible in China* (London: China Inland Mission, 1934), 92.

China in 1911 shifted the balance of power further away from the elite and educated classes, while the *baihua* (= "plain speech") literary movement of 1917 and the May Fourth Movement of 1919 reinforced a cultural shift toward Mandarin already underway, just as the *Wenli* and Mandarin Union Versions were published.

As one of the first complete literary works in vernacular Chinese,[18] the Mandarin CUV became a major force in standardizing the vernacular around northern Chinese idioms through references to it in literature and its inclusion in China's national language curriculum and textbooks.[19] References to the Mandarin CUV also became common in the Chinese literature that sprouted after the May Fourth Movement, even though the prolonged process of translation meant that it sometimes lagged behind vernacular Chinese by the time of its publication.[20] The *Wenli* CUV, by contrast, became irrelevant despite the hopes that its missionary-translators had attached to it. It is revealing that over fifty million copies of the Mandarin CUV were printed over the last century,[21] while the last print run of the *Wenli* CUV was in 1934.[22]

The success of the Mandarin CUV in Chinese history becomes more remarkable considering the three linguistic phenomena already noted for the KJV. First, the committee produced a translation that occasionally imported Western Christian idioms that were less than natural in Chinese. To name just two oddities of "CUV Chinese," normal Chinese never uses "glory" (*rong yao*) as a verb (cf. Mandarin CUV at John 20:19; 1 Cor 6:20), while "grace" (*en, endian*) is usually a verb rather than a verbal object (cf. Mandarin CUV at John 1:16; Rom 12:6; Gal 2:21).[23] However, these expressions have undergone *lexicalization* due to their appearance in the CUV Bible so that Chinese Christians regard them as biblical language even though the first generation of its readers noted their strangeness (much as non-Christians and new converts would today). Wang Mingdao, one of the most important Chinese Christian

---

18. The Mandarin vernacular was then called *guanhua* or *baihua*, but is now known as *putonghua* in China, *guoyu* in Taiwan, and *huayu* in the Mandarin-speaking diaspora in Asia. The general term for the Chinese language without reference to geography is *hanyu*.

19. Mak, *Protestant Bible Translation*, 2–6.

20. Lianhua Zhou, "He he ben yi ben yuan ze he ping gu," in *Zi shang di shuo han yu yi lai: he he ben sheng jing jiu shi nian*, eds. Pingran Xie and Qingbao Zeng (Hong Kong: CABSA, 2010), 6.

21. Zhou, "He he ben yi ben," 16.

22. Tsai, *Sheng jing zai zhong guo*, 364.

23. Ralph Covell, "Bible Translation in the Asian Setting," *The Bible Translator* 15 (1964): 134, 140.

leaders in the twentieth century and a champion of biblical preaching, noted already in the 1930s that the CUV read at times like the work of Western translators who viewed Chinese as a foreign language and evidently struggled to communicate with their native assistants.[24]

Second, the translation committee members were more proficient in Greek than in Hebrew.[25] This limitation means that the OT of the Mandarin CUV tends to be a direct rendering from the ERV, complete with the issues that a translation of a translation would introduce.[26] The ERV of Judges 6, for instance, incorrectly renders that Gideon was threshing wheat in the winepress "to hide it from the Midianites" (v. 11), thereby overturning the Hebrew narrator's portrayal of him as someone hiding himself in fear. The Mandarin CUV moralizes further the ERV's portrayal of Gideon by depicting him as a sentinel motivated by a desire to "guard against" (*fang bei*) Midian. The ubiquity of youth fellowships named "Gideon Fellowship" (*jidian tuanqi*, perhaps also due to Heb 11:32) in the Chinese Christian world attests to the power of *sacralization* in the Mandarin CUV's transmission of a flawed interpretation. It is telling that the Revised Mandarin CUV published in 2010 corrected this mistake as part of a translation philosophy to change the Mandarin CUV only when necessary.[27]

Third, the language shifts that began in early twentieth-century China made the Mandarin CUV a victim of its own success to a degree. Among the Union Versions, it was intended to be the most accessible so that common people could understand it when read aloud. This criterion meant that ease of understanding for non-Christian hearers tended to override the assumptions about translational accuracy, repeated reading, liturgical use, and suitability for academic study which a later Christian readership usually holds about the

---

24. Rouyu Zhuang, *Ji du jiao sheng jing zhong wen yi ben: quan wei xian xiang yan jiu* (Hong Kong: International Bible Society, 2000), 22–23.

25. Zetzsche, *Bible in China*, 309–10.

26. Delin Yu, "Xie zai zi wo mo sheng he gui shun de bian xian shang: he he ben suo cheng zai de yuan sheng shen xue, wen hua xing ji qi shen xue wen fa de (bu) ke neng xing," in Xie and Zeng, *Zi shang di shuo han yu yi lai*, 194. Mak (*Protestant Bible Translation*, 139–40) notes that the 1890 Shanghai Missionary Conference passed a resolution to translate from the original languages, but in practice the OT was translated either from the ERV or with Bishop Joseph Schereschewky's 1902 translation from the Hebrew as a reference (Lihi Yariv-Laor, "Linguistic Aspects of Translating the Bible into Chinese," in *Bible in Modern China: The Literary and Intellectual Impact*, ed. Irene Eber, Monumenta Serica Monograph Series 43 [Nettetal: Steyler Verlag, 1999], 102).

27. The second translation principle of the Revised CUV is to maintain the Mandarin CUV whenever possible (Lianhua Zhou, "Fu bian: zhong wen sheng jing he he ben xiu ding ban zhi yuan qi he guo cheng," in Xie and Zeng, *Zi shang di shuo han yu yi lai*, 17).

Bible.[28] Within a generation, the Mandarin CUV's relationship to the vernacular became similar to that of the *Wenli* CUV and its literary bent which lost ground as China entered the modern era. Consequently, the favor that the Mandarin CUV still enjoys leads to the irony that it sometimes becomes an instrument in its own *defamiliarization.* Chinese Christians tend to regard its familiar wording as authoritative even when they are unsure what it means or acknowledge that it can be inaccurate.

Not unlike with the KJV, the archaisms of the Mandarin CUV that impart the air of a "literary classic" (*jing* in Chinese, one of the characters in *shengjing*, i.e. the Bible) also make Chinese Christians resistant to revisions and new translations. Deviations from the Mandarin CUV can sometimes be perceived as threats to biblical authority itself.[29] The cost of esteeming the Mandarin CUV, however, is that Chinese Christians in the twenty-first century face major struggles in using the Bible to communicate their faith. It becomes difficult to reproduce the Mandarin CUV's original function as contextual theology for evangelizing the Chinese people. The Mandarin CUV's contemporaneity for the republican Chinese context is ironically what can make it obsolete for the modern Chinese world, especially youth and children or those in the diaspora who are less proficient in literary Chinese.[30]

CHINESE CONTEXTUAL THEOLOGY
AND THE MANDARIN CUV

Historical factors make it likely that the Mandarin CUV will remain the preferred Bible of Chinese Christians. The futility of another round of Chinese "Bible wars"[31] makes it better to do Chinese contextual theology from within the Mandarin CUV tradition. On this note, the Mandarin CUV's ongoing relevance for the Chinese world lies in revisiting its message for a pre-Christian audience in republican China which has numerous similarities with the non-Christian Chinese world today. Like all Christian communities whose

---

28. Kuo-Wei Peng, "Contemplating the Future of Chinese Bible Translation: A Functionalist Approach," *The Bible Translator* 63 (2012): 9.

29. Zhuang, *Ji du jiao sheng jing zhong wen yi ben*, 91, 93, 104.

30. Kuo-Wei Peng, "Cong yi ben shi lun wei lai zhong wen sheng jing yi ben zhi chu yi," *China Evangelical Seminary Journal* 1 (June 2008): 43–44.

31. Much like in North America, the 1980s were the heyday of the "Bible wars" in the Chinese world. Several contemporary versions of the Chinese Bible were released in the 1970s (Chinese New Version, Contemporary Chinese Bible, Today's Chinese Version). Interestingly, these Bibles have rather different philosophies of translation but one thing in common: all encountered strident criticism from advocates of the Mandarin CUV.

discourse about faith undergoes lexicalization and sacralization, Chinese Christians have often become linguistically adrift from the Chinese societies around them. Even so, much of the linguistic potential for defamiliarization and refreshing the voice of Chinese Christianity already lies within the Mandarin CUV.

Perhaps the greatest barrier in (re)translating the Bible's *message* of the gospel for the ethnic Chinese has been the perception that the Mandarin CUV, like most other Chinese Bibles, has chosen the wrong *word* for "sin" (*zui* in Mandarin) to describe the human condition. Alexander Chow summarizes,

> When the average East Asian hears the word for "sinner" or, in Chinese, "*zui ren*" – 罪人 – this can very easily be misunderstood as describing a criminal or a convict. In contemporary usage, it is sometimes recognised as part of the vocabulary of a type of "Christianese" – the language of the Christian subcultures of South Korea or China. But for the most part, a *zui ren* is a criminal who has been captured, charged and declared guilty of a crime.[32]

Adrian Chan expresses a stronger version of this position by speaking of a clash between the humanism of Chinese culture and the theocentric worldview of Judaism and Christianity: "That the Chinese language does not have the word *sin* is also because of the cosmogony of that culture. It has no over-arching creation narrative that is comparable to these Abrahamic cultures."[33] These cultural differences have commonly led to the conclusion among Chinese thinkers that the Christian doctrine of sin and its lexicalization as *zui* in Chinese theology (as epitomized by the Mandarin CUV) are essentially Western constructs.[34]

At the same time, it is revealing that proposals to address this issue tend to take the NT Greek word *hamartia* (usually rendered "sin" in English, *zui* in Chinese) as their point of departure.[35] However, focusing on this term and its

---

32. Alexander Chow, "The East Asian Rediscovery of Sin," *Studies in World Christianity* 19 (2013): 127.
33. Adrian Chan, "The Sinless Chinese: A Christian Translation Dilemma?," in *Translating Sensitive Texts: Linguistic Aspects*, ed. Karl Simms, Approaches to Translation Studies 14 (Amsterdam: Rodopi, 1997), 239, italics original.
34. E.g. Chan, "Sinless Chinese"; Jinping Zhuo, "Original Sin in the East-West Dialogue: A Chinese View," *Studies in World Christianity* 1 (1995): 80–86.
35. E.g. Mark Strand, "Explaining Sin in a Chinese Context," *Missiology: An International Review* 28 (Oct. 2000): 427–41.

supposed etymology as "missing the mark"[36] privileges the more abstract notion of sin represented in the NT, as opposed to the more Eastern and concrete understanding of sin that the OT contains. Even Chinese theologians who acknowledge that the OT's worldview stands closer than the NT's to Chinese ideas still tend to work with theological categories drawn from Paul's letters and how the doctrine of sin has been developed in the Western tradition.[37]

It would be incorrect, however, to follow the view of Adolf von Harnack, Jürgen Moltmann, and others that the NT is a Hellenized distortion of a pristine Hebrew worldview. The fallacy of correlating supposed distinctions in Hebrew and Greek ways of thinking with features of their respective languages has been well demonstrated by James Barr.[38] Instead, the modest claim here is that the Mandarin CUV translators were correct to translate the Hebrew Bible's metaphors as transparently as possible so that their newness to Chinese would convey meaning on their own.[39] As a result, revisiting the concreteness of the Mandarin CUV will reverse the processes of lexicalization and sacralization which make it difficult for Chinese Christians to conceptualize sin in anything but the standard theological abstractions of the Protestant tradition.[40] The Hebrew language supplies the raw material for such a contextual Chinese theology by including Protestantism's characteristic focus on juridical ideas while also probing the relational objects and actions that lie behind them. As

---

36. Studies of *hamartia* typically state this etymology as if it unlocks the meaning of the term. Nevertheless, Moisés Silva observes that "the only passage where perhaps it could be argued that the vb. [verb] reflects the notion 'miss the mark' is Rom 3:23, but even here the clause 'fall short of the glory of God' clearly refers not to the *nature* of sin but rather to its *consequences*. Instead, the actual images associated with the concept of sin incl. [include] rebellion, corruption, violation, trespassing, disobedience, etc." (*NIDNTTE*, s.v. *hamartanō*, 1:259, italics original).

37. E.g. Dongjie Zhuang, *Kua yue hong gou: zai hua ren wen hua chu jing zhong quan shi zui* (Hong Kong: Taosheng Publishing, 2009), 452–53. An earlier chapter of the book does discuss the Hebrew terms for sin, but this section unfortunately contains many errors and plays a minimal role in the overall analysis.

38. James Barr, *The Semantics of Biblical Language* (Oxford: Oxford University Press, 1961).

39. Broomhall credits the native Chinese assistants of the committee for urging the Mandarin CUV translators to keep the Bible's metaphors intact even though they were strange in Chinese (*Bible in China*, 93). Zhou indicates that the committee's ninth translation principle was the need to keep metaphors and comparisons intact as much as possible ("He he ben yi ben," 11).

40. To mention one example, it is commonplace to cite an OT statement such as "righteousness and justice are the foundations of his throne" (Ps 97:2b) as biblical support for the divine attributes of righteousness and justice. However, the underlying Hebrew terms *mishpat* and *tsedaqah* entail concrete *actions* of right relating and just judging rather than abstract qualities (John Goldingay, *Key Questions about Christian Faith: Old Testament Answers* [Grand Rapids, MI: Baker Academic, 2010], 213–15).

Paul Ricoeur observes, the "split-reference" nature of metaphor as both figurative *tenor* and literal *vehicle* requires that it operate on both levels.[41]

THE CONCRETENESS OF HEBREW METAPHORS FOR SIN

Recent work on Hebrew metaphors for sin has highlighted their concreteness which is usually overlooked. As Gary Anderson observes,

> Sin is not just a thing . . . but a particular kind of thing. When someone sins, something concrete happens: one's hands may became stained, one's back may become burdened, or one may fall into debt. And the verbal expressions that render the idea of forgiveness follow suit: stained hands are cleansed, burdens are lifted, and debts are either paid off or remitted. It is as though a stain, weight, or bond of indebtedness is created ex nihilo when one offends against God.[42]

The concreteness of these OT metaphors contrasts markedly with the tendency to consider "sin" in English and *zui* in Chinese more as abstract concepts.

The Anglican theologian J. I. Packer provides one such example. He influentially wrote that "we are not sinners because we sin, but rather we sin because we are sinners, born with a nature enslaved to sin."[43] Packer's assertion that sin comes from human nature is theologically sound, but may also reflect a Greek philosophical tendency to essentialize things as invisible universals before considering them as visible particulars. The discipline of cognitive linguistics has advocated the opposite direction of travel, however, since things can become philosophical abstractions in the human mind only after they have been experienced in their physical concreteness.[44] As in any language, it is natural for Hebrew to conceptualize sin (or any other concept) in its literal dimensions before lexicalization enables meaning in its figurative dimensions. This linguistic reality is parallel to how the Mandarin CUV's original audience

---

41. Paul Ricoeur, *The Rule of Metaphor: The Creation of Meaning in Language*, trans. Robert Czerny with Kathleen McLaughlin and John Costello, SJ, Routledge Classics (London: Routledge, 2006), 353, 370, *passim*.

42. Gary A. Anderson, *Sin: A History* (London: Yale University Press, 2010), 4.

43. J. I. Packer, *Concise Theology* (Wheaton, IL: Crossway, 2020), 83. I would affirm that humanity is sinful by nature, but simply observe that the nature of Packer's rhetorical contrast privileges abstractness over concreteness even though it was Adam and Eve's act of sin that first made humanity sinful by nature.

44. George Lakoff and Mark Johnson, *Philosophy in the Flesh: The Embodied Mind and Its Challenge to Western Thought* (New York: Basic, 2010).

would have perceived the unfamiliarity of Hebrew sin-metaphors upon first encountering them in Chinese.

Besides the work of Gary Anderson, Joseph Lam shows that Hebrew sin-metaphors employ several verbal idioms which creatively vary their subjects and objects.[45] Previous studies of the OT's depiction of sin were mired in the *etymological fallacy* that a word's historical origins establish a "root meaning" which underlies all instances of a word's usage. The three main Hebrew terms for sin were thought to have etymologies that dictated their sense, with (1) *ḥēṭʾ* as "missing the mark," (2) *ʿāwōn* as "perversion," and (3) *pešaʿ* as "transgression, rebellion." But the theoretical root meanings for these words never exist in the abstract,[46] since actual occurrences of the terms exhibit the phenomenon of *lexicalization* already mentioned. Lam offers numerous examples of how sin-words have become interwoven in the Hebrew Bible as threads within a broader tapestry of sin-concepts.

Lam nonetheless also shows that lexicalization does not completely negate the value of etymologies in how the OT depicts the concept of sin. Their legacy lives on in four Hebrew metaphors to each of which Lam's book devotes a chapter: (1) sin as a *burden*, (2) sin as an *accounting* or *record*, (3) sin as a *path* or *direction*, and (4) sin as a *stain* or *impurity*. To Lam's list, we will add the OT's fifth depiction of sin as a *breach of trust* which will be especially important for contextualizing sin in Chinese culture. Lexicalization leads to all these metaphors contributing to a broader concept of sin (thereby relativizing the value of individual etymologies), though each metaphor offers a unique emphasis which uses a different mental mechanism for conceptualizing sin as a thing. As noted earlier, cognitive linguistics has confirmed that the brain uses the same mechanisms to process metaphors as one's interactions with the physical world. The priority of concreteness is especially relevant in translating unfamiliar metaphors since lexicalization and sacralization would not yet have been operative in the Mandarin CUV's renderings until "Christian Chinese" flattened the distinctions between concrete sin-metaphors into a more uniform set of abstractions which Christians then read back into the Bible. In summary,

---

45. Joseph Lam, *Patterns of Sin in the Hebrew Bible: Metaphor, Culture, and the Making of a Religious Concept* (New York: Oxford University Press, 2016).

46. To be precise, Hebrew is a Semitic language in having triconsonantal roots whose verbal and nominal derivatives are grouped together in lexicons. However, positing the notion of "root meaning" that inheres in the triconsonantal root is to commit the category fallacy of imposing a real semantic value upon a taxonomic construct. Strictly speaking, the triconsonantal root does not mean anything, only the real Hebrew words relating to it do (Barr, *Semantics*, 100–103).

both sides of the disagreement over whether "sin" is properly rendered as *zui* tend to fall into three common fallacies: (1) overvaluing the role of etymologies in meaning; (2) neglecting the reality of language shift and lexicalization over time, both for Hebrew and Chinese; and (3) conflating words with concepts as if they existed within a strictly one-to-one relationship. The pervasiveness of these issues makes it essential to defamiliarize both sin-terms and sin-concepts as a precursor to a Chinese theology of sin that is both biblically faithful and contextually relevant.

FOUR KINDS OF HEBREW SIN-METAPHORS

Joseph Lam's first metaphorical category of sin as *burden* is handled appropriately by the Mandarin CUV. For the Hebrew idioms *nāśā ḥēṭ'* ("bear [one's] sin") and *nāśā 'āwōn* ("bear [one's] iniquity"), the Mandarin equivalents are *dandang [ta de] zui* (Lev 24:15) and *dandang [ta de] zui nie* (Ezek 4:6). The Chinese verb *dandang* is a literal rendering of Hebrew *nāśā* ("bear, carry, lift"), faithfully reproducing the word-picture of sin as a weight upon the sinner.[47] In Genesis 18:20, the Mandarin CUV hews closely to this Hebrew metaphor by characterizing the wickedness of Sodom and Gomorrah as *zui e ji zhong* ("very heavy [in] iniquity"). By contrast, the English Revised Version follows the KJV in rendering "their sin is very *grievous*," using an archaic meaning of "grievous" as "pressing heavily upon a person . . . burdensome, oppressive." The *Oxford English Dictionary* lists examples of this usage only till the mid-nineteenth century, while noting that the definition of "grievous" has shifted toward the psychological sense of "causing mental pain or distress" and "exciting grief or intense sorrow."[48] The Mandarin CUV's literal rendering of sin as a burden appears to have stood the test of time better than the renderings of modern English Bibles.[49]

Nonetheless, the Mandarin CUV opts for lexicalization in rendering a different use of the same idiom. Interestingly, sin's portrayal as a burden means that forgiveness of sin is conceptualized as the lifting of that burden – its mirror image. The verb *nāśā* does double duty in Hebrew as an upward action of some kind, whether the "carrying/bearing" of sin's weight by a weak subject

---

47. The verb *dan dang* is used in other Chinese idioms from the same conceptual field, such as *dan dang ze ren* ("to bear responsibility").

48. "Grievous, *adj.*," OED Online, March 2022, Oxford University Press, https://www.oed.com/view/Entry/81409.

49. NLT: "their sin is so *flagrant*"; 2011 NIV: "their sin [is] so *grievous*"; 1974/1995/2020 NASB: "their sin is exceedingly *grave*"; NRSV: "how very *grave* [is] their sin!" (all italics added).

or its "lifting off" by a strong one:[50] *nāśā ḥēṭ'* is "to lift off [one's] sin-burden" (e.g. Gen 50:17; Exod 10:17), *nāśā 'āwōn* is "to lift off [one's] iniquity" (e.g. Exod 34:7; Mic 7:18), and *nāśā peša'* is "to lift off [one's] transgression" (e.g. Exod 23:21; Job 7:21).

Unfortunately, the Mandarin CUV renders these *nāśā* idioms as *raoshu* ("to pardon") or *shemian* ("to forgive") in construing sin as a legal offense. This reflects the English Bible tradition's departure from the literal Hebrew idiom in favor of a conventionalized legal sense of "pardon" or "forgive." It is true that forgiveness always involves God absolving the sinner of an offense (cf. 1 John 1:9–10; 3:4), but that aspect of the biblical depiction is less important in this sin-metaphor than the sinner's experience of a heavy burden that only God can lift.[51] As forgiveness is lexicalized into Chinese (and English before it) with sin's wrongness before God in the foreground more than its unattractiveness for the sinner, it becomes natural to think that a properly theocentric view of sin excludes the notion of human self-interest.[52]

The second metaphor of sin as an *accounting* or *record* is also better treated by the Mandarin CUV than by the ERV that underlies it. One of the main Hebrew idioms to communicate this image from financial bookkeeping uses the root *pāqad* ("to render, repay, call to account"). This verb features in the OT's assertion that Yahweh will "render/return the sins/iniquities" of ancestors to their children (e.g. Exod 20:5; 34:7; Num 14:18) or back upon sinners themselves (e.g. Lev 26:16; Isa 13:11). The Mandarin CUV reproduces this metaphor using the verb *zhuitao*, a financial idiom that typically refers to seeking payment or settling debts. For the Mandarin CUV to use the verb *zhuitao* means that the Hebrew sin-metaphor and its Chinese equivalent in these passages is not framed as a merely legal matter, even though *zui* or some derivative of it is the object of the verb. In the ERV, however, the courtroom is the implied background when the means of punishment is described as God "*visiting* the iniquity of the fathers upon the children" (e.g. Exod 20:5; Deut 5:9) or that he will "*visit* their transgression with the rod, and their iniquity with stripes" (e.g. Ps 89:32).[53] The Mandarin CUV translators pro-

---

50. Anderson, *Sin*, 18–21.
51. Lam, *Patterns of Sin*, 86.
52. Cf. Chongrong Tang, *Zui e yuan tou de tan tao* (Hong Kong: STEMI Ltd, 2012), 71–103.
53. The OED Online entry for "visit" notes that this verb was used to denote some form of judgment, punishment, or testing in English Bibles even before the KJV ("visit, *v.*," OED Online, March 2022, Oxford University Press, https://www.oed.com/view/Entry/223958).

vided a commendable rendering for this idiom which departed from their own Bible traditions.

The third picture of sin as *path* or *direction* fares especially well in the Mandarin CUV. As the Chinese missiologist Enoch Wan observes, the Mandarin CUV's frequent use of the term "way" (*dao*) echoes signature motifs in the main Chinese religions, such as the Buddhist journey of the Eightfold Path, the Taoist quest for harmony with the *Dao*, and the Confucian path to self-improvement.[54] Chinese Christian scholars have often noted the synergy of these Chinese ideas with the NT's identification of Jesus as the divine *dao* (i.e. the Chinese translation of Greek *logos*). In fact, the OT's journey metaphors exhibit a greater diversity than the NT and provide a more comprehensive match with the Chinese language's countless idioms about the directionality of life.

In the OT, sin as a deviation is just one aspect of life as a journey with God and others. For example, intimacy with the divine is described as "walking with God" (*yushen tongxing*; e.g. Gen 5:22; 6:9). The ethical requirements of such a journey can be seen when Yahweh directs Abraham and his descendants "to follow [*zunshou*] my way [*dao*] and walk [*xing*] in my righteousness" (Gen 18:20; cf. 17:1; 24:40). Similarly in Deuteronomy, Moses often warns Israel to continue "walking [*xing*] in Yahweh's ways" (e.g. Deut 10:12; 26:17) even after "going/walking" to Canaan is complete – the figurative journeys that Yahweh's people must continue even after their literal arrival in the land.

The book of Proverbs expresses a similar need for vigilance. The entirety of life is portrayed as an ongoing decision between two opposing paths that others have already taken, as when the prologue of the book exhorts the wise to "walk together in the one way [*tongxing yidao*]" rather than following fools and walking "their paths [*zou tamen de lu*]" (1:15). The rest of Proverbs develops this binary contrast between life and death (e.g. 11:19; 12:28), in one instance even reducing life to not two paths, but to a single path that requires "fixing your gaze straight in front of you" (*xiangqian zhiguan*; Prov 4:25).

The flexibility of the OT's journey metaphors is also evident in how other OT passages join them with other kinds of motion. The prophet Jeremiah, for instance, urges his hearers to exhibit the right combination of stopping and moving: "Stand at the crossroads [*lushang*] and look; ask for the ancient paths [*gudao*], ask where the good way [*shandao*] is, and walk [*xing*] in it, and you will find rest for your souls. But you said, 'We will not walk in it'" (Jer

---

54. Enoch Wan, "Tao: The Chinese Theology of God-Man," *His Dominion* 11 (1985): 24–27.

6:16). Standing, asking for directions, walking, resting, and wandering make successive appearances in this verse. Joseph Lam notes a good number of such expressions, but his chapter on sin as a path or direction mainly explores the spatial dimensions of the metaphor. This leads to a neglect of how the OT also uses the journey metaphor to depict a community that marches figuratively according to a set of shared values. Later we will explore the need for a fifth way of conceptualizing sin in more relational and communal terms.

On this note, a characteristically Western emphasis on sin in its individual dimensions seems at work in Lam's fourth and final category of sin as *stain* or *impurity*. He offers a helpful analysis of the verbs for cleanness (*ṭhr*) and uncleanness (*ṭmʾ*), outlining the flexible roles that their idioms play in metaphors of ritual and moral dirtiness. However, his focus on these Hebrew roots overlooks a variety of passages which use other terms to describe sin as a contagious *action* that spreads within the community. In Deuteronomy, for example, a single sinner can pose such a threat in attracting others that it becomes necessary "to purge the evil from among you" – addressing diverse cases such as a sweet-talker who advocates idolatry (13:5), a worshiper who tries to pass off a blemished animal as perfect (17:7), an outspoken person who refuses to heed the priest (17:12), several sexual sins (22:21, 22, 24), and various crimes associated with human trafficking (24:7). Impurity of a cultic or moral nature, both of which remain hidden, fails to explain the need to supply a visible deterrent in these cases. Since non-punishment would embolden others to follow suit, Moses directs the community to purge the sin or sinner so that "all Israel will hear and be afraid, and no one among you will do such an evil thing again" (13:11; cf. 17:13; 19:20; Josh 6:24–25).

Also related to Lam's fourth category, the Mandarin CUV captures a Hebrew feature of these Deuteronomic laws which English translations are unable to. The Chinese language has distinct second-person pronouns for the singular (*ni*) and plural (*nimen*), unlike English which now uses "you" for both. This allows the Mandarin CUV to reproduce the alternation between singular and plural reference which often characterizes the speeches of Moses in Deuteronomy. OT scholars have shown that, somewhat paradoxically, singular second-person pronouns in Deuteronomy refer to the entire people as a communal entity as well as speaking directly to singular "you," while plural second-person pronouns address the community as a group of individuals.[55]

---

55. Timothy A. Lenchak, *Choose Life! A Rhetorical-Critical Investigation of Deuteronomy 28,69 – 30,20*, Analecta Biblica 129 (Rome: Pontifical Institute, 1993), 13.

When these pronouns appear in the same passage, the rhetorical effect is that of emphasizing the community's obligation to correct individual sins as well as the individual's obligations to safeguard the community's standards. For the punishment clause of Deuteronomy 13:5 (13:6 MT), to cite one instance, the Mandarin CUV correctly reflects the Hebrew's conceptual link between singular and plural in this passage: "You [sg. *ni*] must put to death the [false] prophet; this is to purge the evil from among you [pl. *nimen*]." By differentiating pronouns, the Mandarin CUV improves conspicuously upon the renderings of the *Wenli* CUV which uses the same archaic forms throughout: "So shalt *thou* [er] put away the evil from the midst of *thee* [er]." This overlooks how the Hebrew grammar of the passage provides a theological statement about the reciprocity of individual and community.

Here and elsewhere, the OT of the Mandarin CUV supplies much of the raw material for a Chinese theology of sin that is more communal and relational in orientation. Although Chinese theologians and philosophers have recognized such a theology would be more appropriate for Chinese culture, their perspective can be skewed by a fixation on the Mandarin CUV's use of *zui* which leads to categories for sin that veer toward the individual and legal. Joseph Lam has provided a helpful start in moving beyond terms for sin to metaphors and idioms, but his work still limits itself to the four word-pictures that Hebrew etymologies were once thought to represent – sin as burden, sin as accounting or record, sin as a path or direction, and sin as a stain or impurity.

Sin as Breach of Trust

Lam is correct about the OT's four "root metaphors" for the concept of sin.[56] Surrounding all these metaphors, however, is the soil of sin as *breach of trust*. Just as soil is hidden but plays an essential role for plants, the worldview of a culture represents the fundamental cultural assumptions that may not always find expression in words. Or to illustrate using a concept from social anthropology, Hebrew and Mandarin Chinese are both *high-context* languages in which much communication lies "below the surface," in contrast to languages like English and Greek which tend to be *low-context* in relying on explicit statements.[57] This cultural difference means that Western perspectives on sin, along with those of Chinese Christians to a certain extent, tend to examine

---

56. Lam, *Patterns of Sin*, xi.
57. Edward T. Hall, *Beyond Culture* (New York: Anchor, 1976), 91–92, contrasts Chinese as high-context with Western languages as low-context. It should be noted, though, that the

the OT's root metaphors of sin without always penetrating to their soil of relationships with God and others which supports and nourishes them all. The aspect of communality in sin is rarely stated because it is part of the OT's cultural scenery which is always there.

Since it cannot be confined to a set of terms or idioms, the OT's fifth conceptualization of sin as a *breach of trust* assumes numerous forms. The most common of these is a sin of omission which, by definition, typically does not use a sin-term or sin-idiom since it involves something good that Israel has failed to do. For example, the OT prophets repeatedly use negations of the verb *šāmaʿ* (cf. Deut 6:4) in condemning Israel's failure to "listen." Refusal to "hear" and "heed" Yahweh will eventually result in Yahweh's refusal to "listen" to his people (e.g. Isa 1:10; Jer 11:14). The English language has distinct words for "hearing," "listening," "heeding," and "obeying" which each fall within the semantic domain of *šāmaʿ*, forcing English Bibles to use different terms to render wordplays on this Hebrew root.[58]

A distinctive feature of Mandarin grammar, in contrast to both English and the literary Chinese found in the *Wenli* CUV, is that collocations of two Chinese characters fix one character while varying the other or adding an adverbial particle to produce related expressions. This semantic flexibility results in the Mandarin CUV's translation of Jeremiah, for example, using collocations centered on the same character (*ting*) to create a network of idioms. These include the physical ability to hear (*tingjian*; e.g. 6:24; 18:2), heeding or giving a summons (*dangting, ting a*; e.g. 25:36; 28:7), the spiritual ability to listen for the sake of obedience (*tingcong, tinghua, tingwen*; e.g. 3:13; 6:19; 7:13; 48:29), believing gullibly what one hears (*tingxin*; e.g. 29:8), and requesting a superior to hear (*chuiting*; e.g. 37:20). The lack of such collocations in English Bibles and the *Wenli* CUV obscures these wordplays on *šāmaʿ*, making the Mandarin CUV uniquely suited to highlight Jeremiah's portrayal of a people torn between the voices of Yahweh, true prophets, and false prophets. This is in keeping with the OT's repeated castigation of covenant neglect, a sin that is functionally similar to how Chinese culture understands a lack of filial piety.

---

literary language of *Wenli* is even higher-context than Mandarin since the former, as a literary language, relies on literary context rather than on collocations and adverbial particles to express shades of meaning.

58. For example, Jeremiah 11 contains four identical *šāmaʿ* imperatives in close proximity. However, even a Bible as literal as the NASB is forced to render them as both "hear" (vv. 2, 6) and "listen to" (vv. 4, 7). Overall, the root occurs 9x in the chapter, but the English term "obey" occurs only once (v. 8) even though this connotation is clearly present in all the instances.

For example, the prophets' accusation that Israel has "not listened to my word" has special resonance in Chinese as *buting wodehua* – the Hebrew idiom is rendered with a Chinese parent's typical way of scolding a rebellious child.

Breaching trust is also described as a sin of commission – the OT's frequent accusation that Israel has broken its kinship bonds with Yahweh. In Ezekiel, for example, a special people who bear Yahweh's "name" (cf. Exod 20:7; Deut 28:10) have desecrated "my holy name" (4x in Ezek 36:20–23). The Mandarin CUV renders this passage's address to "the house of Israel" explicitly in kinship terms (*yiselie jia*), rightly underscoring that Israel's conduct as a shameless family among the nations has led to shame for Yahweh's "reputation/name" (as Chinese *ming* and Hebrew *šēm* both denote). Such shamelessness must be turned upon itself – Israel will suffer shaming through exile which pricks its hardened conscience, ends its self-reliance, and restores its dependence on Yahweh (Ezek 36:31–32). Interestingly, the OT's frequent description of rebellion against God as bringing its own punishment mirrors the concept of homeopathy (*yidugongdu*, lit. "using poison to fight poison") in traditional Chinese medicine. This yields a creational alternative to conceiving sin and punishment in the mainly legal terms which are common in Western theology.

The motif of sin as ingratitude and treachery against God is evident in penitential prayers of the OT as well. In Ezra 9, for instance, the historical context is that Judah's returnees from exile have failed to keep their vows to return to Yahweh (ch. 8), instead choosing to intermarry with pagan peoples who led them astray. The leaders have been first in this act of "unfaithfulness" (*ma'al*), a Hebrew term that denotes the relational failures of disloyalty, deception, and breaking faith. However, the Mandarin CUV renders Ezra 9's three instances of the Hebrew root using *zui* (v. 4) and two of its related idioms, *zuikui* ("archcriminal"; v. 2) and *zuinie* ("guilt requiring retribution"; v. 6).[59] This choice probably reflects the ERV's use of "trespass" (vv. 2, 4) and "guiltiness" (v. 6) to render *ma'al*, leading the Mandarin CUV to imply that Ezra 9 focuses on Judah's guilt when it actually devotes more space to talking about shame.

However, the relational theme of shame has greater prominence through the passage's opening allusion to Ezekiel 36, when Ezra describes himself as

---

59. Yingyu Ou (*Ezra*, Tien Dao Bible Commentary [Hong Kong: Tien Dao Publishing House, 1998], 267) concurs that the Mandarin CUV's renderings of *zui* obscure the relational thrust of the Hebrew.

"ashamed and humiliated" (Ezra 9:6) in precisely the manner that shameless Israel had failed to demonstrate (cf. Ezek 36:32). Tragically, the disregard that Israel/Judah showed for Yahweh's international reputation makes necessary the public spectacle of "open shame" (Ezra 9:7; cf. Dan 9:8–9). Legal ideas are certainly present in Ezra's confession (e.g. vv. 6, 11, 13–15), but it is significant that the chapter's thrust is that rebelling against Yahweh in the sight of the nations must meet its consequence of being handed over to ridicule by the same community of nations. Yahweh's choice to entwine his reputation with Israel's results in the possibility that he might be shamed, leading to Yahweh severing his reputation from Israel's to vindicate his own.[60] In this penitential context, the emotional urgency of prayer stems from Yahweh's covenant with Israel which offers yet another chance after a cycle of failure and forgiveness. The breaking and restoration of a relationship before the watchful eyes of the nations are the focus, rather than the dispassionate legal principle that the exile will repeat itself if Israel fails to repent.

RETHINKING A CHINESE THEOLOGY OF SIN FROM THE OT

Psalm 32 illustrates both the promise and the challenges of the Mandarin CUV for developing a Chinese theology of sin. All the themes discussed above are found in this psalm since it contains the Bible's highest concentration of sin-terms and sin-concepts in a single place. A literal translation of the first two verses from Hebrew into English is given below:

> [1] Oh, the good fortune of the one whose *transgression* is lifted
> off [*nāśā*],
> whose *sin* is covered over!
> [2] Oh, the good fortune of the one for whom Yahweh does not
> count *iniquity*,
> and in whose spirit there is no *deceit*!

The italicized words are the English equivalents of four different Hebrew terms for sin. The first three are common in the OT and have already been discussed: (1) *peša'* ("transgression"; v. 1a), (2) *ḥăṭā'â* (a synonym of *ḥēṭ'*, "sin"; vv. 1b, 5a, 5d), and (3) *'āwōn* ("iniquity"; vv. 2b, 5d). As Lam observes, the etymologies of these sin-terms are less important than the fact that they appear

---

60. Lyn M. Bechtel, "The Perception of Shame within the Divine-Human Relationship in Biblical Israel," in *Uncovering Ancient Stones: Essays in Memory of H. Neil Richardson*, ed. Lewis M. Hopfe (Winona Lake, IN: Eisenbrauns, 1994), 87–89.

interchangeably in sin-idioms, as in Psalm 32's metaphors of "transgression" as a burden to be "lifted off" (v. 1a), "sin" to be "covered over" (v. 1b), and "iniquity" as an accounting entry to "not count" (v. 2a), that is, to strike from the record. It is significant, however, that the final sin-term in the opening two verses is *remiyâ* ("deceit, treachery"), a word denoting betrayal that accords with our proposal that sin is also a breach of trust. Though this sin-idiom falls outside Lam's categories, his fourth category of sin as path or direction does appear later in the psalm (vv. 7–8). Psalm 32 thus contains all five of the word-pictures for conceptualizing sin that this chapter has discussed.

Before commenting further on the Mandarin CUV's rendering of the first two verses, it is necessary to preview the next three verses since they bear upon one's rendering of the first two. Lam's view about the lexicalization of *nāśâ* sin-idioms as "forgive" may be correct elsewhere, but the literal rendering of Psalm 32:1a as sin being "lifted off" (*nāśâ*) finds support in how the word-picture of sin as weight continues in the psalm. Its next section depicts the various burdens that result from refusing to converse with God:

> ³ When I kept silent, my bones wasted away
>   through my anguish all the day.
> ⁴ For by day and night
>   your hand was heavy upon me.
>   My strength waned in the heat of summer.
> ⁵ My sin I made known to you,
>   And my iniquity I did not cover
>   And you lifted off [*nāśâ*] the iniquity of my sin.

The silence of the psalmist caused sin's weight to bring both physical suffering (v. 3) and the spiritual burden of God's hand of judgment (v. 4) – perhaps two sides of the same coin. But when the supplicant no longer attempts to "cover" the sin (v. 5b; the same verb appears in v. 1b) and confesses it instead (vv. 5a, 5c), the second appearance of a *nāśâ* sin-idiom marks the "lifting off" (*nāśâ*) of the weight (v. 5c). The Mandarin CUV translates these *nāśâ* sin-idioms as "forgive" (in following the ERV), but such a rendering introduces a legal picture instead of highlighting the word-picture of sin as a burden which imparts coherence to Psalm 32:1–5. The literal picture of "sin-lifting-as-forgiveness" accords better with the psalm's own flow than the opposite direction of "forgiveness-as sin-lifting," as implied by rendering the *nāśā* sin-idioms figuratively. As John Goldingay affirms, "Yhwh pays the price of our forgiveness in being willing to 'carry sinful wrongdoing [v. 5].'"[61]

The premature lexicalization of "forgive" in Psalm 32 has led to another misunderstanding of Psalm 32. In v. 3 of the Mandarin CUV, the Hebrew's sense of not-speaking ("when I kept silent") has come into Chinese as the sin of failing to confess in the first place (*wobikou burenzui deshihou*) due to a verb that means "to admit guilt" (*renzui*) in legal contexts. This notably diverges from the literal translation ("when I kept silence"), confirming that the translators of the Mandarin CUV imported a juridical context despite this not being present in the passage. In reality, Psalm 32 never specifies the sin that leads to suffering, for verse 3's meaning in context involves the contrast between silence and talking to God rather than between confessing guilt and hiding it.[62] Otherwise, the psalm is turned upside down.

The rest of Psalm 32 confirms that reconciliation with God and the lessons this imparts for the community are the primary themes at hand. Though this psalm is classified among the so-called "penitential psalms," individual confession and the forgiveness received (v. 5) are a rather brief moment compared with a communal summons to prayer (v. 6), an expression of praise (v. 7), God's reassurance of guidance (v. 8) and warning not to wander dumbly like domestic animals (v. 9), a wisdom saying about the better way of trusting Yahweh (v. 10), and a communal call for rejoicing (v. 11). Even for a passage such as this which contains such an abundance of sin-terms, the category of sin as a breached trust that has now been restored possesses greater significance than the four sin-idioms studied by Lam. In addition, the fact that Psalm 32 is about the "happiness" (vv. 1–2) of reconciliation with God more than the legal transactions of admitting guilt and receiving forgiveness is clear in the Mandarin CUV despite the infelicities of translation already noted. The Mandarin CUV rightly translates this Hebrew term (*ăšrê*) into Chinese as "having good fortune" (*you fu de*), using a character (*fu*) that expresses the desire for happiness, prosperity, and well-being which is proverbial in Chinese culture.[63] The anticipation of the Christian "gospel" (*fu yin*) is hard to miss. Thus, the

---

61. John Goldingay, *Psalms: Volume 1 (1–41)* (Grand Rapids, MI: Baker Academic, 2006), 457. This view also reflects his rendering of v. 1a as "The good fortune of the one whose rebellion is *carried*" (451, italics added).

62. Goldingay, *Psalms*, 455.

63. During Chinese New Year celebrations, for example, the character *fu* is displayed everywhere in an inverted configuration to generate a pun. The phrase *fu daole* in spoken Chinese means both that "*fu* has arrived" and "*fu* is upside down."

question of whether the Mandarin CUV erred in rendering sin-terms using *zui* becomes moot when OT passages such as Psalm 32 are defamiliarized to speak afresh in their concreteness.

CONCLUSION

As with many early translations of the Bible, the Mandarin CUV has become an act of contextual theology in its own right. Its impact in providing Chinese Christians the language to indigenize their faith has been incalculable. Though its publication over a century ago has imparted a distinctive character to Protestant Chinese Christianity, it was never intended as an authoritative Bible for the Chinese world (unlike the King James Version in English). The translators of the Mandarin CUV always considered their efforts to be provisional until Chinese Christians could take over the work from them.[64]

Ironically, the Mandarin CUV's status of "accidental masterpiece" poses the greatest challenge to its continuing relevance for the Chinese world. It contains renderings that reflect the lexicalization and sacralization of "biblical" idioms, but more as conceived in the theological categories of its Western translators than the yet-to-be-formed categories of its original Chinese readers. With the Mandarin CUV's translation decisions having undergone their own processes of lexicalization and sacralization, what was intended as a contextual theology for pre-republican China has sometimes become a timeless, context-less theology which can be out of step linguistically and conceptually with the modern Chinese world.

Nowhere has the gap been wider than in the perception that sin-terms and sin-idioms in the Bible (= the Mandarin CUV) stand at odds with Chinese ways of thinking. Besides the lexical fallacies of this argumentation, objections to the "biblical notion of sin" typically suffer from an inattention to the contours of the Bible's own witness. Despite some issues of translation, the Mandarin CUV faithfully reproduces the OT's more communal and relational portrayal of sin by rendering the concreteness of the Hebrew Bible's sin-metaphors in ways that resonate with Chinese sin-idioms. Greater attention to Hebrew's rich descriptions of sin as burden, sin as accounting or record, sin as path or direction, and sin as breach of trust would therefore lend balance to a Western theological tendency to talk about sin more as a unitary and individual concept. A passage like Psalm 32 exemplifies how a theocentric understanding

---

64. Joseph Hong, "Revision of the Chinese Union Version Bible (CUV): Assessing the Challenges from an Historical Perspective," *The Bible Translator* 53 (2002): 239.

of sin and the characteristic Chinese notion of *fu* ("good fortune") can coexist happily without conflict.[65]

For this reason, the move to challenge a merely juridical understanding of sin is not necessarily emblematic of theological liberalism or downplaying the Bible's teaching on sin, as some Chinese theologians would claim.[66] It is instead an appeal to allow the Bible to challenge our theological formulations which begin as concrete and contextual before they become abstract and absolute, not unlike how Christ is portrayed as "the Word became flesh and made his dwelling among us" (John 1:14). Theology of this sort increases its own chances of a welcome reception among Christians when it works through a received Bible tradition rather than against it.[67] Thus, the best of Chinese contextual theology can still come from one of the original acts of contextual theology – the Mandarin CUV as a transplantation of the Bible's universal message into a Chinese cultural matrix.

The next two chapters will explore two other kinds of translatability that are of paramount importance for doing contextual theology from the Old Testament. Building on our discussion of how to translate the *human* condition across cultures, chapter 3 will examine the OT's model for translating *divine* terminology across religio-cultural systems, particularly the question of whether Christians and Muslims venerate the same deity. The OT's portrayal of Yahweh using the names and attributes of ancient Near Eastern deities is the forerunner of Asian missiology's "Term Question" concerning the use of indigenous names for deity to denote the God of the Bible. But since translating monotheism across cultures is always an issue of worldview and not merely language, chapter 4 will outline how OT monotheism functions within the pantheons of the ancient Near East, a context whose religious pluralism has numerous similarities with that of modern Asia. In the process we will also investigate the OT's relationship to the "piety-prosperity equation" which has characterized Asian religions from ancient times till now.

---

65. Cf. Zhuo, "Original Sin," 80–81. On a different note, Danny Hsu argues that the usual association between Chinese culture and humanism relies too much on Confucian ideas ("Contextualising 'Sin' in Chinese Culture: A Historian's Perspective," *Studies in World Christianity* 22 [2016]: 105–24). This shows further the risk of oversimplification in positing an East-West divide between optimism and pessimism about human nature.
66. E.g. Lit-Sen Chang, *Asia's Religions: Christianity's Momentous Encounter with Paganism* (San Gabriel, CA: China Horizon, 1999).
67. Cf. Zhuang, *Kua yue hong gou*; Strand, "Explaining Sin."

CHAPTER 3

DIVINE TRANSLATABILITY AND TERM QUESTIONS FOR DEITY

Christians have historically taken several approaches to the contested question of whether the God of Christianity and the God of Islam are the same deity.[1] In the most recent round in 2015, Wheaton College became embroiled in controversy after Larycia Hawkins, a professor of political science, stated that Muslims and Christians worship the same God. In doing so she concurred with Pope Francis's statement as well as President George W. Bush's view from 2003. The resulting furor eventually led her to leave her tenured position at Wheaton.[2] By contrast in the following year, Nabeel Qureshi, a Christian apologist who had converted from Islam, continued to frame the choice between Allah and Jesus in either-or terms, as seen in his book's title *No God but One: Allah or Jesus?* (itself a sequel to his *Seeking Allah, Finding Jesus*).[3] These debates have continued during the last several years with systematic theologians, philosophers of religion, and missiologists all weighing in on the "Same God Question" (SGQ).

Notably missing from this discussion has been the contribution of Old Testament specialists regarding the SGQ.[4] The OT had long ago addressed what missiologists call the "Term Question" (TQ) – the proper way to denote a given deity. In statements such as "Yahweh your God . . . is a lord of lords and a great and awesome El" (Deut 10:17) and "El, God, Yahweh has spoken" (Ps 50:1), Israel's deity is identified by a fourfold combination of (1) personal name ("Yahweh"), (2) category and epithet ("god/God," Heb. *'ĕlōhîm*), (3) title

---

1. An earlier version of this chapter appeared as Jerry Hwang, "Are Yahweh and El/Allah the Same God? The OT's Contextualization of Monotheism," *Trinity Journal* 42 (2021): 59–78.
2. See the summary of events by Brian M. Howell, "Wheaton College, One God, and Muslim-Christian Dialog," *Evangelical Missions Quarterly* Occasional Bulletin (Special Edition 2016): 4–5.
3. Nabeel Qureshi, *No God but One: Allah or Jesus? A Former Muslim Investigates the Evidence for Islam and Christianity* (Grand Rapids, MI: Zondervan, 2016); *Seeking Allah, Finding Jesus: A Devout Muslim Encounters Christianity* (Grand Rapids, MI: Zondervan, 2018).
4. For example, no OT specialists are among the contributors to Ronnie P. Campbell and Christopher Gnanakan, eds., *Do Christians, Muslims, and Jews Worship the Same God? Four Views*, Counterpoints (Grand Rapids, MI: Zondervan, 2019).

("lord," Heb. *'ādôn*), and (4) a term which is both a Semitic high god's name as well as a general Hebrew term for deity ("El/god," *'ēl*).[5] In this earliest of answers to the TQ, the OT portrays Yahweh's uniqueness within the ancient Near Eastern pantheon as both similarities to and differences from deities such as El and Baal.[6] The Semitic term *'ēl* also underlies the Arabic terms *'ilah* ("god, God") and *allāh*. These factors make the OT's solution to the TQ an instructive precursor to modern debates about the SGQ.

Our first section examines the OT's portrayal of Yahweh using compound names with "El" in them. These El-compounds identify him as a Semitic high god, while also polemicizing against characteristics of both El and Baal. The OT's various uses of these terms for deity illustrate the linguistic nuances about monotheism that are lost when the cognate terms Hebrew *'ēl* and Arabic *allāh* are both rendered into English as "God." For these reasons, our second section applies the OT's theological witness to modern languages in which translators have wrestled with the TQ, such as Arabic, Chinese, Korean, and Malay/Indonesian. Arabic and Malay/Indonesian are particularly informative for the SGQ since they are living languages with Islamic connections, being spoken by Christians living in majority-Muslim nations. The reality that Arabic and Malay/Indonesian Bibles have for centuries identified the God of the OT as Allah not only lends the SGQ a rather different resonance for believers in the Muslim world, but can also provide a lens to reexamine the modern West's own posture toward Islam.

YAHWEH AS AND AGAINST EL: THE OT AND THE "TERM QUESTION"

The OT contains numerous statements that Yahweh is an incomparable deity (e.g. Exod 15:11; Deut 33:29; Ps 35:10; 71:19; 89:8; Isa 40:18; 46:5; Jer 10:7).[7] Such assertions nonetheless do not mean that Yahwism was the sole religious tradition represented in Israel. Although the OT is often viewed as unwavering in its monotheism,[8] it contains numerous lines of evidence that Israel originally venerated Yahweh as El, the head deity of the Semitic pantheon.

---

5. These renderings from Hebrew are my own.
6. Edward L. Greenstein, "The God of Israel and the Gods of Canaan: How Different Were They?," in *Proceedings of the Twelfth World Congress of Jewish Studies* (Jerusalem: World Union of Jewish Studies, 1999), 47–58.
7. C. J. Labuschagne, *The Incomparability of Yahweh in the Old Testament*. Pretoria Oriental Studies 5 (Leiden: Brill, 1966).
8. E.g. Regina M. Schwartz, *The Curse of Cain: The Violent Legacy of Monotheism* (Chicago: University of Chicago Press, 1998).

The names of people and places in the patriarchal narratives frequently contain the Hebrew lexeme *'ēl*, as in the patronym "Israel" (Gen 32:28; 35:10) and Jacob's pilgrimage place at "Bethel" (Gen 28:19; 31:13).

This observation raises a question of translation: should Hebrew *'ēl* be rendered "El" as the proper name of a Semitic deity, "god" as a class of spiritual being, or "God" as a title for divinity? These issues are closely related to the OT's careful answer to the TQ of whether Yahweh and El are the same deity. Later in this chapter, we will explore how the issues in every act of religious translation are reflected in how the OT portrays Yahweh both *as* El, as well as *against* El. The distinctiveness of any deity in appropriating the names, titles, and attributes of another comes from a continuum of similarity and difference rather than an absolute contrast. In other words, a bridge between El and Yahweh would never be a candidate for translatability across cultures if these two deities were unrelated and/or diametrically different. The usual definition of monotheism in the West as "the doctrine or belief that there is only one God"[9] is less than appropriate in non-Western contexts due to the reality of cross-cultural contact and translatability between deities.[10]

The OT's Presentation of Yahweh *as* El

The frequency of El-compounds in Genesis presents a first line of evidence for translatability. In the Bible's first use of *'ēl*, Genesis 14 narrates Abra(ha)m's encounter with Melchizedek king of Salem who serves as a priest of El Elyon ("El/God Most High"; Gen 14:18–21). This is an epithet for a deity whom Abram recognizes as synonymous with Yahweh (14:22). Yahweh is also identified later in Genesis as El Roi ("El/God who sees me"; 16:11, 13), El Shaddai ("El/God Almighty"; 17:1; 28:3), El Olam ("El/God of Eternity"; 21:33), El the God of Israel (33:20), El of Bethel ("El/God of the house of El/God"; 35:7), and the El of your father (46:3). Many of these epithets could be rendered as "El" or "God" (and both simultaneously) who possesses particular attributes (e.g. omniscience, eternality),[11] but the unique constructions "El the God of Israel" (33:20) and "the El the God of your father" (46:3) furnish

---

9. This is the first entry under "monotheism, *n.*" at OED Online, March 2022, Oxford University Press, https://www.oed.com/view/Entry/121673.

10. Mark S. Smith, *God in Translation: Deities in Cross-Cultural Discourse in the Biblical World* (Grand Rapids, MI: Eerdmans, 2010), 129–30.

11. David Noel Freedman notes that "while El is a proper noun, the chief name of the chief god of the pantheon, it is also a general term meaning any god or the class of divine beings. Thus in a given nation, the principal god would be called by his own name but also by the term

a key to understanding the rest as references to "El." These two epithets both contain the lexeme *'ēl* followed by an appositive with *'ĕlōhîm*. Thus, it is likely that *'ēl* is a proper name rather than an appellative title (i.e. "god/God").[12]

A second line of evidence is that OT narratives after the patriarchal period continue to identify Yahweh using *'ēl* or El-compounds. Foremost among these is Yahweh's reintroduction of himself to Israel as the plagues against Egypt are about to begin: "I appeared to Abraham, to Isaac, and to Jacob, as *El Shaddai*, but by my name, *Yahweh*, I did not reveal myself to them" (Exod 6:3; cf. Gen 17:1; 35:11). This statement indicates that Genesis uses *'ēl* as a proper name rather than the appellative "god/God."[13] Similarly, Joshua depicts the ark of the covenant as a guarantee that Yahweh/El will help Israel defeat its enemies: "Come here and listen to the words of *Yahweh your God* . . . Here is how you shall know that [a/the] living *El* is among you" (Josh 3:9–10a; cf. 22:22). In this passage, the lack of a definite article on *'ēl* (Josh 3:9) makes it possible to render either "*a* living El/God" or "*the* living El/God."[14] However, this hortatory section in Joshua echoes the book of Deuteronomy and its repeated statements that Yahweh is *hā'ēl*, that is, "the [real] God/El" (7:9; 10:7; cf. 3:24; 4:23–24, 31; 6:15; 7:21). Similarly in the "Ritual Decalogue" (Exod 34:11–26), this understanding of translatability is reflected in Yahweh's warning that "you should not worship another El, for Yahweh, whose name is jealous, is a jealous El" (Exod 34:14). More evidence for rendering *'ēl* as "El" will be considered below.

A third line of evidence is found in Hebrew poetry when Yahweh and several El-epithets are set in parallel. This kind of construction was once described as *synonymous parallelism* in which adjacent elements express basically the same idea. However, there is now a consensus in OT scholarship that

---

'ēl' ("'Who Is Like Thee among the Gods?' The Religion of Early Israel," in *Ancient Israelite Religion: Essays in Honor of Frank Moore Cross*, ed. Patrick D. Miller [Philadelphia: Fortress, 1987], 330).

12. Gordon J. Wenham, "The Religion of the Patriarchs," in *Essays on the Patriarchal Narratives*, ed. D. J. Wiseman and Alan R. Millard (Downers Grove, IL: InterVarsity Press, 1980), 168; Thomas E. McComiskey, "The Religion of the Patriarchs," in *The Law and the Prophets: Old Testament Studies in Honor of Oswald T. Allis*, ed. John H. Skilton (Nutley, NJ: Presbyterian & Reformed, 1974), 198; cf. John Van Seters, "The Religion of the Patriarchs in Genesis," *Biblica* 61 (1980): 222, 224.

13. For detailed discussion of the logical relationship between El Shaddai and Yahweh in this verse, see W. Randall Garr, "The Grammar and Interpretation of Exodus 6:3," *Journal of Biblical Literature* 111 (1992): 385–408.

14. Grammatically, it is ambiguous whether *'ēl* is a definite proper noun or an indefinite class noun.

parallel Hebrew lines and terms are never purely identical.[15] Semantic differences remain even when the same term is repeated for emphasis (e.g. Isa 28:10, 14), so this linguistic axiom becomes even more pronounced when different terms are used. Such tension between identity and contrast appears, for instance, when Balaam's poetic speech identifies El with Yahweh as the deity of the exodus: "How can I curse whom *El* has not cursed? How can I denounce whom *Yahweh* has not denounced?" (Num 23:8). Moreover, the fact that Balaam is described across cultures as a "seer of the gods" (as in the Deir 'Alla inscription) and "one who hears the words of *El*, who sees the vision of *Shaddai*" (Num 24:4; *Shaddai* occurs in the Deir 'Alla inscription) suggests that *ʾēl* bridges Israelite and non-Israelite contexts for the sake of divine translatability.[16] Similarly, poetic parallelism in the Prophets and Writings continues to use *ʾēl* as a lexical bridge to specify Yahweh's identity in several ways: (1) as the El for Israel (e.g. Isa 43:10; Ps 82:1; 99:8); (2) as the Semitic deity by this name (Isa 14:13; Ps 36:7[6]; Job 8:3); and (3) using *ʾēl* as a general appellative for "God" (Isa 31:3; Ps 5:4–5[3–4]; 31:6). The rich variety of meanings and functions for the Hebrew lexeme *ʾēl* anticipates the diversity of senses for its Arabic cognates *allāh* and *ʾilah*.

The OT's Presentation of Yahweh *against* El

This is not to say, though, that the OT makes a wholesale identification between Yahweh and El.[17] The OT's use of *ʾēl* has sometimes led to the view that the OT's portrayal of Yahweh absorbs Canaanite traditions of El while polemicizing against Baal.[18] But as with Hebrew poetic parallelism, the conceptual and lexical similarities that enable translatability across cultures do not exclude the presence of differences. The identity of a holy, wise, and transcendent Creator who rules over all entities in heaven and earth is certainly predicated of both Yahweh/El in the OT (e.g. Gen 14:19, 22; Ps 19:2[1]; Isa 42:5) and El in

---

15. Adele Berlin, *The Dynamics of Biblical Parallelism*, 2nd ed. (Grand Rapids, MI: Eerdmans, 2008).

16. Smith, *God in Translation*, 129.

17. For a nuanced comparison of Yahweh and El, see John Day, *Yahweh and the Gods and Goddesses of Canaan*, JSOT Supplement Series (Sheffield: Sheffield Academic Press, 2000), 13–41.

18. As argued by e.g. Chelcent Fuad, "El, Baal, and Allah: The Translatability of Divine Names in Ancient Israel and Contemporary Indonesia," *International Review of Mission* 108 (June 2019): 178–93; F. M. Cross, *Canaanite Myth and Hebrew Epic: Essays in the History of Religion of Israel* (Cambridge, MA: Harvard University Press, 1973), 44–75.

Ugaritic literature (e.g. *KTU* 1.2; 1.16; 1.128).[19] At the same time, there are several important respects in which the OT's depiction of Yahweh assumes a posture against El rather than for El.

First and most importantly, the OT never describes Yahweh as having a consort. This contrasts with the Ugaritic description of El's dealings with the goddess Asherah.[20] Interestingly, though, a potsherd found at Kuntillet 'Ajrud (an archaeological site in the Sinai) describes the heterodox Israelite community there venerating "Yahweh of Samaria and his Asherah."[21] An inscription such as this provides evidence that translatability between Yahweh and El could be enticing enough to veer into syncretism. However, El not only has a divine consort, he also has two human wives with whom he begets the gods Dawn and Dusk as part of his sovereignty over the created order.[22] So at least in his sexual behavior, El resembles his son Baal with his numerous consorts (though scholars often contrast sharply these two Canaanite deities).

Another significant difference between Yahweh/El in the OT and El at Ugarit lies in the realm of iconography. El is depicted at Ugarit using a bull, and the close identification between Yahweh and El already in the patriarchal period is likely one reason why it was easy for both the Israelites at Sinai (Exod 32:4, 8) as well as King Jeroboam of the northern kingdom several centuries later (1 Kgs 12:28, 32; Hos 8:5) to depict Yahweh using bovine imagery.[23] There are a handful of biblical passages that use bovine imagery as a metaphor for Yahweh's strength (e.g. Gen 49:25),[24] but the OT is unique in the ancient

---

19. W. Herrman, "El," in *DDD*, 275.

20. Meindert Dijkstra, "El, YHWH and Their Asherah: On Continuity and Discontinuity in Canaanite and Ancient Israelite Religion," in *Ugarit – Ein ostmediterranes Kulturzentrum im Alten Orient: Ergebnisse und Perspektiven der Forschung*, eds. Manfred Dietrich and Oswald Loretz, Abhandlungen zur Literatur Alt-Syrien-Palästinas 7 (Münster: Ugarit-Verlag, 1995), 43–73.

21. See discussion in Richard S. Hess, *Israelite Religions: An Archaeological and Biblical Survey* (Grand Rapids, MI: Baker Academic, 2007), 319–21.

22. David Toshio Tsumura, "Kings and Cults in Ancient Ugarit," in *Priests and Officials in the Ancient Near East: Papers of the Second Colloquium on the Ancient Near East – The City and Its Life, Held at the Middle Eastern Culture Center in Japan (Mitaka, Tokyo)*, ed. Kazuko Watanabe (Heidelberg: Universitätsverlag C. Winter, 1999), 215–38.

23. Tryggve N. D. Mettinger, "The Elusive Essence: YHWH, El and Baal and the Distinctiveness of Israelite Faith," in *Die Hebräische Bibel und ihre zweifache Nachgeschichte: Festschrift für Rolf Rendtorff zum 65. Geburtstag*, ed. Erhard Blum (Neukirchen-Vluyn: Neukirchener Verlag, 1990), 398–99.

24. Dijkstra, "El, YHWH and Their Asherah," 61.

Near East for its insistence that Yahweh himself cannot be physically represented in an image (e.g. Exod 20:4–5).[25]

The third and final divergence is that Yahweh/El in the OT takes on the roles of divine warrior and storm god with an immanence of presence that resembles Baal, the son of El, more than the distant transcendence of El himself. Strikingly, several passages in the OT describe Yahweh using a combination of the titles of El and the functions of Baal. Psalm 29 furnishes one such polemical instance in asserting that Yahweh is the "El of glory" (v. 3) but also like Baal in thundering through the skies (vv. 3–5) and ruling over the waters of chaos below (vv. 10–11). The echoes of Canaanite imagery are significant enough that a preeminent scholar such as Frank Moore Cross could even say that "Psalm 29 fills a real gap in the extant *Canaanite* literature."[26] Yet as Dennis Pardee observes, conspicuously absent in Psalm 29's allusions to the Baal Cycle are any references to Baal's death, descent into the underworld, and restoration to life.[27] This argument from silence is reinforced by the OT's overt opposition to Baal in many passages (e.g. Num 25; 1 Kgs 18; Hos 2). Thus, the OT adds the functions of Baal to its depiction of Yahweh as El while excluding Baal epithets and the foibles that characterized both of these Canaanite deities.[28] Or to restate this in linguistic terms, the OT's approach of using El-compounds but redefining El's nature and functions operates more on the level of description and predicates (i.e. connotation) than that of reference and subject (i.e. denotation). This approach yields a polemic toward El that is more subtle than overt hostility to Baal but nonetheless present.[29] In our final section, we will return to this issue by comparing epithets for El and Baal with those predicated of Yahweh and Allah.

---

25. Tryggve N. D. Mettinger, *No Graven Image? Israelite Aniconism in Its Ancient Near Eastern Context*, Coniectanea Biblica: Old Testament Series 42 (Stockholm: Almqvist & Wiksell International, 1995), 196.

26. Frank M. Cross, "Notes on a Canaanite Psalm in the Old Testament," *Bulletin of the American Schools of Oriental Research* 117 (1950): 19, italics added.

27. Dennis Pardee, "On Psalm 29: Structure and Meaning," in *The Book of Psalms: Composition and Reception*, eds. Peter W. Flint et al., Supplements to Vetus Testamentum 99 (Leiden: Brill, 2005), 165–66.

28. Israelite personal and place names occasionally contain "Baal" (e.g., "Jerubbaal" as one of Gideon's names in Jdgs 6:32) and some Israelites apparently addressed Yahweh as "my Baal" (Hos 2:16). However, both these uses come in historical contexts of Israel's apostasy and the OT depicts them as distinctly in the minority.

29. Cf. Fuad, "El, Baal, and Allah," 184.

The Old Testament, Monotheism, and the Term Question (TQ)

To anticipate the next section's discussion of Arabic *allāh*, the fact that Hebrew *'ēl* can be translated as "El," "god," and "God" has significant implications for addressing whether Yahweh and Allah are the same deity. As seen above, the OT uses the lexeme *'ēl* to expand the usual definition of monotheism to describe Yahweh as both ontologically unique as well as functionally superior to Ugaritic El's sovereignty over heaven and earth.[30] Therefore, monotheism in the OT centers on Yahweh as an El and a member of the class of divine beings known as Elim (Exod 15:11), even as no other El is like Yahweh (Ps 29:1).[31]

It is useful to summarize this understanding of monotheism in the linguistic and missiological categories that pertain to the TQ. Linguistically, the meaning of *'ēl* shifts in both *sense* and *reference*, to borrow Gottlob Frege's famous categories for how to distinguish between two related entities.[32] In the second millennium BC, the reality of Canaan's many deities indicates that the Ugaritic lexeme *'ēl* possesses a unity of sense and reference for the high god over the pantheon and the Canaanite chief deity named El.[33] As this lexeme passes into the Hebrew language, the sense and reference of *'ēl* begin to diverge with Yahweh's entrance into the narrative and historical picture. The Pentateuch attests a change of reference for *'ēl* when Yahweh goes from being venerated as "El" (the proper name *'ēl*) to the recognition that he is the only "god" (the class *'ēl*) who merits the title "[the] God" (the appellative use of *'ēl*). These transitions in usage are consistent with how a common noun for deity can become a proper name only when a monotheizing tendency leaves no possibility of confusing this deity with others.[34] The OT identifies this as the period after Yahweh is shown to be sufficiently distinctive among the "gods" to merit the title "God." In the same manner, the superiority of Yahweh over the entire pantheon is reinforced by the *sense* of Hebrew *'ēl* taking on attributes

---

30. Daniel I. Block, "Other Religions in Old Testament Theology," in *Biblical Faith and Other Religions: An Evangelical Assessment*, ed. David W. Baker (Grand Rapids, MI: Kregel, 2004), 58.

31. This modifies the formulation of Michael S. Heiser: "Yahweh was an *'ĕlôhîm*, but no other *'ĕlôhîm* was Yahweh – *and never was nor could be*" ("Monotheism, Polytheism, Monolatry, or Henotheism? Toward an Assessment of Divine Plurality in the Hebrew Bible," *Bulletin for Biblical Research* 18 [2008]: 29, italics original).

32. Gottlob Frege, "Sense and Reference," *The Philosophical Review* 57 (May 1948): 209–30.

33. This corresponds to Frege's exploration of how proper names typically function with unity of sense and reference ("Sense and Reference," 214).

34. Cf. H. C. Brichto, *The Names of God: Poetic Readings in Biblical Beginnings* (New York: Oxford University Press, 1998), 27.

and activities of Canaanite Baal, but without using this Canaanite deity's titles which would allow *reference* to Yahweh as Baal.

Missiologically, the complexity of rendering Hebrew *'ēl* illustrates how every form of the SGQ (Same God Question) is likely to mislead. Even the attempt to strike a middle ground to the question as commonly framed, by answering both Yes and No,[35] suffers from oversimplifications which will be discussed further in the final section of this chapter. To speak of "El" only as a proper name, as in the formulation "Are Yahweh and El the same God?," overlooks the diachronic development of Hebrew *'ēl* as well as effacing the ambiguity in how the lexeme can simultaneously mean "El," "god," and "God." Similarly, the SGQ's use of "God" as an appellative title privileges a synchronic usage which, coupled with the use of English capitalization, reflects a Western understanding of monotheism that is unable to conceive of any other "gods" as a real possibility. Interestingly, both Western and Islamic definitions of monotheism have tended toward this more philosophical approach. The category confusion that results is the topic of our next section on the TQ in both English and Arabic.

IS YAHWEH THE SAME GOD AS ALLAH? THE OT AND THE "SAME GOD QUESTION"

Besides linguistic issues related to *'ēl*, the question of translatability between Yahweh and Allah also hinges on how English uses these two terms for deity. In other words, the theology of the "Same God Question" (SGQ) is closely tied to the linguistics of the "Term Question" (TQ). This is even more the case in English than in Arabic since discussions on the SGQ often employ several Arabic terms without due consideration for whether adequate English equivalents are being used. The interreligious nature of the TQ and SGQ means that they always run parallel in joining matters of linguistics with theology.

Term Questions in English and Arabic

Two disagreements about the TQ between Christians and Muslims are particularly confusing. The first is that readers of English Bibles are unaccustomed to naming Israel's deity as "Yahweh" or the unvocalized tetragrammaton "YHWH." This is despite Jewish and Christian scholars of the Hebrew Bible generally having no qualms in doing so (notwithstanding the third item in the

---

35. E.g. Howell, "Wheaton College," 5.

Decalogue).[36] Yet when the Holman Christian Standard Bible (1999, 2009) bucked five centuries of tradition by rendering select instances of the tetragrammaton as "Yahweh," outcry from readers eventually led Broadman & Holman Publishing to eliminate this practice in the Christian Standard Bible (2017) and revert to the KJV's renderings of the tetragrammaton as "LORD" (using small capitals) and Hebrew *'ădōnay* as "Lord." In sum, retaining familiarity has generally been more important for English Bibles than distinguishing the name "LORD" from the title "Lord." Confusion inevitably results when reading aloud a passage such as Psalm 110:1a, "The LORD says to my Lord" (cf. Matt 22:44; Mark 12:36; Luke 20:42; Acts 2:34).

Related to this is how the English word "god" is not intrinsically sacred but has Teutonic origins. It has also assimilated elements from Greek *theos* and Latin *deus*. Nonetheless, pagan origins have not kept the capitalized form "God" from lexicalization in monotheistic systems and Western philosophy to mean "the Supreme Being, regarded as the creator and ruler of the universe."[37] English thus uses "God" with the synchronic sense of a proper name for a sole deity despite its diachronic origins as the title and category of (a) pagan "god(s)." The norm of addressing "God" coupled with the infrequency of the tetragrammaton means that Anglophone Christians can often be unaware of religious diversity outside the Judeo-Christian tradition. They have simply never considered the TQ in English before. However, the starting point of assuming that capitalized "God" refers to the deity of the Bible turns the SGQ into a category fallacy which rules out a genuine comparison between Christianity and Islam.[38]

The issue of balancing synchronic and diachronic elements in the TQ also features in a second area of linguistic confusion. This is a kind of conflation in which Islamic thinkers and some Western Christians both understand "Allah" synonymously with the deity of Islam. On the one hand, the Qur'an directs

---

36. However, the Catholic Church decreed in 2008 that "Yahweh" is not to be used in liturgical contexts and Bible translations. See Catholic News Agency, "'Yahweh' Not to Be Used in Liturgy, Songs and Prayers, Cardinal Arinze Says," 3 September 2008, accessed 8 December 2020, https://www.catholicnewsagency.com/news/yahweh_not_to_be_used_in_liturgy_songs_and_prayers_cardinal_arinze_says.

37. "God, *n.* and *int.*," OED Online, March 2022, Oxford University Press, https://www.oed.com/view/Entry/79625.

38. For example, Albert Mohler, Jr. asserts, "In common English we use the word God as both a proper name and a noun. We differentiate between the two usages by capitalizing the word when we mean to refer to the specific personal God of the Bible, and by not capitalizing generic uses of the word ("What Does God Care What We Call Him?," 22 August 2007, https://albertmohler.com/2007/08/22/what-does-god-care-what-we-call-him).

Muslims to address "People of the Book" (i.e. Jews and Christians), "We believe in that which has been revealed to us and revealed to you. And our God [*ilah*] and your God [*ilah*] is one; and we are Muslims [in submission] to him" (al-ʿAnkabūt 29:46).[39] The Islamic understanding that all monotheists venerate the same deity, whose name is Allah, is codified in the first part of the Shahadah, the Muslim's confession that "there is no God [*ilah*] but Allah." Interestingly, Western Christians for whom "Allah" is a foreign word often concur that this term always has the God of Islam in view, despite the circularity of reasoning that Islamic monotheism must be directed at the wrong deity because of the differing name "Allah."[40]

Unfortunately, this tendency to equate "Allah" with the god of Islam overlooks the evolution of the lexeme *allāh*. Simply put, the historical development of Arabic reveals that *allāh* (i.e. the lexeme) used to *mean* "god" as a title or category for divinity, but the issue has now become whether Allah (i.e. the lexicalized, capitalized term) *is* God as a divine name. Prior to the advent of Islam in the seventh century AD, the generic word *allāh* was already in use by Nabataean Arabs, following the influence of Aramaic and Syriac Christians who referred to deity as *alaha* or *alah* (= "the god"/"God"; e.g. Ezra 4:24; 5:8).[41] This convention persists today among Arab Christians since they use *allāh* for the God of the Bible while challenging this term's potential Islamic associations.[42] The fact that Arab Christians long ago settled the TQ but are still addressing the SGQ shows that the latter contains a characteristic mixture of theology and terminology. Many would view the SGQ through only one lens or the other, as Kenneth Thomas observes:

> When those whose mother tongue is Arabic and who live among
> Muslims have no problem with the name Allah being used for
> God in the Bible, this raises a question what possible problem

39. Umar F. Abd-Allah, "Do Christians and Muslims Worship the Same God?," *Christian Century* 121 (24 Aug. 2004): 36.
40. Harold A. Netland, "On Worshiping the Same God: What Exactly Is the Question?," *Missiology: An International Review* 45 (2017): 443–44; F. S. Khair-Ullah, "Linguistic Hang-Ups in Communicating with Muslims," *Missiology: An International Review* 4 (1 July 1976): 307; cf. Miroslav Volf, *Allah: A Christian Response* (New York: HarperOne, 2012), 81.
41. Rick Brown, "Who Was 'Allah' before Islam? Evidence That the Term 'Allah' Originated with Jewish and Christian Arabs," in *Toward Respectful Understanding and Witness among Muslims: Essays in Honor of J. Dudley Woodberry*, ed. Evelyne A. Reisacher (Pasadena, CA: William Carey Library, 2012), 147–78; Imad N. Shehadeh, "Do Christians and Muslims Believe in the Same God?," *Bibliotheca Sacra* 161 (2004): 18–20.
42. Martin Parsons, *Unveiling God: Contextualising Christology for Islamic Culture* (Pasadena, CA: William Carey Library, 2005), xxx–xxxi.

there might be with the use of Allah elsewhere in the translation of the Bible. It would seem that those who object to its use do so in order to maintain a radical distinction between the Christian and Islamic concept of the supreme being.[43]

To answer the SGQ meaningfully, it is imperative to compare divine names and attributes with respect to how each predication about deity functions within its own theological system.[44] Previous attempts at interfaith dialogue between Christians and Muslims have instead sought for "lowest common denominators" which catalogue the theological affirmations that could apply to both Yahweh and Allah. This is the approach, for instance, of "A Common Word between Us and You," a document produced in 2007 by Muslim leaders and affirmed by numerous Christian leaders (including Pope Benedict XVI, the Catholic pontiff at the time).[45]

A Comparison of the Divine Epithets El, Yahweh, and Allah

The best way to compare divine names and their predicates across religions is to examine the divine epithets that are shared for El, Yahweh, and Allah. Since each of these is the Semitic name of a deity, the respective epithets given to them in the Ugaritic, Hebrew, and Arabic languages tend to be cognates with one another. When identical divine epithets occur across these Semitic languages, as frequently happens, it is useful to examine the network of associations that each epithet evokes within a larger theological system. Focusing on epithets and their functions has the benefit of being more holistic in moving beyond ontological questions of name, sense, and reference. This approach also avoids the banality of the near-universal agreement among world religions on the primacy of love, as stated in "A Common Word": "The Unity of God, the necessity of love for Him, and the necessity of love of the neighbour is thus the common ground between Islam and Christianity."[46] When generalities about divine love and compassion become the basis for comparisons (à la Max Müller's religious humanism), deeper differences are easily passed over. The

---

43. Kenneth J. Thomas, "Allah in Translations of the Bible," *International Journal of Frontier Missions* 23 (Winter 2006): 173–74.

44. J. Gordon McConville, "Yahweh and the Gods in the Old Testament," *European Journal of Theology* 2 (1993): 109.

45. The Royal Aal Al-Bayt Institute for Islamic Thought, "A Common Word between Us and You" (Jordan, Jan. 2009), https://www.acommonword.com/downloads/CW-Booklet-Final-v6_8-1-09.pdf.

46. "A Common Word," 6.

generic approach to religions leads to tautologies such as the frequent English rendering of the Shahadah as "there is no God but God."

On this note, Semitic languages have a common reservoir of language that is used to describe the mercy and compassion of Semitic deities.[47] Ugaritic literature often portrays the head of the pantheon as "the benevolent one, El, the merciful one" (*ltpn 'il dp'id*). These epithets for El have Arabic cognates that are applied to Allah as "benevolent" (*latif*) and "gracious" (*dū fu'ād*),[48] with "the benevolent one" (*al-latīf*) also serving as one of Allah's ninety-nine traditional "beautiful names."[49] The *bismillah* incipit that opens each qur'anic Sūra is similar for stating, "in the name of Allah, the Compassionate, the Most Merciful" (*bismi llāhi ar-raḥmānu ar-rahīmu*). The *bismillah* has two epithets from the Semitic root *rhm* which echo the OT's frequent statements that Yahweh is "a merciful El" (*'ēl raḥûm*; e.g. Exod 34:6). The interconnections among these Semitic divine epithets within their conceptual world are also evident in how the *bismillah* prefaces several books in Codex 151, the oldest extant manuscript of the Arabic New Testament from the ninth century AD.[50]

Nevertheless, common terminology in Semitic languages does not mean that divine mercy and compassion portray El, Yahweh, and Allah as identical. To borrow a concept from linguistics, cognate terms can sometimes make for "false friends."[51] This principle has a theological counterpart in how divine attributes may not mean the same things in different religious systems even when denoted with the same terms (whether in the same language such as English, or related languages such as Hebrew and Arabic). Particularly for divine mercy and compassion, these traits are expressed in the relationships that sovereign deities have with humans in their frailty and sinfulness.

A closer look at divine mercy and compassion reveals significant differences with respect to El, Yahweh, and Allah. The Ugaritic epithet of El as "the merciful one" (*dp'id*) is linked to El's creative ability as "the father of mankind"

---

47. John F. Healey, "The Kindly and Merciful God: On Some Semitic Divine Epithets," in *"Und Mose schrieb dieses Lied auf": Studien zum Alten Testament und zum alten Orient – Festschrift für Oswald Loretz zur Vollendung seines 70. Lebensjahres mit Beiträgen von Freunden, Schülern und Kollegen*, eds. Oswald Loretz, Manfried Dietrich, and Ingo Kottsieper, Alter Orient und Altes Testament 250 (Münster: Ugarit-Verlag, 1998), 349–56.

48. Day, *Yahweh and the Gods*, 26.

49. Parvez Dewan, *The Name of Allāh* (New Delhi: Penguin Books India, 2003), 37.

50. Shehadeh, "Christians and Muslims," 17.

51. For example, French *sympathique* means "nice, friendly" rather than "sympathetic," while *attendre* means "to wait" instead of "to attend."

(*'ab 'adm*) and "creator of creatures" (*bny bnwt*).[52] These terms emphasize El's transcendent distance from people rather than his accessibility or the capacity for sinners to be reconciled with him. Ugarit's common depiction of El as an elderly and mostly passive deity stands in contrast to young and vigorous Baal who, as already mentioned, is deeply involved in human affairs as a divine warrior and storm god. In sum, Ugarit's benign portrayal of El diverges significantly from the Hebrew Bible's repeated declaration that Yahweh is "a merciful El" (Exod 34:6; cf. Deut 4:31; Ps 86:15) intent on "maintaining love to thousands, and forgiving wickedness, rebellion and sin" (Exod 34:7). Forgiveness is simply not part of El's portfolio since he fits the mold of creator, judge, and king like a typical high god of the ancient Near East.[53]

Much like Ugaritic El, the Islamic depiction of Allah frequently describes his mercy and compassion, but within a theological framework that keeps him at a distance. The utter oneness of Allah (an Islamic doctrine known as *tawhid*) makes him radically inaccessible to humans. Imad Shehadeh observes that "God being 'merciful and compassionate' in Islam describes only what he can *do*, not what he *is*. . . . God's relationship to his people in the Bible is . . . described as that of a spouse, a lover, a father, a brother, a friend, etc. – concepts foreign to Islam, and possibly offensive."[54] In essence, Islam's prohibition on using any human concepts to describe Allah means that his moral attributes are strictly confined within himself as matters of internal *rationality* or *potentiality* rather than external *relationality*.[55] This understanding of divine compassion is deeply at odds with the OT's frequent depiction of Yahweh as a sovereign who is nevertheless willing to be vulnerable and experience pain on behalf of his creatures.[56] Abraham Joshua Heschel rightly concludes,

> For all the belief in divine mercy, Allah is essentially thought of as unqualified Omnipotence, Whose will is absolute, not conditioned by anything man may do. He acts without regard for

52. Cf. Aicha Rahmouni, *Divine Epithets in the Ugaritic Alphabetic Texts*, trans. J. N. Ford, Handbook of Oriental Studies, Section 1: The Near and Middle East 93 (Leiden: Brill, 2008), 205.
53. On the characterization of El at Ugarit, see W. Herrman, "El," *DDD*, 275–77.
54. Imad Shehadeh, review of *Allah: A Christian Response*, by Miroslav Volf, *Themelios* 36 (2011): 375, italics original, https://www.thegospelcoalition.org/themelios/review/allah-a-christian-response/.
55. Ida Glaser, "The Concept of Relationship as a Key to the Comparative Understanding of Christianity and Islam," *Themelios* 11 (Jan. 1986): 57–60.
56. Terence E. Fretheim, *The Suffering of God: An Old Testament Perspective*, Overtures to Biblical Theology (Philadelphia: Fortress, 1984).

the specific situation of man. Since everything is determined by Him, it is a monologue that obtains between Allah and man, rather than a dialogue or a mutuality as in the biblical view. Not the relation between Allah and man, but simply Allah himself is central to Islam.[57]

The uniqueness of Yahweh vis-à-vis El and Allah comes to the fore especially in the OT's protest literature. Yahweh's mercy and compassion not only entail his willingness to suffer, as noted above, but even the invitation that his people should argue with him about their own suffering. In a passage such as Psalm 77, the poet both engages his "El" while questioning divine faithfulness at the same time: "Will the Lord [*ădōnay*] reject forever? Will he never show favor again? Has his unfailing love [*hesed*] vanished forever? Has his promise failed for all time? Has God [*'ēl*] forgotten to be gracious? Has he in anger withheld his compassion [*rahămîm*]?" (Ps 77:7–9[MT 8–10]). It is striking how the the entire psalm to this point refers to deity in the third person in all but one instance (v. 4 [MT 5]), and only using either generic terms (e.g. *'ĕlōhîm, 'ădōnay*) or "El" with his epithets (e.g. *'ēl, 'elyōn*). The name of Yahweh is not (yet) mentioned, as in much of the "Elohistic Psalter" in Psalms 73–83. Suddenly, the poet switches to the first use of second-person address as well as mentioning the tetragrammaton: "I shall remember the deeds of Yahweh; surely I will remember your wonders of old. . . . Your way, O God [*'ĕlōhîm*], is in holiness; Who is a great El [*'ēl*] like [our] God? You are the El [*hā'ēl*] who works wonders, you have made known your strength among the peoples" (Ps 77:11, 13–14[MT 12, 14–15]).

Psalm 77's juxtaposition of protest (vv. 1–10[MT 2–11]) and faith (vv. 11–20[12–21]) is representative for employing familiar motifs in ironic and countercultural ways.[58] Against Ugaritic El, the poet's bemusement that "El" may have forgotten about his plight (v. 9[10]) alludes to the possibility that he may be too detached to care. But the self-rejoinder is that Yahweh is incomparably "a great El" (v. 13[14]) and "the El who works wonders" (v. 14[15]) because he is present, powerful, and active in the life of Israel (v. 15[16]). Not only is Yahweh "the [real] El" (v. 15[16]; cf. Deut 7:9–10) who is better than

---

57. Abraham J. Heschel, *The Prophets*, 2 vols. (New York: Harper & Row, 1962), 2:21.
58. Dominik Markl, "Divine Mercy in the Ancient Near East and in the Hebrew Bible," in *Rahma: Muslim and Christian Studies in Mercy*, eds. Valentino Cottini, Felix Körner, and Diego R. Sarrío Cucarella, Studio arabo-islamici del PISAI 22 (Rome: PISAI, 2018), 46, observes that this is the Hebrew Bible's unique contribution to the ANE.

El of Ugarit, he also surpasses Baal by putting the waters to flight without any struggle (vv. 16–17[17–18]). Yahweh rather than Baal sends thunder and lightning to the earth (v. 18[19]), and rescues Israel through the exodus from Egypt (vv. 19–20[20–21]).[59] Much like Psalms 74 and 89, Psalm 77 depicts Yahweh's triumph over both historical and mythic powers but without any of the conflict that characterizes ancient Near Eastern cosmogonies such as *Enuma Elish* or the Baal Cycle.

A comparison between Yahweh and Allah in the light of Psalm 77 yields similar results. The doubt exhibited within Psalm 77 about the extent of "tender mercies" (*raḥămîm*; v. 9[10]), a plural of intensity or abstraction in Hebrew,[60] would be simply incoherent within Islam. "The Compassionate" (*ar-raḥmānu*) and "the most Merciful" (*ar-raḥīmu*) are foremost among Allah's ninety-nine names.[61] The Semitic root *rḥm* underlying both terms is evidently related to the "womb" (Heb. *reḥem*, Arab. *rahim*) with its connotation of motherly love. However, such a give-and-take relationship is impossible for the Muslim due to Allah's decree of strict predestination (Arab. *al-Qadr*). The corollary to such determinism is that Islamic spirituality generally views divine mercy and compassion as reasons for submission to Allah's will in a manner akin to fatalism.[62]

Dissatisfaction with such a detached view of deity was what caused the existential crisis of the Pakistani poet Daoud Rahbar. Before his conversion from Islam to Christianity, Rahbar completed a PhD on divine justice in Islamic theology. As David Cashin summarizes, Rahbar's research led him to realize

> that the nature of God in the Qur'an was one of absolute justice. That is to say, "mercy" and "grace," which are terms really only functionally understood through relationship, remain unsubstantiated titles for God in the Qur'an. The words "*bism'illah ar rahman ar rahmin*" . . . are on the lips of every Saudi/Isis/al-Qaida/Yemeni/Pakistani executioner as they slice off the heads of their inmates/hostages/yeziddis. The words are meaningless

---

59. The psalm contains allusions to other ANE myths (as noted by Michael Fishbane, *Biblical Myth and Rabbinic Mythmaking* [Oxford: Oxford University Press, 2005], 44–47), but only those about El and Baal concern us here.

60. Markl, "Divine Mercy," 40.

61. Dewan, *Name of Allāh*, 8–9.

62. Helmer Ringgren, "Islamic Fatalism," in *Fatalistic Beliefs in Religion, Folklore, and Literature: Papers Read at the Symposium on Fatalistic Beliefs Held at Abo on the 7th–9th of September, 1964*, ed. Helmer Ringgren (Stockholm: Almqvist & Wiksell, 1967), 59–60.

titles, something hoped for but never demonstrated. He later became a Christian.[63]

The practical implications of Allah's radical transcendence and sovereignty thus leave a practical void which popular Islam fills with other means of making contact with or seeking help from spiritual powers.[64] In contrast to Islamic theology, Israelite faith frequently makes divine mercy and compassion the grounds for appealing to God in lament rather than retreating from God in fatalism. Yahweh is unique among Semitic deities for fulfilling the ancient Near East's functions of a high god's power (like Allah and Ugaritic El) but also a family god's compassion (like the patriarchs' deity which Genesis sometimes identifies with El-compounds).[65] Regarding the character of one's deity, whether mercy is paired with intimacy or only with power becomes the determining factor in whether a suffering or sinful worshiper exhibits a posture of engagement or one of resignation.

The Same God Question and the Term Questions in Chinese, Korean, and Indonesian

The preceding discussion shows how fraught with potential misunderstanding is the answer to whether Yahweh and El/Allah are the same God. Though "Yes and No"[66] does some justice to the question as usually posed, it would be more accurate to say, "It depends," because of how speakers and hearers of living languages perceive the nature of sameness and deity differently even within the same community of faith.[67] That is to say, the move beyond viewing names of deity as timeless ontological markers has a close counterpart in the methods of Bible translation. Language itself also plays an important role in both shaping and communicating understanding over space and time. Parallel to the SGQ, the history of mission illustrates how "the Interminable Term

---

63. David Cashin, "I Cannot Worship a God Who Does Not Understand Human Suffering," *Evangelical Missions Quarterly* Occasional Bulletin (Special Edition 2016): 9.

64. Bill A. Musk, "Popular Islam: The Hunger of the Heart," in *The Gospel and Islam: A 1978 Compendium*, ed. Don M. McCurry (Monrovia, CA: Missions Advanced Research and Communication Center, 1979), 218; Max Weber, *The Sociology of Religion*, trans. Johannes Winckelmann, 4th ed. (Boston: Beacon Press, 1963), 575.

65. Jean-Marc Heimerdinger, "The God of Abraham," *Vox Evangelica* 22 (1992): 41–55. This theme will receive special attention in the next chapter.

66. See n. 34 above.

67. Netland, "Worshiping the Same God," 452.

Question"[68] quickly becomes unresolvable when translators work with static models of language, especially for an issue as important as naming deity.[69] Since languages and their users exist in a dialogical relationship to one another, meaningful communication ultimately hinges on both the *semantics* of words and the *pragmatics* of words in their cultural context.

The issues raised by the TQ in Chinese, Korean, and Malay/Indonesian illustrate the strengths and weaknesses of using a culture's pre-existing terms for deity. In turn, an examination of Bible translations in these languages can impart a sharper perspective on the SGQ than is available solely via English and other European languages. This is true for two reasons. First, the Judeo-Christian heritage of Western civilization means that the TQ in Western languages is already a distant memory. Despite the rise of religious diversity in what was formerly Christendom, the starting point for interfaith dialogue tends to remain Judeo-Christian terminology. Second, the ready availability of Bibles and critical mass of Christians in Western cultures means that new converts to Christianity in the West usually associate "God" with the Christian God without conflating this term with their previous deity or deities. By contrast, the TQ and SGQ are often one and the same issue for the first generation of Christians in non-Western cultures. They are typically a religious minority but share terminology about "God" with the dominant culture and language around them. As Christians beyond this first generation of converts emerge and become more numerous, they begin to resemble Western Christians in being linguistic insiders who understand shared divine terms in their Bibles with fewer of their previous associations.

The SGQ/TQ in Chinese and Korean are entwined for historical reasons.[70] On the Chinese side of the SGQ/TQ, Protestant missionaries debated for most of the latter nineteenth century over the proper term for God to use

---

68. This is the title of Irene Eber's essay which is itself taken from the "translation wars" over the Chinese Bible in the late nineteenth and early twentieth centuries ("The Interminable Term Question," in *The Bible in Modern China: The Literary and Intellectual Impact*, ed. Irene Eber, Monumenta Serica Monograph Series 43 [Nettetal: Steyler Verlag, 1999], 135–61).

69. The discipline of *relevance theory* helpfully moves beyond these problems. For applications of relevance theory to biblical studies, see Gene L. Green, "Relevance Theory and Biblical Interpretation," in *The Linguist as Pedagogue: Trends in the Teaching and Linguistic Analysis of the Greek New Testament*, ed. Stanley E. Porter and Matthew Brook O'Donnell (Sheffield: Sheffield Phoenix, 2009), 217–40; Karen H. Jobes, "Relevance Theory and the Translation of Scripture," *Journal of the Evangelical Theological Society* 50 (Dec. 2007): 773–97.

70. Sung-Deuk Oak, "Competing Chinese Names for God: The Chinese Term Question and Its Influence upon Korea," *Journal of Korean Religions* 3 (Oct. 2012): 89–115.

in Chinese Bible translations.[71] One school of thought, composed mainly of American missionaries, favored the term *shen*. This generic term for "god" could describe any kind of spirit or deity (like Heb. *'ĕlōhîm*, Gk. *theos*), even though this left the possibility of confusion with polytheism. The other camp of largely European missionaries advocated the term *shangdi* ("high ruler/Ruler"). This term for supreme deity had roots in Chinese mythology which led Sinologist translators such as James Legge to argue for an "original monotheism" in Chinese culture.[72]

It is telling that Chinese Christians were largely bystanders while others argued on their behalf. The Western translators tended to overlook "how Chinese convert-teachers and their listeners – both educated and illiterate – understand the terms for God."[73] When a belated survey was attempted before the pivotal Shanghai Missionary Conference of 1877, it turned out that Chinese Christians had a range of conflicting associations for *shangdi* and *shen*, depending on their level of education, dialect, religious background, and local customs.[74] The lack of resolution for this stalemate was ultimately reflected in the publication of the Chinese Union Version of the Bible of 1919 in both *shangdi* and *shen* editions, a practice that continues to the present day. Despite this bifurcation in Chinese Bibles, it is common not only to find *shangdi* and *shen* used interchangeably by Chinese Christians nowadays, but to find each term used as both proper name and appellative title. Multiple generations of Chinese Christians have grown accustomed to "biblical" vocabulary from both kinds of editions. Interestingly, the only term for the Bible's deity that is uncommonly used in addressing God (besides in Scripture reading) is *yehehua*, the Chinese transliteration for "Jehovah" (which is, interestingly, an "impossible form" for representing the tetragrammaton).

The Korean TQ had a simpler resolution compared with the Chinese TQ. Scottish missionaries in northeast China and Manchuria, adjacent to Korea, were advocates of the Chinese term *shangdi*. This led them to adopt its Korean equivalent of *hanănim* in their translations of the Bible for this reason.

---

71. For the sake of drawing out similarities and differences between Chinese and Korean versions of the TQ, this study passes over the Catholic TQ from two centuries prior during the Chinese Rites Controversy. The options for terms presented at that time included *shangdi* (by the Jesuits) and *tianzhu* ("the Lord of Heaven," by Dominicans and Franciscans).
72. For a full account of the Chinese TQ in the latter nineteenth century with a particular focus on James Legge, see Norman J. Girardot, *The Victorian Translation of China: James Legge's Oriental Pilgrimage* (Berkeley, CA: University of California Press, 2002).
73. Eber, "Interminable Term Question," 152.
74. Eber, 152–54.

More than *shangdi* and its literary flavor in Chinese, though, the Korean term *hanănim* was a vernacular term that denotes a supreme deity over the pantheon who is nonetheless universally seen as the progenitor of the Korean people and their culture.[75] Korean Protestants have thus been nearly unanimous on *hanănim* as the preferred term for deity.[76] The direct connection of *hanănim* to Korea's origin myths and the greater homogeneity of Korean culture overall have gone hand in hand as significant factors in the explosive growth of the Korean church.[77] At the same time, the mythic heritage of the term *hanănim* means that Korean Christianity both at home and abroad can sometimes retain elements of shamanism in its beliefs and practices.[78]

The Malay and Indonesian languages have several features that offer a rather different test case from Chinese and Korean. First, Malay/Indonesian has a significant number of Arabic loanwords due to the arrival of Islamic traders around the thirteenth century AD. Among these words was *Allah* which, as in ancient and modern Arabic Bibles, has been the standard term for God since the Gospel of Matthew was first published in Malay in the early seventeenth century and the complete Malay/Indonesian Bible was published in the eighteenth century. Second, *Allah* has become fully absorbed as a native word for "god/God" (unlike in Western languages). It no longer follows the grammar and inflection of its Arabic precursor, even to the point of taking suffixes which are impossible in Arabic since *Allah* has become a proper name.[79] Third and along these lines, the use of *Allah* by Christians and Muslims was shared without controversy for over three centuries. This linguistic reality only became a problem in recent decades with the rise of Islamism, especially in Malaysia when local authorities went so far as to prohibit any Christian usage of Allah, including distributing Malay versions of the Bible that already referred to God in this way.[80] No such issue is found in the neighboring country of Indonesia,

75. Oak, "Chinese Names for God," 101–6.
76. Sung-Wook Hong, *Naming God in Korea: The Case of Protestant Christianity*, Global Theological Voices (Oxford: Regnum, 2008), 138.
77. Bong Rin Ro, "Communicating the Biblical Concept of God to Koreans," in *The Global God: Multicultural Evangelical Views of God*, ed. Aída Besançon Spencer and William David Spencer (Grand Rapids, MI: Baker, 1998), 222–23.
78. Tae-Ju Moon, "The Korean American Dream and the Blessings of Hananim (God)," in *The Global God: Multicultural Evangelical Views of God*, eds. Aída Besançon Spencer and William David Spencer (Grand Rapids, MI: Baker, 1998), 240–42.
79. Daud Soesilo, "Translating the Names of God: Recent Experience from Indonesia and Malaysia," *The Bible Translator* 52 (2001): 419.
80. Eugene Yapp, "The 'Copyright' Controversy of 'Allah': Issues and Challenges of the Malaysian Church (A Case Study)," in *The Church in a Changing World: An Asian Response – Challenges*

interestingly, even though the Malay and Indonesian languages largely share the same Bible. The difference between Malaysia and Indonesia shows that the SGQ in these Islamic nations hinges on divergent *perceptions* of what "Allah" means (or perhaps must mean) rather than any linguistic *necessity* that limits this term's denotation to the God of Islam.

The history of the TQs in China, Korea, Malaysia, and Indonesia illustrates that the SGQ about Yahweh and El/Allah is primarily for linguistic outsiders and first-generation linguistic insiders who are concerned with naming the "Other" properly (i.e. matters of reference). Following this initial contact between religions, however, the Same God Question fades in importance for second-generation linguistic insiders due to the tendency to conflate the name and titles for deity (i.e. matters of description). At the same time, the reality of syncretism indicates that using the same word for "god" does not mean that people are worshiping the same God, any more than a wrong name indicates that people are worshiping the wrong God (e.g. the erroneous vocalization of "Jehovah" preserved in many languages, English included). And since linguistic insiders are ultimately the ones with the most at stake, it is for them to determine what a term like "Allah" means for their own community of faith, whether Christians or Muslims, rather than linguistic outsiders.[81] Synchronically it is true that "Yahweh" functions similarly to "Allah" in Islam, but diachronically Allah became a divine name because of Islamic usage.

CONCLUSION

Christianity has always been characterized by translatability. This contrasts with Islam, in which converts are required to adapt to Islamic norms and Arabic as its religious language.[82] The case is usually made with reference to the NT, but applies all the more to the OT and Israelite faith. It is unfortunate, however, that Western Christians who lack historical perspective and missiological awareness can be more secular than they realize in considering biblical monotheism to require a monopoly on God-language. Instead, the OT records how Yahweh can be identified using El as both divine name and appellative, as well as by appropriating many other epithets which denote the

---

from the Malang Consultation on Globalization, eds. Bruce Nicholls, Theresa Roco Lua, and Julie Belding (Quezon City, Philippines: Asia Theological Association, 2010), 147–56.
81. Mark Naylor, "Who Determines if Allah Is God? A Contextual Consideration of the Use of the Term 'Allah' for the God of the Bible," *Evangelical Missions Quarterly* Occasional Bulletin (Special Edition 2016): 21.
82. Sanneh, *Translating the Message*.

power of both El and Baal. The uniqueness of Yahweh comes more in taking over the terms and functions of ancient Near Eastern deities than in merely denying their existence (although the OT does opt for the latter at times). Parallel to this, the fact that Allah is an Arabic derivative of Semitic *ʾēl* and its related terms suggests that Yahweh is big enough to encompass Allah and his epithets without compromising monotheism.

Looking beyond Islam and returning to the English language, the translatability of Yahweh can be seen in the controversy about Hinduism following the breakup of the Beatles in 1969. George Harrison released "My Sweet Lord" in 1970 as his first single. This immediately became a hit and proved to be the most popular song of Harrison's solo career. Among Christians, reaction to the song was mixed since "My Sweet Lord" involved a collision of worldviews. The song praises the singular deity, "my sweet Lord," using two clashing sets of background vocals: "Hal-le-lu-jah" (a Hebrew exclamation of praise to Yahweh), and "Ha-re-krish-na" (a Vedic mantra that reflected Harrison's conversion to Hinduism). Christian leaders tended to advocate a boycott of the song, while Christian musicians often took a different approach in singing the song with the Hindu mantra taken out. Cultural appropriation was the original impetus for "My Sweet Lord," in fact, for Harrison admitted later that the African-American spiritual "Oh Happy Day" had been his inspiration. His use of the same *title* of "Lord" for deities with the differing *names* of Yahweh and Krishna is consistent with the OT's own witness that divine translatability is both powerful enough to enable contextualization as well as vulnerable enough to permit syncretistic misunderstandings. A monotheism that can be understood by other cultures demands no less, since this is the only kind that could be meaningful and comprehensive enough to declare of Yahweh that "among the gods there is none like you, Lord; no deeds can compare with yours" (Ps 86:8). The next chapter will explore how OT monotheism works within a pluralistic context when multiple religions, each with their official and popular expressions, are in contact with one another. Foremost among these is the prosperity theology that has become commonplace in Asian Christianity.

CHAPTER 4

OFFICIAL RELIGION, POPULAR RELIGION, AND PROSPERITY THEOLOGY[1]

The Prayer of Jabez was a blockbuster immediately upon its publication in 2001.[2] A stay of several months atop the *New York Times* #1 bestsellers list reflected its sales in the millions and even spawned a side industry of Jabez merchandise. In this short book of ninety-two pages, readers are introduced to an obscure character whose only appearance in the Bible comes in the middle of a genealogy: "Jabez cried out to the God of Israel, 'Oh, that you would bless me and enlarge my territory! Let your hand be with me, and keep me from harm so that I will be free from pain.' And God granted his request" (1 Chr 4:10). The author of *The Prayer of Jabez*, Bruce Wilkinson, testified that learning to repeat Jabez's fourfold petition transformed his life and multiplied his ministry several times over. Internet websites that collect personal testimonies of using Jabez's prayer spoke of similar results. The popularity of *The Prayer of Jabez* extended beyond the West to the Majority World as well, as when it was translated into some Asian languages that have hardly any Christian literature. The Thai version of *The Prayer of Jabez* appeared already in 2003, for example, while St. Augustine's *Confessions* was not translated into Thai until 2018.

The fad of Jabez's prayer has run its course, yet the Chronicler's characteristic theme of reward and punishment as the will of God continues to find a welcome audience in Asian Christianity.[3] In a booklet widely circulated in Singapore, for example, Yahweh's words to Solomon were adopted as the

---

1. This chapter draws on material published as Jerry Hwang, "The Book of Jeremiah as Case Study in Asian Contextual Theology," *Asia Journal of Theology* 35 (2021): 25–37; and Jerry Hwang, "Syncretism after the Exile and Malachi's Missional Response," *Southern Baptist Journal of Theology* 20 (2016): 49–68.
2. Bruce Wilkinson, *The Prayer of Jabez: Breaking through to the Blessed Life* (Sisters, OR: Multnomah, 2001).
3. For discussion of this theme in Chronicles, see Raymond B. Dillard, "Reward and Punishment in Chronicles: The Theology of Immediate Retribution," *Westminster Theological Journal* 46 (1984): 164–72.

theme for Christians to pray for revival in anticipation of the country's ju-bilee celebration of independence in 2015: "If my people, who are called by my name, will humble themselves and pray and seek my face and turn from their wicked ways, then I will hear from heaven, and I will forgive their sin and will heal their land" (2 Chr 7:14). To the extent that Christians in Asia are acquainted with 1–2 Chronicles (some of the most overlooked books of the Bible), it is striking that the most well-known verses relate to pragmatic concerns for blessings, life, and health.

First and Second Chronicles offer more than this, of course, but it is true that they mirror the rest of the OT in connecting the life of faith to its material aspects. Norman Gottwald famously notes that "only as the full materiality of ancient Israel is more securely grasped will we be able to make sense of its spirituality."[4] The earthiness of Israel's life in a real land dots every page of the OT, in contrast to the NT's account of how the Christian church begins as a scattered Jewish diaspora and grows among Gentiles in a manner less bound by geography. As a consequence of its this-worldly nature, the OT occupies a central place in the argument that God decrees material abundance for his chosen people, as in the different forms of *prosperity theology*.[5] On the human side of the so-called "piety-prosperity equation," followers of God can expect blessings for keeping up their end of the arrangement through ritual obser-vance. The arrival of suffering or one's lack of prosperity can only mean that the worshiper lacks obedience in some way.

Reward and punishment are essential parts of every religio-philosophical system of justice. Because the OT's *retribution principle* resembles at first glance the universe's principle of cause and effect which characterizes both Eastern religions and folk Christianity, it is necessary to explore how Israelite faith is distinctive in relating human piety in ritual observance to God's will in blessing the believer. Morality cannot be reduced to the transactional matter of seek-ing rewards and avoiding punishment,[6] since the dynamism of relating to a personal God transcends the impersonal notion of *karma*, here understood in its philosophical sense as the moral causality that "each person makes his own fate, and all suffering happens for a reason. There is no arbitrary or meaningless

---

4. Norman K. Gottwald, *The Tribes of Yahweh: A Sociology of the Religion of Liberated Israel, 1250–1050 BCE* (Sheffield: Sheffield Academic Press, 1999), xxv.

5. Brent A. Strawn, *The Old Testament Is Dying: A Diagnosis and Recommended Treatment* (Grand Rapids, MI: Baker Academic, 2017), 131–55.

6. Sigmund Mowinckel, *Religion and Cult: The Old Testament and the Phenomenology of Religion*, ed. K. C. Hanson, trans. John F. X. Sheehan (Eugene, OR: Cascade, 2012), 24–28.

suffering in the world."[7] Karma in this broader perspective is not unique to Hinduism, Buddhism, and Jainism, the three major Eastern religions that originated on the Indian subcontinent, but is part of how grassroots adherents view the function of piety in every religion.

OFFICIAL RELIGION AND POPULAR RELIGION IN THE ANCIENT NEAR EAST

On this note, missiologists and anthropologists have observed that every system of belief is a combination of *official religion* and *popular religion*.[8] Official religion (or "high" religion) centers on institutions that are supported by priests, temples, and rituals. Its formal character tends to erect a distance from regular people. This leaves a gap for the accessibility of popular religion (also called "low" religion) to address everyday issues such as sickness, infertility, or making decisions. Societal tensions are typical between official religion and popular religion since each makes competing demands of authority over people's lives. In theological terms, however, both are integral since official religion's focus on transcendence addresses what is distant and lies outside oneself, while popular religion emphasizes immanence and answers urgent questions about the near, here, and now. When contact between different cultures is frequent, as when tiny Israel subsisted among larger empires or when Christianity arrived in East Asia with its already established religions, the stage is well set for a mixture of old and new, at both the official and popular levels.

Polytheistic systems address the distinction between official religion and popular religion by way of different deities handling different areas of life. In the ancient Near East, for example, gods and goddesses can be loosely classified as national deities, nature deities, and personal deities. These categories are not mutually exclusive, since in a polytheistic and multicultural world, the number of deities could always increase when deities were promoted in status or borrowed between peoples. National deities typically belonged to the realm of official religion, personal deities were clan-based and operated more at the level of popular religion, while nature deities could often have one foot in both since their roles in the cosmos had everyday significance for people. The status of a deity could also vary by region or social grouping, such

---

7. Whitley R. P. Kaufman, "Karma, Rebirth, and the Problem of Evil," *Philosophy East & West* 55 (Jan. 2005): 18.
8. Paul G. Hiebert, R. Daniel Shaw, and Tite Tiénou, *Understanding Folk Religion: A Christian Response to Popular Beliefs and Practices* (Grand Rapids, MI: Baker, 1999), 73–92.

as when a manifestation of Baal is the local deity of a particular place ("Baal of [the] Lebanon") but is a nature deity elsewhere ("Baal of the heavens").[9] The example of Baal shows that the relationship between official and popular religion is more of a spectrum than a dichotomy.

This diversity of roles for deities (including Yahweh to some extent, as we will explore below) reflects how their worshipers in the ancient Near East viewed them more in terms of function (i.e. what they do) than essence (i.e. who they are). Such nonontological ways of thinking are not as foreign to modern minds as it might seem, for a functional view of deities is analogous to how people typically understand stocks and react to their vicissitudes in financial markets. Rare is the investor who understands the details of what a company does or how it operates, since the focus is typically on whether the stock's price is rising rather than falling. Individual investors tend to buy when a stock is rising but sell when it is dropping, a psychological tendency that institutional investors use to their advantage. Deities in a polytheistic system are likewise trusted when their power is operative but abandoned or exchanged for other deities who apparently still have power. For both deities and stocks, the nature of power can be somewhat mysterious, but questions about their essence remain in the background as long as the stakeholders receive the results they seek.

Monotheism presents a special set of challenges for the usual distinction between official and popular religion. In contrast to polytheistic systems which do not expect a given deity to be everything to everyone, the nature of monotheism is that a single deity is understood to bridge the theological poles of transcendence and immanence (however comprehensively or incomprehensively). In ancient Near Eastern categories, this kind of singularity meant that Israelite monotheism understood Yahweh to cover the three general categories of a personal deity, national deity, and nature deity. Only then could Yahwism provide an adequate equivalent to a pantheon in which near and far deities each had their own functions. In modern Asia, similar challenges in bridging official and popular religion have led to folk Christianity, folk Islam, folk Buddhism, and folk Hinduism taking their place at the popular level alongside the official versions of these religions.

This is not to say, though, that Israelite monotheism requires that Yahweh be experienced uniformly and simultaneously as personal deity, national deity, and nature deity. Instead, the storyline of the Old Testament shows how

---

9. W. Herrman, "Baal," *DDD*, 133.

Yahweh is an amalgam of all three kinds of deity, thereby covering all the functions that are usually divided between official and popular religion. The following sections will discuss how Yahweh possesses a unique combination of presence and power which transcends the typical categories for deity in the ancient Near East: (1) a personal deity who also becomes a family deity during the patriarchal era in Genesis, (2) a national deity in the Mosaic Yahwism which is inaugurated by the exodus events, and (3) a nature deity for when Israel begins life in Canaan. Along the way and building on the previous chapter, we will also explore occasions when the OT's account of monotheism was contextualized against the backdrop of various kinds of syncretism in ancient Israel.

These theological categories will set the stage for a case study on Jeremiah, the OT book that deals most comprehensively with magical and karmic understandings of God's will for his people. The statement of Jeremiah 29:11 that God has "plans to prosper you and not to harm you, plans to give you a hope and a future" is perhaps the most common expression of this view, as attested by how this verse is regularly identified by both the Bible Gateway website and the YouVersion Bible app as the most frequently bookmarked.[10] However, the frequent understanding of Jeremiah 29:11 as God's unconditional promise to bring prosperity and blessing is nearly the opposite of what it meant for despondent Jewish refugees in Babylon. The prophet who was the most strident in criticizing the prosperity theology of his time has ironically become its most vocal advocate in the hands of modern interpreters, such as the prosperity teachers who exert outsized influence among some Asian Christians.

Yahweh as Personal Deity (and More)

Devotion to a personal deity is well documented in the ancient Near East, especially in Mesopotamia.[11] Unlike nature and national deities which were too remote to be worshiped, ANE peoples venerated personal gods and goddesses who were thought to act like parents and assist with mundane affairs such as a wife's fertility, blessing on crops, or healing from sickness. The nearness of their concern was expressed in how their worshipers often kept them close by as icons in the home, as when Rachel stole her father's *teraphim* which were kept

---

10. Griffin Paul Jackson, "The Top Bible Verses of 2018 Don't Come from Jesus or Paul," *Christianity Today*, 10 December 2018, https://www.christianitytoday.com/news/2018/december/most-popular-bible-verse-2018-youversion-app-bible-gateway.html.
11. Thorkild Jacobsen, *The Treasures of Darkness: A History of Mesopotamian Religion* (New Haven, CT: Yale University Press, 1976), 147–64.

in the family tent (Gen 31:34–35). Such intimacy entailed certain limitations of power, however, so that the inefficacy of a personal deity might impel the worshiper to seek the greater power of a more remote deity. Nevertheless, people's first recourse in times of trouble would be to their family deity or deities to whom they owed moral and ritual duties. With the passing of generations, the personal deity would become known as "the god of [my] father" and thus a family deity as well.

The previous chapter noted that the book of Genesis frequently describes Yahweh using El-compounds such as El Elyon ("El/God Most High"; Gen 14:18–21) and El Shaddai ("El/God Almighty"; 17:1; 28:3). But unlike Ugaritic El and the official rituals of El religion, the patriarchal narratives in Genesis depict their characters venerating Yahweh mostly without priests and always without temples (e.g. Gen 16:11; 17:1; 28:3; 33:20).[12] He is the El-deity of the patriarchs who accompanies them in their journeys while also promising them future blessings of land and fertility (Gen 21:33; 31:13; 35:7), just as an ANE personal deity would.[13] Beyond the first generation, Yahweh assumes epithets such as "the God of my father, the God of Abraham, and the fear of Isaac" (Gen 31:42) as well as "the mighty One of Jacob" (Gen 49:24). The narrative frame of Genesis certainly presents Yahweh as the creator of heaven and earth, but the Israelite patriarchs' own speech to or about Yahweh reflects their experience of a personal/family god whom they typically name with El-compounds.[14] The book of Genesis hints in this way that Israel is a people who are privileged to enjoy the immanence and care of "the god of my father[s]" (Gen 31:5, 42; 32:9) but with the transcendence and power of an El-deity who is the eternal creator of all things (Gen 14:22; 21:33).

The theme of Yahweh as personal deity also appears frequently in OT poetic texts. As a contrast to the Genesis narratives about promises made, the wisdom and lament psalms are intriguing for how they use the personal-deity motif to protest about promises broken instead of praising God for promises kept. Psalm 73 furnishes an outstanding example of this type. The passage begins with a summary statement affirming the OT's retribution principle:

---

12. It is true that Abram needs to approach El Shaddai through the mediation of Melchizedek the priest, but this is because he is in an unfamiliar place with an existing priest rather than due to patriarchal religion itself having a priesthood. Most of the time, however, the patriarchs build their own altars wherever God happens to meet with them.

13. Heimerdinger, "God of Abraham," 43–45.

14. It is for this reason that R. W. L. Moberly calls the patriarchal narratives and their description of patriarchal religion "The Old Testament of the Old Testament" (*The Old Testament of the Old Testament*).

"Surely God is good to Israel, to those who are pure in heart" (v. 1). But in what follows, the psalmist recounts the process of losing faith in his personal deity. Envy threatens to overwhelm when he sees the prosperity and arrogance of the unrighteous (vv. 2–10), who dare even to taunt God (v. 11) since their wealth accumulates despite their evil (v. 12). Is Yahweh their personal deity rather than his?

Bitterness sets in as the psalmist concludes that the retribution principle is false (vv. 13–14). The complaint that "in vain I have kept my heart pure" (v. 13) contradicts the psalm's opening statement (cf. v. 1), while the frustration that "all day long I have been afflicted, and every morning brings new punishments" (v. 14) represents the ultimate injustice of retribution for the righteous and a reward for the wicked. It is not only that the psalmist's personal deity has been absent or slower to act than usual, for that would have been a matter of appealing for him to pay attention. A multitude of lament psalms do exactly this (e.g. Pss 5; 25; 61). Instead, the theological problem in a wisdom psalm like Psalm 73 is worse in that the psalmist claims, at least for a moment, that Yahweh is present and active in breaking his own laws of morality. Before wandering too far, the psalmist turns toward God and addresses him as "you" for the first time while acknowledging how rash it would have been to verbalize these complaints to the congregation of Israel (v. 15). The psalmist then comes into God's presence and realizes that the retribution principle still holds (vv. 16–17). God has allowed the wicked to remain so that their eventual destruction will be beyond question and total (vv. 18–20).

More is happening in Psalm 73, in fact, than a simple reaffirmation of the retribution principle. For the psalmist, the desperation from suffering unjustly (vv. 21–22) has served the pedagogical function of increasing his awareness of the personal god's guidance (vv. 23–24). The desire for justice now pales in comparison to the desire for the presence of a God who has no equal in heaven or on earth (vv. 25–26). It is true that the wicked will eventually get their due (v. 27), but the psalmist's definition of what is "good" has shifted dramatically: "But as for me, it is good to be near God. I have made the Sovereign LORD my refuge; I will tell of all your deeds" (v. 28).[15] Here is the countercultural shape of OT monotheism: Israel's personal deity has loving purposes for suffering that could not be learned if Yahweh had granted the psalmist's request for relief as an ANE personal deity was expected to. The contrast with Jabez's expectation that "I will be free from pain" (1 Chr 4:10) could not be greater.

---

15. James Luther Mays, *Psalms*, Interpretation (Louisville, KY: John Knox, 1994), 243–44.

Yahweh as National Deity (and More)

The OT's identification of Yahweh as national deity builds upon Genesis's portrayal of the personal/family deity of the patriarchs. At the pivotal moment of reintroducing the God of Israel to Moses, the narrative of the burning bush states that Yahweh is "the God of Abraham, the God of Isaac and the God of Jacob" (Exod 3:6, 15) as well as "the God of your father[s]" (Exod 3:6, 13, 15) and El Shaddai (Exod 6:3). The clan deity who is "the God of the Hebrews" (Exod 3:18; 5:3) has also become "the God of Israel" (Exod 5:1; cf. Gen 33:20). In taking a stand against Pharaoh and the (other) gods of Egypt (Exod 12:12),[16] Yahweh has proven himself to be a worthy national deity by defeating the entire Egyptian pantheon (9:16; 14:4). The purpose of the exodus is for both Israelites as well as Egyptians to "know that I am Yahweh" (6:7; 7:5, 17; 8:22; 10:2; 14:17–18). The OT then moves to identify Yahweh as "the God of Israel" (e.g. Exod 34:23; Josh 7:13; Judg 5:5; 1 Sam 10:18; 1 Kgs 8:20), a title for national deity which is juxtaposed with titles for family deity such as "our/your God" (e.g. Josh 24:23–24), "the God of your ancestors" (e.g. Josh 18:3), and "the God of Jacob" (Ps 46:7; 146:5).

As with the personal/family deity, however, the OT portrays Yahweh as a national deity whose sovereignty remains intact in both success and failure. This paradox is perhaps most evident in 1 Samuel 4–7, the narrative about the Philistines' capture and return of the ark of the covenant. This passage demonstrates humorously how a missionary God responds to people who have animistic beliefs about sacred objects, whether Israelites or Philistines. Following an initial defeat against the Philistines, the Israelites regard the presence of the ark as a talisman that can guarantee victory in battle: "Let us bring the ark of the LORD's covenant from Shiloh, so that he may go with us and save us from the hand of our enemies" (1 Sam 4:3). Yet the ark offers little help, for not only is Israel defeated again by the Philistines, but the ark itself is captured and the two sons of Eli the priest die in battle (1 Sam 4:11). To lose both the visible symbol of Yahweh's presence and the future leaders of Israel means the death of the national deity as well as the demise of the nation itself.[17]

Israel has given up faith because its superstition about Yahweh's ark has failed, but the national deity of Israel is just getting started. The Philistines

---

16. See discussion of Pharaoh's central role in the Egyptian pantheon by James K. Hoffmeier, *Israel in Egypt: The Evidence for the Authenticity of the Exodus Tradition* (Oxford: Oxford University Press, 1999), 149–55.

17. Walter Brueggemann, *First and Second Samuel*, Interpretation (Louisville, KY: John Knox, 1990), 33.

who take the ark quickly see that the real battle is about superstition. They first do as victorious armies in the ancient world typically would in moving the symbol of their enemy's god into the temple of their own god (1 Sam 5:2). To the Philistines, Dagon their national god is clearly stronger than Yahweh since Israel lost the battle. On this point the Israelites would likely have agreed with the Philistines. But the next morning, the Philistines find Dagon flat on his face before the ark of Yahweh. Wondering if perhaps Dagon was positioned improperly on his throne, the Philistines return Dagon to his place. The next morning, Dagon is lying prostrate again, but his head and hands are broken off (1 Sam 5:4). The national deity of Israel has ensured that this time is neither accident nor coincidence, for his hand of judgment is heavy against the Philistines (1 Sam 5:6, 7, 9, 11).[18]

The ensuing chapters contain a rather unique account of strength and weakness with reference to national deities. Yahweh has allowed the ark to be taken because of the superstition of the Israelites. But the ark has undertaken a "mission trip" of sorts to defeat the superstition of the Philistines![19] The humbled Philistines show more respect for the ark than the Israelites did earlier to the symbol of their national deity: "What shall we do with the ark of the god of Israel?" (5:8; cf. 4:3). Ironically, the God of Israel has hidden himself from his people but reveals his power in Philistia. When the Philistines realize that they are on the losing side just as Pharaoh and the Egyptians were (6:6), they determine to rid themselves of the ark that they had brought back as victors in battle. When the ark arrives by oxcart in Beth Shemesh, the Israelites who welcome the ark home from Philistia foolishly open the ark and look inside, only to be struck down for their sin. If the men of Beth Shemesh had at least believed that the ark was holy, as the superstitious Israelites did in 1 Samuel 4, they would not have dared to open the ark. But because they reject the old superstition, they open the ark and thereby mock the holiness of their national deity. The consequences for them are fatal.

First Samuel 7 brings the story of the ark full circle. The Philistines still pose a problem for the Israelites, but the prophet Samuel implores Israel not to enter battle with the same misunderstandings about the relationship between piety and success: "If you are returning to the LORD with all your hearts, then rid yourselves of the foreign gods and the Ashtoreths and commit yourselves

---

18. Brueggemann, *First and Second Samuel*, 37.
19. A. Stirrup, "'Why Has Yahweh Defeated Us Today before the Philistines?' The Question of the Ark Narrative," *Tyndale Bulletin* 51 (2000): 93–94.

to the Lord and serve him only, and he will deliver you out of the hand of the Philistines" (7:3). What is notable about Israel's response to Samuel is that the people have finally learned to seek Yahweh rather than his deliverance: "We have sinned against the Lord. . . . Do not stop crying out to the Lord our God for us, that he may rescue us from the hand of the Philistines" (7:6, 8). The ark narrative has concluded with the national deity of Israel saving his people from the Philistines, but in a surprising manner that utilizes both strength and weakness. Yahweh's redemptive purposes are accomplished through human agents on both sides of the battle in a manner that demonstrates how he is both the national deity of his people as well as being supreme over other national deities. The countercultural combination of presence and power shown by Yahweh in 1 Samuel 4–7 exemplifies how

> it is only Israel that decisively extended the attitude of personal religion from the personal to the national realm. The relationship of Yahweh to Israel – his anger, his compassion, his forgiveness, and his renewed anger and punishment of the sinful people – is in all essentials the same as that of the relation between god and individual in the attitude of personal religion.[20]

Yahweh as Nature Deity (and More)

While portraying him as a distinctive synthesis of personal and national deity, monotheism in Israel also regards Yahweh as the ultimate nature deity. The OT's linking of these categories can be seen in the confrontation between Yahweh and Ashur, the national deity of Assyria, during the narratives of Jerusalem's siege in the eighth century BC (2 Kgs 18–19; Isa 36–37). The Assyrian envoy insults his Judahite counterparts with the taunt that Yahweh, King Hezekiah, and Judah's ally Egypt are all equally helpless by the standards of international power politics (Isa 36:4–9). The logical conclusion to draw from Judah's repeated defeats by Assyria is that Yahweh their national deity has turned against his own people (Isa 36:10).

When the Judahite officials try to hush the envoy by requesting that he speak in Aramaic (Isa 36:11–12), he turns to address the eavesdropping crowd in Hebrew (36:13). The envoy not only repeats the threat that he made semi-privately to the officials, but he also changes his tune briefly by offering the propaganda that the king of Assyria would be a kind patron:

---

20. Jacobsen, *Treasures of Darkness*, 164.

> Make peace with me and come out to me. Then each of you will
> eat fruit from your own vine and fig tree and drink water from
> your own cistern, until I come and take you to a land like your
> own – a land of grain and new wine, a land of bread and vine-
> yards, a land of olive trees and honey. Choose life and not death!
> (2 Kgs 18:31–32; Isa 36:16–17; cf. Deut 30:19)

The envoy is well acquainted with both Israel's geography and covenant traditions, for he proposes that his patron king and deity will supply the same
kind of creational abundance that Yahweh had repeatedly promised as a better
nature deity than Baal (e.g. Deut 8:8; 26:15; Hos 2:8, 16–23[MT 10, 18–25]).

The Assyrian official concludes his brief aside about nature deities and
shifts back to the theme of dueling national deities. Recent history indicates,
he asserts, that the gods of various peoples cannot resist the Assyrian king who
does the bidding of Ashur the national god:

> Has the god of any nation ever delivered his land from the hand
> of the king of Assyria? Where are the gods of Hamath and Arpad?
> Where are the gods of Sepharvaim, Hena and Ivvah? Have they
> rescued Samaria from my hand? Who of all the gods of these
> countries has been able to save his land from me? How then can
> the LORD deliver Jerusalem from my hand? (2 Kgs 18:33–35)

The poignant reference to the exiled kingdom of Samaria demonstrates the
envoy's impeccable logic by ANE standards: the splitting of Yahweh's national
estate meant that he was unable to defend its northern half, so what chance
would the southern half stand against the Assyrian onslaught?

A similar mixture of ANE traditions about deity can be found in Psalm
121. This familiar passage begins by referring to Yahweh as a nature deity:
"I will lift up my eyes to the mountains – where does my help come from?
My help comes from the LORD, the Maker of heaven and earth" (vv. 1–2).
Usually overlooked, though, is that the opening question is actually a rhetor-
ical question which expects a negative answer – no, not from the mountains![21]
The logic of the first two verses contrasts with the interpretation popularized
by *The Sound of Music* in viewing them as nature's reminder of divine help.[22]
Many worship songs based on Psalm 121 are similarly reflective of Western

---

21. Hans-Friedmann Richter, "Von den Bergen kommt keine Hilfe: Zu Psalm 121," *Zeitschrift
für die alttestamentliche Wissenschaft* 116 (2004): 406.
22. Jerome F. D. Creach, "Psalm 121," *Interpretation* 50 (1996): 47.

culture's long association between nature and the sublime (e.g. Henry David Thoreau's *Walden*).

But if it were true that Yahweh showed his special presence in the mountains (v. 1), the psalmist would not proceed to challenge himself that Yahweh is actually the "Maker of heaven and earth" (v. 2). Modern and urban people tend to regard mountains as places of rest and refuge, but this anachronism clashes with the view of ancient people that they were instead the place where fearful powers dwelled.[23] The Arameans harbored such a superstition about Yahweh (1 Kgs 20:27–29). Israel had its own version of this misunderstanding in attempting to worship Yahweh at the "high places" (e.g. 1 Kgs 3:2–4; 12:31–32; 2 Kgs 17:7–12; cf. Num 33:52; Deut 12:2) which were formerly used to venerate Canaanite nature deities such as Baal and Asherah. In such a historical context, the beginning of Psalm 121 is a declaration about Yahweh's rule over a polytheistic world of nature gods and mythological powers, rather than the sort of contrast between finite mountains and their infinite Creator which a modern/Western monotheist would draw.[24]

The rest of the passage continues this antisuperstitious trajectory. Unlike other ANE nature deities, Yahweh is alert enough to keep the suppliant from falling because he does not slumber and sleep (vv. 3–4), in contrast to Baal who needs to die annually in "sleep" and "wake" again as part of regenerating the natural world. It was for this reason that Elijah mocked the prophets of Baal by accusing their god of being too drowsy or dead to hear their cries and see their self-inflicted wounds (1 Kgs 18:27). And joining Mesopotamian motifs to its polemic against Canaanite motifs, the psalm identifies Yahweh as Israel's real guardian (v. 5) by proclaiming that "the sun [*šemeš*] will not harm you by day, nor the moon [*yārēaḥ*] by night" (v. 6). Here the Hebrew terms are cognates to the names for the Akkadian sun-god Shamash and Ugaritic moon-god Yarikh, lending this passage a mythological flavor that tends to be lost on modern people who view these celestial bodies as balls of gas and rock.[25] The real power ascribed to the sun and the moon in Israel's popular religion can be seen in the many references to the practice of venerating them

23. Leonard P. Maré, "Psalm 121: Yahweh's Protection against Mythological Powers," *Old Testament Essays* 19 (2006): 716.
24. Eugene H. Peterson, *A Long Obedience in the Same Direction: Discipleship in an Instant Society*, 20th anniversary ed. (Downers Grove, IL: InterVarsity Press, 2000), 41–42. Chapter 8 of this book will address creation themes in more detail.
25. The modern predilection to think of the sun and moon in physical terms is reflected in the suggestion that v. 5 speaks of their harmful rays from which Yahweh provides shade (e.g. Anthony R. Ceresko, "Psalm 121: A Prayer of a Warrior?," *Biblica* 70 [1989]: 507).

(e.g. Deut 4:19; 2 Kgs 23:5, 11; Ezek 8:16), as well as in proper names like Samson ("little sun") and the aforementioned Beth Shemesh ("house of the sun/Shamash").[26]

Psalm 121's confession of trust in Yahweh thus occurs against the backdrop of other ANE nature deities rather than in the theological distinction between Creator and creature. Yahweh is not only the ultimate nature deity, for he is also the best among personal deities for possessing a unique ability to "guard" (*šmr*) his people throughout time and space: "The LORD will keep [*šmr*] you from all harm – he will watch [*šmr*] over your life; the LORD will watch over [*šmr*] your coming and going both now and forevermore" (vv. 7–8). The two closing verses add three references to the Hebrew root *šmr* (cf. vv. 3, 5) to express the constancy of Yahweh's protection against every manner of evil. To experience this blessing requires the kind of repentance that turns away from other powers and toward Yahweh. However, since psalms of individual trust have been used to support the view that God unconditionally prevents harm from coming to the believer (as in some uses of Psalms 91 and 121 during the COVID-19 pandemic), it becomes essential to take a broader look at how the OT portrays the relationship between piety and prosperity, sin and suffering. The next section will undertake this examination of why Israel's exile happened. Did all those who were deported to Babylon truly deserve their punishment – individually, corporately, and across generations? During the sixth century BC, the book of Jeremiah in particular engaged critically with ideas about reward and retribution in Israelite popular religion which mirror those in Eastern religions and folk Christianity.

THE NATURE OF DIVINE REWARD AND RETRIBUTION: A CASE STUDY ON JEREMIAH

Judah's last four decades of existence spanned the chaotic events from King Josiah's reforms to Babylon's sacking of Jerusalem and the deportation of the city's inhabitants. During this period in the late seventh and early sixth centuries BC, the prophet Jeremiah was both witness to and participant in theological debates about the exile which competed for Judahite hearts and minds. The book that bears his name reveals how Yahwism addresses three kinds of Israelite popular religion, along with the different understandings of divine reward and retribution which are wrapped up in them: (1) revival and repentance in light of fatalism; (2) prosperity theology in light of pragmatism;

---

26. Maré, "Psalm 121," 719–20.

and (3) cosmic justice in light of suffering. Jeremiah's critical engagement with these forms of Judahite popular religion will supply a hermeneutical guide for how the Old Testament can respectively address some of the characteristic ideas of Islam, folk religion, and Buddhism. By applying the OT's depiction of Yahweh as personal, national, and nature deity to the real-world problems faced by Judah in exile, the book of Jeremiah provides an appropriate contextual theology that bridges official and popular expressions of religious piety, especially with reference to the divine will.

Revival and Repentance in Light of Fatalism: Jeremiah and Islam

As just noted, Judah's greatest moments of revival and repentance lie in the background of Jeremiah. The superscription to the book (Jer 1:1–3) indicates that the prophet ministered from King Josiah's thirteenth year (627 BC) until the fall of Jerusalem in King Zedekiah's eleventh year (587 BC). The four decades of Jeremiah's ministry began just before King Josiah initiated his religious reforms in 622 BC which temporarily overturned centuries of apostasy (2 Kgs 22–23).

Apostasy in Judah quickly returned when Josiah's son Jehoiakim reversed the reforms of his father and resumed the apostasy that had already led the northern kingdom of Israel into exile. Correspondingly, repentance faded as a possibility when a significant number of the people couched their *refusal* to repent as an *inability* to repent. It was not so much that Judah denied the fact of sinfulness (cf. Jer 2:31; 16:10–11), but rather accused Yahweh of failing to make a genuine offer of restoration in the first place: "Why do we sit still? Gather together, let us go into the fortified cities and perish there; for the LORD our God *has doomed us to perish*, and has given us poisoned water to drink, because we have sinned against the LORD" (8:14 NRSV). This lament indicates that Judah blamed the inevitability of exile on the trap created by Yahweh's holiness on the one hand, and his unwillingness to offer forgiveness on the other. After the exile Judah also blamed the ancestors for their sins which brought retribution on their descendants: "The parents have eaten sour grapes, and the children's teeth are set on edge" (31:29; cf. Ezek 18:2). With self-centered statements such as these, the "tragic fatalism" of Judah claimed that the combination of a distant deity and wicked ancestors meant that destruction had always been unavoidable.

The fatalism of Judah just described has certain resonances with Islam, the world religion that finds its largest number of adherents in modern Asia.[27] It is important not to generalize fatalism among Muslims as a universal or uniform phenomenon,[28] but predestination (Arab. *al-Qadr*) is certainly among Islam's six core beliefs.[29] The absoluteness of divine omnipotence and omniscience in Islam means that "God is the creator of all the acts of his servants, even as he is the creator of their essences[;] all that they do, be it good or evil, is in accordance with God's decree, predestination, desire and will."[30] While the concepts of human freedom and repentance for sin do exist in official Islam (e.g. Sūras 10:44; 13:11, 31), the practical implications of Allah's radical transcendence and sovereignty leave an existential void which popular Islam fills with other means of making contact with or seeking help from spiritual powers.[31] Precisely for this reason, the debate on how to reconcile *al-Qadr* with human agency has continued among Islamic thinkers till the present day.[32]

The book of Jeremiah addresses the theological predicament of fatalism by presenting Yahweh's transcendence as the *basis* and *motivation* for repentance rather than being opposed to it, as popular religion often holds it to be. In the sign-act narrative of Jeremiah 18, Yahweh declares his authority to revoke a previous decree of destruction if an unrighteous nation repents of its evil, while a righteous nation can still face destruction if it proceeds to do evil (18:7–11). That is, Yahweh wills his prior declarations of a nation's fate to be contingent upon its responsiveness, yet his sovereignty encompasses both the original decree to destroy as well as his subsequent decision to relent.[33] By combining the traits of authority and flexibility without compromising sovereignty, the God of Jeremiah makes a genuine invitation to repentance which contrasts with the near-determinism found in at least one statement of

27. Charles E. Farhadian, *Introducing World Religions: A Christian Engagement* (Grand Rapids, MI: Baker Academic, 2015), 416–17.
28. Gabriel A. Acevedo illustrates how Islam's relationship to fatalism must include examination of local factors such as income and education level. Overall, however, his cross-cultural analysis demonstrates that Islamic societies have a higher degree of fatalistic orientation than others (Gabriel A. Acevedo, "Islamic Fatalism and the Clash of Civilizations: An Appraisal of a Contentious and Dubious Theory," *Social Forces* 86 [2008]: 1737–40).
29. Shaik Kadir, *Islam Explained* (London: Marshall Cavendish, 2007), 164.
30. Ringgren, "Islamic Fatalism," 59.
31. Musk, "Popular Islam," 218; Weber, *Sociology of Religion*, 575.
32. Zakaria Wanfawan, "Qadar in Classical and Modern Islamic Discourses," *International Journal of Islamic Thought* 7 (2016): 39–48; Ahmet T. Karamustafa, "Fate," in *Encyclopaedia of the Qur'ān*, ed. Jane Dammen McAuliffe (Leiden: Brill, 2001), 2:185–88.
33. Terence E. Fretheim, "The Repentance of God: A Study of Jeremiah 18:7–10," *Hebrew Annual Review* 11 (1987): 81–92.

the Qur'an that makes reward and retribution the sole prerogative of Allah: "There is no calamity that befalls the earth or your own selves but in accordance with the law [of causation] before We make it evident" (Sūra 57:22).[34] As thus understood in the kind of Sunni Islam which is common in Southeast Asia (where the world's most populous Islamic nation, Indonesia, is located), the result of *al-Qadr* is that "although it is human beings who act, agency is created by God, because God creates all things."[35]

In addition, Jeremiah addresses the complaint of Judah's popular religion of Judah which viewed divine sovereignty about reward and retribution as an indication that any human response to Yahweh was futile: "It is no use! We will follow our own plans, and each of us will act according to the stubbornness of our evil will" (18:12 NRSV). Yahweh responded that because the people felt that repentance was impossible, their misunderstanding would soon become a reality when destruction by Babylon's hand arrived (18:13–17). Yet this irony occurred not because retribution was part of an impersonal God's unchangeable decree, but because the people made a self-fulfilling prophecy that rationalized their disobedience toward Yahweh. In sum, Jeremiah 18 challenges fatalism in both its Israelite and Islamic forms by showing that apostasy comes from human unwillingness to repent rather than a divine unwillingness to accept it. Yahweh is not so arbitrary that reward or retribution will happen to people regardless of how they respond to him.

Prosperity Theology in Light of Pragmatism: Jeremiah and Folk Religion

The previous section about Jeremiah's relevance to Islam and Hinduism primarily concerned the realm of official or "high" religion. But as noted already, popular or "low" religion tends to occupy the void when felt needs go unmet by the complexity of institutions or rituals which adherents perceive in its more formal counterpart. The primal urgency of immanence over transcendence in such contexts typically gives rise to trying an eclectic mixture of inputs for the "piety-prosperity equation" so that worshipers may receive blessing and avoid curse.

---

34. This rendering comes from Ahmed Ali, *Al-Qur'ān: A Contemporary Translation* (Princeton, NJ: Princeton University Press, 2001), 471.
35. Fauzan Saleh, *Modern Trends in Islamic Theological Discourse in 20th Century Indonesia: A Critical Study*, Social, Economic, and Political Studies of the Middle East and Asia 79 (Leiden: Brill, 2001), 118.

Jeremiah 44 addresses precisely this scenario of the Jewish refugees after they leave their homeland. In this narrative set in Egypt, the Jewish community reveals its pragmatism concerning which deity it will choose as they begin their diaspora existence. The people have evidently not learned the lesson that Jerusalem fell due to their apostasy from Yahweh (vv. 2–9). Thus they fail to heed Jeremiah's warning that history will soon repeat itself in Egypt (vv. 10–14), insisting instead that their veneration of other gods yielded better results than repentance toward Yahweh ever did (vv. 15–17). They are particularly contemptuous toward Josiah's reforms which did away with other deities such as the "queen of heaven": "But from the time we stopped making offerings to the queen of heaven and pouring out libations to her, we have lacked everything and have perished by the word and by famine" (v. 18 NRSV).

Because the queen of heaven was a Babylonian fertility deity thought to rule the heavenly hosts, it is no accident that Jeremiah 44 refers four times to the God of Israel as "the LORD *of hosts*" or "the LORD God *of hosts*" (vv. 2, 7, 11, 25 NRSV) rather than "your God" as the preceding chapters tend to do (e.g. 40:2; 42:2–5, 13, 20, 21). As Judah misinterpreted its recent history in the exile, the *correlation* between venerating the queen of heaven and experiencing prosperity has hereby been conflated with the *causation* that suffering must be the effect of rejecting her in favor of Yahweh.

Such a mechanistic worldview is common in Asia for reducing the supernatural (whether conceived as impersonal forces or personal deities) into a means toward practical ends such as prosperity, health, and fertility. Because people continue to pay homage to their own god or gods in syncretism, two conclusions quickly follow: that the experience of blessings becomes proof of one's piety, while the opposite experience of curses can be nothing other than impiety. This may sound like the OT's retribution principle that sin generally leads to suffering, but it has actually reversed it and hardened it into an absolute law – all suffering comes from sin, while all prosperity comes from righteousness.[36] This is not the OT's own understanding of causality, but the Eastern religious law of *karma* with which Job's friends concluded that his suffering proved that he had sinned.

More will be said below on karma, reward, and retribution in the discussion of Jeremiah and Buddhism. But it is pertinent to note that a pragmatic

---

36. On the impossibility of flattening the OT's various depictions of retribution, see Stephen B. Chapman, "Reading the Bible as Witness: Divine Retribution in the Old Testament," *Perspectives in Religious Studies* 31 (2004): 171–90.

approach to the sacred is common in societies influenced by Chinese folk reli-gion with its mixture of Confucianism, Taoism, Buddhism, ancestor worship, and animistic elements.[37] Even in a more Westernized society like Singapore, for example, the nation's core values of *meritocracy* and *self-determination* reflect a synthesis of ancient Chinese humanism and the modernizing presence of Western and/or Christian institutions.[38] As a result, this city-state has witnessed the *religious* pragmatism of seeking a variety of powers or deities joining forces with the *secular* pragmatism of Western capitalist principles and education in Christian-heritage mission schools to ensure prosperity for the nation.[39]

Against a similar line of pragmatic thinking, however, the God of Jeremiah reminds his people that he is not a force to be manipulated nor one of many deities with whom they can hedge their bets. The burning question of the Jewish community, "Was it ever worth it to follow Yahweh?," is certainly natural and not irrelevant. Jeremiah 44 nonetheless refutes such logic in a comprehensive manner both by asserting the uniqueness of Yahweh as "God of Israel" and by having him take over the queen of heaven's perceived powers and benefits as "God of hosts" (v. 7) – military, celestial, or otherwise.[40] In sum, the narrative depicts Yahweh as powerful and patient enough to allow syncretism to deconstruct itself via the futility of seeking whichever source of power is convenient at the moment (v. 28).

Cosmic Justice in Light of Suffering: Jeremiah and Bud-dhism

Along with Ecclesiastes, the book of Jeremiah is particularly suited to the existential questions of reward and retribution in Buddhism. The intensity of Jeremiah's multifaceted exploration of evil, suffering, and theodicy is mirrored by these being some of Buddhism's main themes. As Farhadian observes, "The

---

37. Farhadian, *Introducing World Religions*, 256; Winfried Corduan, *Neighboring Faiths: A Christian Introduction to World Religions*, 2nd ed. (Downers Grove, IL: IVP Academic, 2012), 410.

38. Clive S. Chin, *The Perception of Christianity as a Rational Religion in Singapore: A Missiological Analysis of Christian Conversion*, American Society of Missiology Monograph Series 31 (Eugene, OR: Pickwick, 2017), 82–88.

39. Brett McCracken, "How the Gospel Takes Root in 'Crazy Rich' Singapore," The Gospel Coalition, 24 September 2018, https://www.thegospelcoalition.org/article/gospel-takes-root-crazy-rich-singapore/.

40. In fact, the overlap between Yahweh and the "queen of heaven" is significant to the extent that some scholars wonder if Jeremiah 44's polemic against idolatry undermines itself because these two deities are too similar (e.g. Teresa Ann Ellis, "Jeremiah 44: What If 'the Queen of Heaven' is YHWH?," *Journal for the Study of the Old Testament* 33 [2009]: 465–88).

seriousness with which Buddhism recognizes and addresses suffering makes it an eminently appealing tradition for many. Everyone suffers. What is striking about Buddhism is the acute attention the tradition pays to analyzing and providing a cure for the universality of suffering."[41]

A comparison of suffering in Buddhism and Jeremiah will illustrate certain similarities between them. Like Siddhartha's Four Sights of *dukkha* (i.e. suffering) which led him to seek answers about the cause and solution for suffering in the Four Noble Truths, the ministry of Jeremiah begins with two visions which concern his work as the one who undeniably suffers the most among the OT prophets (1:11–18). As Siddhartha grew into the Lord Buddha, the pathway to enlightenment which he advocated in the Eightfold Path (in Chinese, the *ba zheng dao*) has notable similarities with Jeremiah's insistence that he is no theological innovator. Similarly to other Eastern religions, Jeremiah instead enjoins Judah to proceed along a well-known *Dao* (i.e. "way, path"): "Stand at the crossroads and look, and ask for the ancient paths [*gu dao*], where the good way [*shan dao*] lies; and walk [*xing*] in it; and find rest for your souls" (6:16 NRSV).[42] But as the prophet's failures and setbacks drive him to utter despair, he cries out, "Why did I come forth from the womb to see toil and sorrow [*lao lü chou ku*], and spend my days in shame?" (20:18 NRSV).[43] All this is not to argue that Buddhism and Jeremiah supply the same answers to life's questions, but simply to note that the act of translating Jeremiah into an Asian language such as Chinese inevitably brings the book into the same lexical field of suffering, evil, and retribution as Buddhist terminology. One major difference in Jeremiah's use of these terms, for example, is to express frustration that the expected links between sin and retribution as well as righteousness and reward are missing (as in the prophet's "Confessions" of chs. 11–20).

On this note, the prominence of retribution themes in Jeremiah suggests a conceptual bridge with the varied belief systems which come under the label "Buddhism." The concept of karma provides an entrée into all schools of Buddhism, as Damien Keown observes, since "belief in karma is a constant which underlies the philosophical diversity of the many Buddhist schools, and it is one of the few basic tenets to have escaped major reinterpretation over the course of time."[44] The nature of karmic justice varies in different

---

41. Farhadian, *Introducing World Religions*, 138.
42. On the commonality of *Dao / Tao* across Chinese religions, see Wan, "Tao."
43. The quotations in brackets are from the Chinese Union Version of the Bible.
44. Damien Keown, "Karma, Character, and Consequentialism," *Journal of Religious Ethics* 24 (1996): 329.

Buddhist systems, but always contains the feature that reward (i.e. good karma) and retribution (i.e. bad karma) for one life's actions are passed on to the next through *samsara* (i.e. reincarnation).[45] The fact that suffering is both the outgrowth of past karma and an opportunity to improve future karma leads Buddhists (and often Asians in general) to a paradoxical question: is suffering in one's present life a shameful burden to be rejected or a meritorious gift to be embraced?

This paradox receives a nuanced answer in Jeremiah's interaction with the misunderstandings of divine retribution in his time. Particularly in chapters 28–29, the book of Jeremiah affirms that suffering happens because punishment is necessary, but redemption and restoration are possible in this life rather than the next. On the one hand, Jeremiah 28 addresses the presumption of the false prophet Hananiah that the exile is unnecessary and will soon be reversed. Hananiah sets forth a "positive" version of karmic theology which conflates divine power to save with divine willingness to do so (28:2–4), resulting in the false expectation that Yahweh must end the deportation of the Judahites and Jehoiachin their king on Hananiah's terms (that is, within two years). On the other hand, Jeremiah 29 contains a letter of reassurance to the exiles who have fallen into "negative" karmic theology – the notion that restoration is impossible because Yahweh is either unwilling or unable to deliver his people from Babylon (29:8–9). Jeremiah responds that exile was not only a punishment, but also an act of preservation for the refugees in Babylon (29:10–14).

In his response to both forms of karmic theology, Jeremiah's multifaceted message could perhaps be framed in Buddhist terms: *dukkha* is real because the law of karma must apply for sins committed, but karma results from the intervention of a personal God rather than the causality of an impersonal universe. Because of this relational involvement, the punishment of karma is intended to bear good fruit in one's present existence rather than only a future one, making *samsara* across lives unnecessary for redemption to take place. The exile will be neither short nor forever, yet aims toward the greater purpose of restoration from exile.

Or in Chinese Buddhist terms, the common proverb about retribution that "vice begets curse, virtue begets blessing" (*e you e bao, shan you shan bao*) is challenged when Jeremiah asserts that the putatively simple one-to-one relationship between cause and effect is actually a many-to-many relationship.

---

45. Bruce R. Reichenbach, "The Law of Karma and the Principle of Causation," *Philosophy East and West* 38 (1988): 399–410.

Though the vice of apostasy begets the curse of exile, exile is not an end in itself but another opportunity for virtue, as when the Jewish refugees in Babylon are implored to use their humiliation as an opportunity to learn virtue rather than vice. Moreover, the curse of exile is a blessing in disguise since life in Babylon offers a sanctuary for the refugees (29:4–7) who would otherwise not survive the final destruction of Jerusalem. The *retributive* aspect of suffering therefore continues to function but contains a this-worldly *restorative* aspect. Not only this, but the prophet who was predestined for suffering (1:17–19) becomes a theological symbol because of his Creator God's suffering, weeping, and messy involvement with his own creatures in the drama of redemption (9:1–3).

Jeremiah's depiction of multiple purposes for the exile demonstrates how cosmic justice by its nature requires multiple causes and effects. This conclusion undercuts both Western and non-Western approaches to reward and retribution, though in different ways. In the West, redaction criticism tends to fragment Jeremiah's variety into supposedly irreconcilable literary layers rather than keeping them in dialogical tension.[46] Judgment and deliverance are then reckoned to different periods of Jeremiah's message. Interestingly in the non-Western world, religions like Buddhism share this tendency to treat reward and retribution as monolithic concepts which are mutually exclusive, except that the separation between supposedly contradictory ideas occurs across human incarnations instead of literary layers.[47] In both parts of the world, however, such understandings of suffering offer unsatisfying answers for why the righteous often suffer and the unrighteous often prosper. The ensuing reductionism often becomes a forced choice between prosperity theology and blaming the victim.

CONCLUSION

The people of Yahweh in every age have been prone to misunderstand official Yahwism and turn it into the popular religion of trying to manipulate him like a magical power or diminish his justice into a karmic force. Because this impersonal understanding of retribution differs little from animism or karma, Edwin Good rightly observes, "The chief enemy of faith in the Old Testament

---

46. Cf. Robert P. Carroll, "Synchronic Deconstructions of Jeremiah: Diachrony to the Rescue? Reflections on Some Reading Strategies for Understanding Certain Problems in the Book of Jeremiah," in *Synchronic or Diachronic? A Debate on Method in Old Testament Exegesis*, ed. J. C. de Moor (Leiden: Brill, 1995), 39–51.
47. Cf. A. R. Wadia, "Philosophical Implications of the Doctrine of Karma," *Philosophy East and West* 15 (1965): 145–52.

is magic,"[48] by which he means the superstition that "the right deed at the right moment, or the wrong deed at the right moment, will inexorably be followed by results good or bad."[49] Throughout the history of Israel but especially after the shattering event of exile, the experience of defeat or weakness among the nations led Yahweh's people to seek ways of seizing control over their destiny instead of walking by faith with the personal, cosmic, and nature deity who promised to uphold all aspects of their lives. The official religion which promised blessings as long as Israel did not seek them for their own sake was compromised by the popular religion of using God as a selfish means to their own ends.

The allure of such syncretism is hardly unique to OT times. For in the modern technological world, in both Minority and Majority World contexts, the primal temptation to humanism remains present in the impulse to control one's destiny through science and other myths about self-actualization – what Lesslie Newbigin has labeled the Enlightenment's illusion to have become an autonomous possessor of "the secret of knowledge and therefore the secret of mastery over the world."[50] In this regard, Yahwism stands equally against the animist's rituals to control the natural world and the technologist's quest to harness the scientific universe in the name of human progress. The missional God of Israel promises to draw near to his people with a unique blend of presence and power which dethrones the presumption that human causation is the key that unlocks the Creator's domain.

When this essential lesson goes unlearned, however, what Roger Olson said of folk Christians in the West is all the more true of Christians in Asia when they misuse the OT in prosperity theology: "To the extent that Christianity is reduced to folk religion, it ghettoizes itself from the wider culture and fails to be an influence in the public square."[51] For these reasons, the next chapter will explore how the OT's distinctive teaching on covenant, law, and kinship supplies the theological resources for Asian Christians to understand their relationship with God using familial concepts that are more native to their cultures than the Western legal categories of conditionality and unconditionality.

---

48. Edwin M. Good, *Irony in the Old Testament*, 2nd ed., Bible and Literature Series (Sheffield: Almond Press, 1981), 196.
49. Good, *Irony in the Old Testament*, 197–98.
50. Newbigin, *Foolishness to the Greeks*, 23.
51. Roger E. Olson, *Questions to All Your Answers: The Journey from Folk Religion to Examined Faith* (Grand Rapids, MI: Zondervan, 2008), 18.

CHAPTER 5

COVENANT, LAW, AND KINSHIP

Disney's animated films provide a window into how the West relates to the cultures of "the rest." Particularly in the 1990s, the trio of *Aladdin* (1992), *The Lion King* (1994), and *Mulan* (1998) offered an introduction of sorts to the Middle East, Africa, and Asia, respectively. Each film was acclaimed by its target audience in North America, but people in the cultures depicted were often less enthusiastic due to the feeling that they had been "Disneyfied," that is, reduced to catchy songs that appeal to Western sensibilities. *Aladdin* did poorly in Arab countries and its use of racist stereotypes has come to be acknowledged by Disney itself. *The Lion King* continues to arouse mixed feelings among Africans, as in their exasperation at Disney's move to trademark the Swahili expression "Hakuna matata" which the film made famous. *Mulan* also fell flat in the Chinese world due to its distorted portrayal of courtship, honor, and shame.

Disney has been forthcoming about its past of cultural blinders.[1] However, the problem of the West's caricatures of non-Western societies has a long history which is difficult to overcome. This is especially the case in understanding and contextualizing the Bible, for the challenge of historical distance makes it impossible to employ Disney's strategy of using native consultants to provide an insider's view of living cultures. Western scholars of the Bible and mission thus face a constant struggle with what social scientists call *reification* – the imposition of overly broad and abstract models onto concrete cultures without attending to their specific features and differences. Or to restate this problem in Disneyesque terms, the 1998 *Mulan* movie was presented as an appreciation of Chinese culture, but it blended a Western narrative of self-actualization

---

1. On its Disney+ streaming service, Disney recently added the disclaimer that *Aladdin* contains "negative depictions and/or mistreatment of people and cultures" (Samuel Gelman, "Disney+ Updates Offensive Content Disclaimer for Aladdin, Peter Pan and More," CBR, https://www.cbr.com/disney-plus-update-disclaimer-aladdin-peter-pan/). It is revealing that all the other Disney films with this disclaimer are much older than *Aladdin* (1992), such as *Fantasia* (1940), *Dumbo* (1941), *Song of the South* (1946), *Peter Pan* (1953), and *Lady and the Tramp* (1955).

with a Middle Eastern understanding of honor and shame. The original tale's emphasis on filial piety and loyalty was lost.[2]

The Old Testament institutions of covenant, law, and kinship have been similarly distorted in Western scholarship due to cultural biases toward individualism and libertarianism. In addition, the move to group these three institutions together may come as a surprise to readers with a Protestant instinct to view covenant through the juridical lens of law rather than the familial lens of kinship. Since such tendencies appear in both Western biblical scholarship and missiology, an Asian perspective on the authority and kinship structures of traditional societies will be profitable to situate them better within their original OT context and to draw interpretive analogies for modern Asia. As we will see, the OT is uniquely holistic in its world for subordinating legal stipulations to the familial framework of Yahweh's covenant with his people. The so-called "law codes" of the OT are family matters of the community more than legal matters of the court, in much the same way as Asian societies typically conceive of themselves as an extension of the family. At the same time, we would be mistaken to apply an overgeneralized understanding of kinship, honor, and patronage to the OT or to extrapolate these cultural values to the entire non-Western world, as biblical scholars and missiologists in the West have sometimes done. The need for contextualization that reflects OT covenant and law's balance between objectivity and relationality will inform the case studies on the cultural values of Chinese *guanxi* ("connections") and Filipino *utang na loob* ("debt of gratitude") which conclude this chapter.

COVENANT AND LAW IN WESTERN PERSPECTIVE

Certain Western assumptions about *covenant* and *law* in the OT are encoded in the usual definitions of these terms. "Covenant" is the standard rendering of Hebrew *bĕrît* (287x in the OT), but the English word carries the legal connotation of "contract" at the expense of the kinship ideas underlying the Hebrew term which we will explore below. It has thus become common in Western OT scholarship to classify covenant as a subcategory of law even though they sprang from discrete cultural traditions of the ancient Near East. The fact that covenant and law are already blended in the OT makes it easy for readers to miss how uniquely it has synthesized these traditions.

---

2. Qing Yang, "Mulan in China and America: From Premodern to Modern," *Comparative Literature: East & West* 2 (2018): 45–59.

"Law" is the usual English translation of Hebrew *tôrāh*. This follows a trend in the West that dates from the renderings of *nomos* in the Greek Septuagint and *lex* in the Latin Vulgate. The term *tôrāh* nonetheless denotes the pedagogical idea of "instruction" more than the legal idea of "law." The Torah (i.e. the Hebrew name for the Pentateuch) contains far more narrative than legal material, showing that all "law" is pedagogical but not all "instruction" is legal. But when a narrow definition for "law" is joined to a juridical understanding of "covenant," the result in OT scholarship and Christian theology has been a fixation on the legal ideas of unconditionality and conditionality in conceiving of God's relationship to people. Popular-level Christianity conceptualizes this relationship most frequently using the legal category of "God's *unconditional* love." Such a formulation is not unique to the West, since the Enlightenment's axiom of the individual's freedom from tradition has special appeal for those weary of the patron-client expectations that often govern relationships in Asian cultures – an instance of cultural diffusion and hybridity to which this chapter will return later.

The epitome of Western distortions of covenant and law can be found in the work of Julius Wellhausen, the German scholar of the OT best known for his JEDP "documentary hypothesis." His view of the Pentateuch's three-stage composition of Yahwist-Elohist (JE),[3] Deuteronomic (D), and Priestly (P) sources is in the minority today. Yet the directions charted in his 1878 book *Prolegomena to a History of Israel* remain influential in OT scholarship. Wellhausen described his method as the task of exposing the *Zeitgeist* ("spirit of the age") of the Bible,[4] but historians of OT scholarship have come to recognize that he reflects the German intellectual culture of the nineteenth century. The torrent that was Wellhausen's *Prolegomena* gained strength from several tributaries of German history, among which were philosophical naturalism, Romanticism, and anti-Semitism. The interconnectedness of these streams will become especially apparent in our discussion of anti-Semitism in Wellhausen's work.

Upon the release of *Prolegomena*, its bias of philosophical naturalism was immediately recognized by Franz Delitzsch, the conservative German OT scholar mentioned in chapter 1. Delitzsch observed that "Wellhausen's

---

3. The J signum in JEDP comes from "Jahwe/JHWH," the German spelling of "Yahweh/YHWH."
4. Julius Wellhausen, *Prolegomena to the History of Israel* (Cleveland, OH: World Publishing Company, 1957), 82.

speculations [were] merely applications of Darwinism to the sphere of theology and criticism."[5] The fact that Wellhausen used several evolutionary terms led many to associate him with Georg Wilhelm Friedrich Hegel's hypothesis of societal progress.[6] Evidence for Wellhausen's philosophical naturalism also comes from his statements about the gradual development of monotheism. In nineteenth-century Europe where monotheism was commonly considered a higher and therefore later form of religion than polytheism,[7] Wellhausen identified the same trajectory toward "ethical monotheism"[8] in his documentary hypothesis. His reconstruction of Israel's history viewed the introduction of *bĕrît* terminology by the eighth-century prophets (e.g. Amos) as part of a theological revolution in which "the [previously unconditional] relation of Jehovah to Israel was conditioned by the demands of His righteousness, as set forth in His word and instruction."[9] The carefree religion of the patriarchal age in the JE sources supposedly devolved through the demands of the D and P sources "to familiarise the Jewish mind with the idea that the covenant depended on conditions, and might possibly be dissolved."[10]

Related to Wellhausen's evolutionary scheme was his appropriation of German Romanticism. As just hinted, Wellhausen's primary criterion for classifying Pentateuchal texts as early was the degree to which they exhibited a character that was free from institutional organization and religious ritual. The elaborate sacrifices, instructions, and regulations of the P source were the outcome of the strictness of Mosaic Yahwism in the "Deuteronomic" (D) source. The final form of the Pentateuch in the Second Temple period reflected what Wellhausen disdained as "the Judaising tendency to remove God to a distance from man."[11]

---

5. Rudolf Smend, "Julius Wellhausen and His Prolegomena to the History of Israel," trans. A. Graeme Auld, *Semeia* 25 (1982): 14.
6. Wellhausen's use of terms such as "denaturalization," "process," and especially the word "evolution" itself touched off a debate over whether "Hegel begat Vatke, Vatke begat Wellhausen." Though Wellhausen's system was frequently linked with Hegel's hypothesis of societal progress, his view of humankind's decline rather than rise differs significantly from Hegel (Albert de Pury, "Le Pentateuque en question: position du problème et brève histoire de la recherche," in *Le Pentateuque en question*, eds. Thomas C. Römer and Albert de Pury, 3rd ed. [Geneva: Labor et Fides, 2002], 28).
7. See discussion in Gerald Bray, *Biblical Interpretation: Past and Present* (Downers Grove, IL: IVP Academic, 1996), 302–3.
8. Julius Wellhausen, *Sketch of the History of Israel and Judah* (London: Adam & Charles Black, 1891), 88.
9. Wellhausen, *Prolegomena*, 418.
10. Wellhausen, 419.
11. Wellhausen, 79.

An example of how Romantic influences steered Wellhausen's thought and thereby shaped OT scholarship can be found in his treatment of Exodus 34. Bernard Levinson has shown that Wellhausen was powerfully moved by Johann Wolfgang von Goethe's suggestion a century prior that Exodus 34 contained the earliest Decalogue.[12] Goethe had proposed that Exodus 34:6–7 preserved an early Decalogic tradition of Yahweh's benevolence as "compassionate and gracious, slow to anger, abounding in lovingkindness in truth." As such, this version of the Decalogue was universally offered to all and devoid of the particularism that Goethe and Wellhausen found repugnant in later Jewish thought. Levinson concludes, "What motivates Wellhausen's appropriation of this model [is] primarily a romantic yearning for originality and antiquity."[13]

The twin streams of philosophical naturalism and German Romanticism led to the third and most troubling feature of Wellhausen's thought: his hostility toward Jews. Wellhausen's contempt for the law is evident on *Prolegomena's* first page when he summarizes his investigation as "the question whether . . . [the] law is the starting-point for the history of ancient Israel or rather for that of Judaism."[14] Similarly in the 1881 edition of *Encyclopedia Britannica*, Wellhausen's scathing article on Israel oozes with contempt for the Priestly code which he regarded as the basis of Judaism:

> Judaism . . . is an irregular product of history. . . . [It is] every-where historically comprehensible, and yet it is a mass of antin-omies. . . . We meet with a pedantic asceticism which is far from lovely, and with pious wishes the greediness of which is ill-con-cealed; and these unedifying features are the dominant ones of the system. . . . The Creator of heaven and earth becomes the manager of a petty scheme of salvation; the living God descends from His throne to make way for the law. The law thrusts itself in everywhere; it commands and blocks up the access to heaven; it regulates and sets limits to the understanding of the divine

---

12. Bernard M. Levinson, "Goethe's Analysis of Exodus 34 and Its Influence on Wellhausen: The *Pfropfung* of the Documentary Hypothesis," *Zeitschrift für die alttestamentliche Wissenschaft* 114 (2002): 212–23; cf. Julius Wellhausen, *Die Composition des Hexateuchs und der historischen Bücher des Alten Testaments*, 4th ed. (Berlin: Walter de Gruyter, 1963), 84, 95.
13. Levinson, "Goethe's Analysis," 222, n. 36.
14. Wellhausen, *Prolegomena*, 1.

> working on earth. As far as it can, it takes the soul out of religion
> and spoils morality.[15]

Wellhausen's disdain for the conditionality of OT law continues in his analysis of those who made greatest use of it: the Pharisees of Jesus's time. In a wide-ranging survey of anti-Jewish statements in the Wellhausen corpus, the Israeli scholar Moshe Weinfeld rightly concludes that "Wellhausen continues extolling the Church and denigrating Judaism."[16] Wellhausen was consistent in this regard with the anti-Semitic milieu in nineteenth-century Germany.[17]

It is revealing that Wellhausen's later discussion of Islam reflects the same biases as his work on Judaism. In esteeming Arabs more highly than Islam itself, Wellhausen opined that the later era of Islam lacked intellectual openness and was governed by fundamentalist law. Wellhausen again found a ready opponent to criticize by exchanging the patriarchal nomads of Canaan for the Bedouin traders of Arabia,[18] both doomed to disappear into the suffocating conditionality of their respective systems. Irrespective of which religion Wellhausen was dealing with, his conclusions regarding each were formally identical. This indicates that his convictions were not a matter of evidence but of an Enlightenment bias toward the autonomy of the individual.

It would be simplistic to say that OT scholarship in the West reproduces Wellhausen's inclinations, even in the characteristically German discipline of literary criticism.[19] Nevertheless, his characteristic dichotomy between unconditionality and conditionality (which presupposes Judaism's fixation on the latter) has endured in modern OT scholarship, even in the aftermath of the Holocaust as the greatest abomination of anti-Semitism. This is not the place to recount the conflicted relationship between OT scholarship and anti-Semitism

---

15. Wellhausen, 508–9. The 1957 reprint of *Prolegomena* appends a reprint of Wellhausen's 1881 *Encyclopedia Britannica* article.

16. Moshe Weinfeld, *The Place of the Law in the Religion of Ancient Israel* (Leiden: Brill, 2004), 5.

17. Lou Silberman, "Wellhausen and Judaism," *Semeia* 25 (1982): 75–82, makes helpful qualifying remarks about the extent of Wellhausen's feelings toward Jews.

18. See the assessment of Wellhausen's attitudes toward Muslim Arabs and Islam in Kurt Rudolph, "Wellhausen as an Arabist," *Semeia* 25 (1982): 115.

19. The early twentieth-century German scholar Walther Eichrodt, for example, argued that covenant was a mutual commitment in which "the relationship with God has the character of a relationship of grace, that is to say, it is founded on a primal act in history, maintained on definite conditions and protected by a powerful divine Guardian" (*Theology of the Old Testament*, 2 vols., Old Testament Library [Philadelphia: Westminster, 1967], 1:36).

in pre–World War II Germany.[20] But it is telling that an implicit association between conditionality, the exilic dating of the P source, and Second Temple Judaism continues to play a significant role today in OT scholarship on covenant and law (though certainly without Wellhausen's anti-Semitic overtones). NT scholarship, by contrast, has undergone a reckoning through advocates of *covenantal nomism*[21] helping to achieve a more balanced picture of Second Temple Judaism as a religion of both grace and law.

The persistence of Wellhausen's categories can be seen in form-critical studies on the links between ANE treaties and covenants in the Hebrew Bible. In a widely cited 1970 article, Moshe Weinfeld argued that ANE political documents could be divided into royal grants which confirmed the suzerain's commitment to the vassal (usually the promise of land or kingship), and suzerainty treaties which codified a vassal's obligations to the suzerain. His interpretation of the ANE data adopted the unconditional-conditional divide popularized by Wellhausen, for Weinfeld asserted that the "promissory type" (i.e. Abrahamic, Davidic) expresses the unconditionality of the royal grant, while the "obligatory type" (i.e. Israelite) reflects the conditionality of the suzerainty treaty.[22] Weinfeld's strict contrast between grants and treaties found wide acceptance,[23] but newer research indicates that these ANE documents cannot be categorized so easily in unconditional and conditional terms.[24] In addition, the legal designations "unconditional" and "conditional" tend to obscure the

---

20. On which see Bernard M. Levinson, "Reading the Bible in Nazi Germany: Gerhard von Rad's Attempt to Reclaim the Old Testament for the Church," *Interpretation: A Journal of Bible and Theology* 62 (July 2008): 238–54.

21. A term coined by E. P. Sanders in his famous 1977 book *Paul and Palestinian Judaism*. For a more recent discussion, see his "Covenantal Nomism Revisited," *Jewish Studies Quarterly* 16 (2009): 23–55.

22. Moshe Weinfeld, "The Covenant of Grant in the Old Testament and in the Ancient Near East," *Journal of the American Oriental Society* 90 (1970): 184–85, 189, 195–96.

23. E.g. Eugene H. Merrill, *Everlasting Dominion: A Theology of the Old Testament* (Nashville, TN: Broadman & Holman, 2006), 238–45, 432–42; Graham Davies, "Covenant, Oath, and the Composition of the Pentateuch," in *Covenant as Context: Essays in Honour of E. W. Nicholson*, eds. A. D. H. Mayes and R. B. Salters (Oxford: Oxford University Press, 2003), 71–83; Bruce K. Waltke, "The Phenomenon of Conditionality within Unconditional Covenants," in *Israel's Apostasy and Restoration: Essays in Honor of Roland K. Harrison*, ed. Avraham Gileadi (Grand Rapids, MI: Baker, 1988), 129–39; Walther Zimmerli, "Sinaibund und Abrahambund: Ein Beitrag zum Verständnis der Priesterschrift," in *Gottes Offenbarung: gesammelte Aufsätze zum Alten Testament* (Munich: C. Kaiser, 1963), 205–16.

24. Gary N. Knoppers, "David's Relation to Moses: The Contexts, Content and Conditions of the Davidic Promises," in *King and Messiah in Israel and the Ancient Near East: Proceedings of the Oxford Old Testament Seminar*, JSOT Supplement Series (Sheffield: Sheffield Academic Press, 1998), 91–118; "Ancient Near Eastern Royal Grants and the Davidic Covenant: A Parallel?," *Journal of the American Oriental Society* 116 (1996): 670–97.

relational aspects that inhere in all covenants and treaties. These problems made it natural for studies of OT covenant and law to draw on social concepts such as patronage and kinship, though again not without certain Western biases.

PATRONAGE AND KINSHIP IN WESTERN PERSPECTIVE

In a 1998 essay on "Kinship and Covenant in Ancient Israel," Frank Moore Cross issued an important corrective to OT scholarship's frequent conflation of covenant with law. This already classic study showed that the tendency to consider familial language as "covenant terminology . . . is to turn things upside down. The language of covenant, kinship-in-law, is taken from the language of kinship, kinship-in-flesh."[25] Though Cross was careful to root his analysis in West Semitic tribal structures, the more typical approach has been the application of a pan-Mediterranean anthropological model which centers on reciprocity, gift-giving and the cultural norms of honor and shame.[26] Nonetheless, the Greco-Roman model that underlies so-called "Mediterraneanism" is more suited to the Hellenistic world of the NT than to the ancient Near Eastern world of the OT.

Several scholars have utilized the concepts of patronage and kinship to OT covenants, both in their divine-human and human-human forms. Niels Peter Lemche, for example, generalizes the Roman model of patronage to describe any "relationship found between people of different standings in decentralized, partly centralized political societies, as well as in centralized states, on the verge of collapse. . . . The patronage system governs the political interplay between various members of such societies."[27] Reflecting this broad definition, a pan-Mediterranean model is evident when Lemche also links ancient Romans with Italian-Americans in the twentieth century by identifying

25. Frank Moore Cross, "Kinship and Covenant in Ancient Israel," in *From Epic to Canon: History and Literature in Ancient Israel* (Baltimore, MD: The Johns Hopkins University Press, 1998), 11; cf. Paul Kalluveettil, *Declaration and Covenant: A Comprehensive Review of Covenant Formulae from the Old Testament and the Ancient Near East*, Analecta Biblica 88 (Rome: Biblical Institute, 1982), 213.

26. E.g. J. Schäder, "Patronage and Clientage between God, Israel, and the Nations: An Investigation of Psalm 47," *Journal for Semitics* 19 (2010): 235–62; Saul M. Olyan, "Honor, Shame, and Covenant Relations in Ancient Israel and Its Environment," *Journal of Biblical Literature* 115 (1996): 201–18. See the history of research in James N. Jumper, "Honor and Shame in the Deuteronomic Covenant and the Deuteronomistic Presentation of the Davidic Covenant" (PhD diss., Harvard University, 2013), 8–41.

27. Niels Peter Lemche, "Kings and Clients: On Loyalty between the Ruler and the Ruled in Ancient 'Israel,'" in *Biblical Studies and the Failure of History*, Changing Perspectives 3 (Sheffield: Equinox, 2013), 201–2.

the mafia relationships in *The Godfather* movie (1972) as a prime example of patronage.[28] In addition, Lemche's example of *The Godfather* illustrates the dilemmas that arise when a client is unable to refuse the patron's demands due to the power differential between them.

Another problem with pan-Mediterranean approaches to patronage and kinship has been the assumption that "limited good" in these societies (whether conceived as material, social, or relational capital) steers all interactions between people to be transactional in nature.[29] Reciprocity between parties is certainly a feature of covenants and agreements between people in the OT,[30] as when David and Jonathan pledge loyalty to one another in a "covenant" (*bĕrît*) of mutual protection from Saul's threats (1 Sam 20). In divine-human covenants, however, Yahweh's favor to Israel is depicted as overwhelming and generous to such an extent that no reciprocity is truly possible.[31] This degree of asymmetricity reflects the unexpected role of Yahweh himself as a covenant partner rather than the usual role of deity as a witness to human-human agreements. Later we will explore how Yahweh's elevation of an entire nation (and not merely a chosen individual, such as a king) to participate in his covenant relativizes the power dynamics which typically operate between patrons and clients.

Third and most problematically, the links drawn between gift-giving, honor, and social status reflect an idealized Western view of patronage and clientage as a relational negotiation which traffics in unspoken expectations. In such a view of "Mediterranean" societies, every act of exchange and counter-exchange becomes a competitive matter since it occurs in full view of the so-called "Public Court of Reputation." Approval from patrons, superiors, or rulers becomes an achievement to be sought at all costs and especially at the expense of others. But to the extent that the need for reciprocity or claims upon honor are a zero-sum game that dominate everyday life in the Mediterranean, such generalizations still overlook how the OT's combination of covenant and law provides a counterculture to the hypermasculinity which such an antagonistic environment inevitably creates. Zeba Crook demonstrates that the equation

28. Lemche, "Kings and Clients," 201.
29. Cf. T. R. Hobbs, "Reflections on Honor, Shame, and Covenant Relations," *Journal of Biblical Literature* 116 (1997): 501–3.
30. Adrian Schenker, "L'origine de l'idée d'une alliance entre Dieu et Israël dans l'Ancien Testament," *Revue biblique* 92 (1988): 184–94.
31. Zeba Crook, "Reciprocity: Covenantal Exchange as a Test Case," in *Ancient Israel: The Old Testament in Its Social Context*, ed. Philip F. Esler (Minneapolis, MN: Fortress, 2006), 84; George E. Mendenhall, *Law and Covenant in Israel and the Ancient Near East* (Pittsburgh: Biblical Colloquium, 1955), 25.

of patronage with covenant neglects how covenants have detailed stipulations that formalize the expectations upon both parties.[32] The frequent view that "patronage is the root metaphor underlying the fundamental idea of covenant in the biblical literature"[33] is not so much incorrect as it is incomplete.

The next section will outline how the OT's posture toward its cultural environment challenges the validity and use of a pan-Mediterranean model. This will likewise suggest that attempts to employ patronage, honor, and shame as neutral concepts for contextualization ultimately go against the biblical grain. While it is generally true that the biblical world is more communal than individual in orientation, approaches to contextualization which overlook the Bible's opposition to hypersensitivity about reciprocity and reputation are unable to resolve problems with collectivism in the Majority World, such as favoritism, corruption, and groupthink. In other words, outsider/etic analyses of patronage and kinship tend to neglect the depth of insider/emic struggles and conflicts about these issues. In both Western OT scholarship and missiology, the use of patronage and kinship in studies of covenant and law sometimes only exchanges one kind of conditionality with another. The main difference is that the one-sidedness of expectations has shifted from legal stipulations (as in Western OT scholarship) to relational demands (as in Western missiology). Therefore, we need to examine how the OT's recasting of covenant and law presents a deeper form of contextualization which includes a cultural critique of reciprocity in addition to engaging it. The next chapter will study matters of reputation, honor, and shame in more detail.

THE OT'S CONTEXTUALIZATION OF COVENANT AND LAW

As noted, covenant and law in the OT have certain resemblances to their respective ANE counterparts in political treaties and legal codes. At the same time, they stand apart since the OT not only joins these institutions together, but also adds notable differences to each which exalt Yahweh as covenant-maker and lawgiver. The result is that the OT undermines the consolidation of power by human patrons and leaders, most notably the Israelite king. To appreciate the nuances of the OT's posture in its world, we will retrace how the OT blends the political institutions of covenant and law to show that Yahweh is

---

32. Crook, "Reciprocity," 84–90.
33. Ronald A. Simkins, "Patronage and the Political Economy of Monarchic Israel," *Semeia* 87 (1999): 129. Cf. Jayson Georges, *Ministering in Patronage Cultures: Biblical Models and Missional Implications* (Downers Grove, IL: InterVarsity Press, 2019), 40.

the ultimate patron and kin to Israel. The book of Deuteronomy brings into sharp relief how the OT draws on familial concepts from the ancient Near East but takes them in new directions. In the process it offers an alternative vision of life as "a Mediterranean counterculture."[34]

Covenants in the ancient Near East take on numerous forms such as loyalty oaths, royal grants, suzerain-vassal treaties, and parity treaties. The OT contains many of these types as well. Remarkably for readers accustomed to the Bible, however, the roughly seventy extant treaty and covenant documents from the ancient Near East typically record a *human-human* agreement. Variations abound in other respects, such as across time and geography (e.g. Hatti in the second millennium BC vs. Assyria in the first millennium), societal contexts (e.g. political treaties vs. religious documents), relational configurations (e.g. relationships between equals vs. unequals), and literary features (e.g. the placement of the witness list in Hittite vs. Assyrian treaties).[35] But with the exception of a third-millennium BC covenant between a man and his deity in Sumer,[36] the notion of a *divine-human* covenant is unique to the OT. And in contrast to the Sumerian example, the OT's presentation of the Israelite covenant is of Yahweh's dealings with an entire nation instead of a single individual.

This aspect of distinctiveness goes hand in hand with several theological innovations in Deuteronomy. First and foremost is that Yahweh takes on the usual role of the king in suzerain-vassal treaties who enjoins loyalty upon his subjects. The OT corpus is also striking for depicting Yahweh both as covenant witness (as in Jacob and Laban's parity treaty in Gen 31) as well as covenant partner (as in the Israelite covenant at Sinai and its renewals). In fact, Exodus and Deuteronomy impart royal authority to the entire polity of Israel by identifying them as "my [Yahweh's] firstborn" (Exod 4:22) and "children of Yahweh your God" (Deut 14:1).[37] This is a democratization of the royal title "son of [the] god[s]" which usually identifies someone as the favored choice of the gods to rule on their behalf, as in the Davidic covenant (2 Sam 7:14–20; Ps 2:7; cf. Exod 19:5–6). By the same token, for Yahweh to identify himself

34. Seth Schwartz, *Were the Jews a Mediterranean Society? Reciprocity and Solidarity in Ancient Judaism* (Princeton, NJ: Princeton University Press, 2010), 31.
35. For a full catalogue of relevant ANE documents, see Kenneth A. Kitchen and Paul J. N. Lawrence, *Treaty, Law and Covenant in the Ancient Near East*, 3 vols. (Wiesbaden: Harrassowitz, 2012).
36. The covenant between King Urukagina of Lagash and Ningirsu his deity is noted by Kenneth A. Kitchen, "Egypt, Qatna, and Covenant," *Ugarit-Forschungen* 11 (1979): 462.
37. Author's translation.

as Israel's father (Deut 1:31; 8:5; 32:6, 18) broadens dramatically the usual scope of covenants so that all Israel becomes Yahweh's kin.

The elevation of all Israel to royalty and family coincides with restrictions on kings in Israel, particularly as expressed in Deuteronomy's "Law of the King" (17:14–20). The Israelite king was forbidden from accumulating horses, wives, and precious metals for himself (17:16–17), with limitations set on his power in the military and economic realms which diverge from other ANE kings.[38] In addition, the stipulation for the Israelite king to copy the Deuteronomic Torah in the presence of the priests (17:18–19) made him subject to the leadership offices of prophets and priests. Prophets and priests were typically subordinate to kings in the rest of the ANE, but they outranked kings in Israel (at least during those times when Israelite kingship was functioning according to the Deuteronomic pattern). To summarize, the requirement for the king to be one of "your brothers"[39] (17:15, 20) uses kinship language to express how kings in Israel were no longer the exclusive mediators between heaven and earth. Such was the case both for speaking God's word to people (as prophets) and for bringing the people's requests before God (as priests). Deuteronomy delegates the former function to the Torah and the prophets who enforce it, and the latter to the Levitical priesthood.

The role of Israelite kings is also curtailed with reference to law as with covenant. Law codes in the ancient Near East typically aimed to celebrate the justice of kings, but OT law differs in this regard for claiming its origin from Yahweh rather than the king. The Code of Hammurabi, for instance, asserts that the king of Babylon is "Hammurabi, the pious prince, who venerates the gods, to make justice prevail in the land, to abolish the wicked and the evil, to prevent the strong from oppressing the weak. . . . I established truth and justice as the declaration of the land, I enhanced the well-being of the people."[40] In the next chapter, we will examine how OT historiography is royal in origin but often anti-royal in theme, unlike its cultural counterparts with their propagandistic agenda to magnify kingly honor and downplay kingly shame. The OT tends to depict authority figures such as kings and ancestors as both negative and positive examples, a marked emphasis on truth-telling

---

38. Daniel I. Block, "The Burden of Leadership: The Mosaic Paradigm on Kingship (Deut 17:14–20)," *Bibliotheca Sacra* 162 (2005): 259–78.
39. Author's translation.
40. "The Laws of Hammurabi," trans. Martha Roth, *COS* 2.131:336–37.

which contrasts with how traditional societies tend to conceive of the present as the outgrowth of an ideal past.

Deuteronomy contains several other features that modify the usual role of law in the ANE. Primary among these is the definition of "law" (*tôrāh*) more as an instructional narrative than as legal stipulations. In the first speech of Moses, the exposition of "this law" (1:5) begins not with an exposition of the statutes received at Sinai/Horeb, but an account of Israel's departure from Sinai/Horeb toward Canaan and the wilderness. Moses goes on to detail how the journey to Canaan's doorstep at Kadesh-Barnea which should have been eleven days (cf. 1:2) instead took thirty-eight years (2:14). Yahweh had offered the people the opportunity to enter Canaan (1:21), but their initial refusal despite Yahweh's promises of success meant they would fail once they attempted to do so in their own power (1:41–46). Yahweh was gracious through their wanderings in the wilderness to give them an alternate route to Canaan via the plains of Moab to the east (chs. 2–3). The travel narrative of Deuteronomy 1–3 is often identified as a prologue which mirrors the Hittite treaties of the second millennium BC, but this passage remains unusual in its world for emphasizing the vassal's disobedience more than the suzerain's favor.

Even after Moses finishes this retrospective and mentions Sinai/Horeb again in chapter 4, his emphasis remains pedagogical rather than legal. Moses mentions in passing the legal statutes (4:1–2) and Decalogue (4:13) but postpones the recitation of their terms until the following chapters for two reasons. First, Israel must realize that the *content* of the legal statutes pales in importance compared with how *obedience* to them demonstrates that Israel is "a great nation" (3x in 4:6–8) with "a god so near" (4:7 NRSV). Here and throughout Deuteronomy 4, the missional attractiveness of Israel and "this whole Law [*tôrāh*]" (4:8 NASB) as signs of Yahweh's presence is given first importance.[41] Second, Israel must recall the sounds and sights of Sinai/Horeb more than the law received there:

> You saw no form of any kind the day the LORD spoke to you at Horeb out of the fire. Therefore watch yourselves very carefully, so that you do not become corrupt and make for yourselves an idol. . . . But as for you, the LORD took you and brought you out of the iron-smelting furnace, out of Egypt, to be the people of

---

41. Peter T. Vogt, *Deuteronomic Theology and the Significance of Torah: A Reappraisal* (Winona Lake, IN: Eisenbrauns, 2006), 129.

his inheritance, as you now are. . . . Be careful not to forget the covenant [*bĕrît*] of the Lᴏʀᴅ your God that he made with you; do not make for yourselves an idol in the form of anything the Lᴏʀᴅ your God has forbidden. (4:15–16, 20, 23)

Deuteronomy's third mention of Sinai/Horeb in chapter 5 finally begins the exposition of the legal stipulations of the Israelite covenant.[42] Yet before repeating Exodus 20's familiar words of the Decalogue (Deut 5:6–21), Moses invites all future generations of Israel to transport themselves to the mountain of theophany: "The Lᴏʀᴅ our God made a covenant *with us* at Horeb. It was *not with our ancestors* that the Lᴏʀᴅ made this covenant, but *with us, with all of us* who are alive here today. The Lᴏʀᴅ spoke to you face to face out of the fire on the mountain" (5:2–4, emphasis added). The first exodus generation actually died in the wilderness (Deut 1:35; 2:14), but Moses addresses his hearers as eyewitnesses of Sinai/Horeb to emphasize the surprising solidarity between dead and living generations – death for those who disobey and re-peat the mistakes of the past, and life for those who obey and enter the land (30:15–20).[43]

The Decalogue that follows in Deuteronomy 5 is constituted by ten pro-hibitions upon "you," not an archaic "thou" as in English, but the usual form of second-person masculine singular address in Hebrew that aims particularly at each patriarch and head of household in the audience. Other ancient Near Eastern codes were almost always constructed in the third person to create distance between the king and the people, between the law code and the cit-izens. The speeches of Moses in Deuteronomy are the opposite – purposely using the second person "you," both to help people hear God's voice and for leaders to know that they must not take the worship that rightfully belongs to their God or usurp the rights of the people below them.[44]

To sum up, the OT's contextualization of covenant and law is characterized by a sharply contrarian emphasis on what modern legal scholars would call, somewhat anachronistically, the "rule of law." King Hammurabi's distinctions

---

42. Norbert Lohfink, "Reading Deuteronomy 5 as Narrative," in *A God So Near: Essays on Old Testament Theology in Honor of Patrick D. Miller*, eds. Brent A. Strawn and Nancy R. Bowen (Winona Lake, IN: Eisenbrauns, 2003), 261–81.
43. For details, see Jerry Hwang, *The Rhetoric of Remembrance: An Investigation of the "Fathers" in Deuteronomy*, Siphrut: Literature and Theology of the Hebrew Scriptures 8 (Winona Lake, IN: Eisenbrauns, 2012).
44. J. Gordon McConville, "Singular Address in the Deuteronomic Law and the Politics of Legal Administration," *Journal for the Study of the Old Testament* 97 (2002): 19–36.

between social classes exemplify this ANE tendency to detail how the *awilu* (i.e. the upper class) and the commoner will receive different treatment:

> If an *awilu* should blind the eye of another *awilu*, they shall blind his eye. . . . If he should blind the eye of a commoner or break the bone of a commoner, he shall weigh and deliver sixty shekels of silver. . . . If an *awilu* should knock out the tooth of another *awilu* of his own rank, they shall knock out his tooth. If he should knock out the tooth of a commoner, he shall weigh and deliver twenty shekels of silver.[45]

On and on it goes: if an *awilu* harms someone in a social class above, the punishment is more severe than if the victim comes from a social class below. So in ancient Babylon, the case of the *lex talionis* (cf. Exod 21:24) does not apply with reference to people of a lower class since a small fine can resolve the issue rather than giving up one's eye or tooth. The value of life is directly dependent on one's economic production, political influence, or belonging to the right class – all these being traits of the *awilu*.

But for Israel, the distinctiveness of its deity leads to a distinctive ethics among the nations. Deuteronomy 10:17 makes this connection clear: "For the LORD your God is the God of gods and the Lord of lords, the great, the mighty, and the awesome God, who does not show partiality, nor take a bribe" (NASB). Yahweh is set apart from his creation as the God above all other gods. Precisely because he is mighty, awesome, and transcendent, he cannot be manipulated or negotiated with. The Hebrew expression "to show partiality" is literally "to lift the face" (*nāśāʾ pānîm*), that is, to observe who is watching and thereby adjust one's effort based on the status of the other party. Susceptibility to "lifting the face" is exactly what happens in patron-client settings since stakeholders in the system weigh the relational stakes before deciding how sincerely, or even whether, to do what is right.

Because the God of Israel is not swayed by social status or impressed by appearance, this is precisely the kind of objective view that can be fully trusted. The next verse continues in saying that the God of Israel "executes justice for the orphan and the widow, and shows His love for the stranger by giving him food and clothing" (NASB). Unlike the gods of the nations who operate in the way patrons usually do, the God of Israel does not play favorites with those who can offer him more. It is for this reason that verse 19 commands

---

45. "The Laws of Hammurabi," *COS* 2.131:348.

the people, "So show your love for the stranger, for you were strangers in the land of Egypt" (NASB). In other words, biblical law and covenant flatten the hierarchical structure of traditional societies so that there must be no preferential treatment for the rich and powerful, nor any stacking of the legal deck against the poor or those too weak to seek justice for themselves. Yahweh is both patron and kin to Israel, but with a countercultural manner of relating that ensures his fairness to all rather than devolving into the kind of favoritism that happens when patronage, kinship, and collectivism are unchecked.

PATRONAGE AND KINSHIP IN ASIAN PERSPECTIVE

The OT's conception of covenant, law, and kinship achieves a balance between objectivity and relationality. Recognizing this balance is essential for critiquing the use of patron-client concepts which assume that the OT and the Majority World share a hierarchical worldview. This position has been common among Western missiologists who propose that the traits of patronage cultures can serve as an ally in missions and cross-cultural ministry. Helpful as these proposals are for those unfamiliar with patronage, they tend to underestimate how much people within these hierarchies deal with the "face fatigue" of cultivating and maintaining a web of relational obligations. It is thus essential to bridge the gap between etic proposals for harnessing patron-client dynamics by Western missiologists, and the emic reservations that are harbored by Asians who live within them.[46] The former group tends to operate with a pan-Mediterranean model which views patronage as a neutral and necessary reality, in contrast to Asian settings where Christians are increasingly vocal about the need for a contextual theology that uses the Bible to move beyond corruption, hierarchy, and facework.[47] The cases of Chinese *guanxi* and Filipino *utang na loob* will illustrate how these cultural norms are useful for contextual theology only if we follow the OT's lead in offering a *critical* contextualization of patronage and kinship.

The Chinese notion of *guanxi* is more extensive than the literal renderings of "connections" or "relationships" would suggest. Liang-Hung Lin observes that *guanxi* pervades all aspects of Chinese culture and comprises three

---

46. Hwa Yung and Tan Soo-Inn, *Bribery and Corruption: Biblical Reflections and Case Studies for the Marketplace in Asia* (Singapore: Graceworks, 2010).
47. For a description of pan-Mediterranean honor, shame, and patronage with a critique of similarities and differences with Filipino culture, see Narry F. Santos, *Turning Our Shame into Honor: Transformation of the Filipino Hiya in the Light of Mark's Gospel* (Manila: Lifechange Pub., 2003), 67–98.

elements: "(1) sharing identities and status with others in a group or mutually having an association with the same person; (2) actual connections and frequent contact between people; and (3) getting close to someone by direct interpersonal interaction. In addition, *guanxi* is considered as interpersonal networks of reciprocal bonds."[48] Because of the hierarchical nature of Confucian societies, the practice of gift-giving by a weaker party is essential to generate trust and open doors in exchange for the access that a stronger party can provide. Ambrose King summarizes the implications in his pioneering sociological analysis of *guanxi*: "To know and to practice *guanxi* is part of learned behavior – of being Chinese. As a sociocultural concept *guanxi* is deeply embedded in Confucian social theory and has its own logic that may be said to form and constitute the social structure of Chinese society."[49]

Because of the undeniable importance of *guanxi*, a massive literature exists in the business world on the relationship of *guanxi* to bribery and corruption in Chinese societies. Interestingly, Western scholars of China seem more apt than Chinese business ethicists to defend the leveraging of *guanxi* through gifts as a cultural necessity distinct from bribes.[50] Such a view of *guanxi* is also found in missiologist Jayson Georges' recent work on patronage cultures when he asserts, "Leveraging *guanxi* in business is not considered bribery but is actually expected. People feel obliged to trade favors and cooperate with others in their *guanxi* network of relationships. This is the nature of social capital."[51] Georges' important book does also assert that patronage must be God-centered and life-giving to be biblical,[52] but its otherwise helpful discussion of the OT is marred by the assumption that patronage is a biblical concept which needs no critique.[53] Similarly neutral views can be found in works by Western mis-

---

48. Liang-Hung Lin, "Cultural and Organizational Antecedents of Guanxi: The Chinese Cases," *Journal of Business Ethics* 99 (Mar. 2011): 441.

49. Ambrose Yeo-chi King, "Guanxi and Network Building: A Sociological Interpretation," in *China's Great Transformation: Selected Essays on Confucianism, Modernization, and Democracy* (Hong Kong: Chinese University Press, 2018), 79.

50. Ling Li, "Performing Bribery in China: Guanxi-Practice, Corruption with a Human Face," *Journal of Contemporary China* 20 (Jan. 2011): 20, notes this strategy finds an ironic parallel among corrupt officials in China who defend their behavior as a legitimate use of *guanxi*, even as the covertness of their behavior proves otherwise. See this tendency in Jacob Harding, "Corruption or Guanxi? Differentiating between the Legitimate, Unethical, and Corrupt Activities of Chinese Government Officials," *Pacific Basin Law Journal* 31 (2014): 127–46.

51. Georges, *Ministering in Patronage Cultures*, 12.

52. Georges, 131–42.

53. Georges, 39–50.

siologists, all of whom are familiar with the Majority World but also bring a Western starting point to the discussion.[54]

Within Chinese Christianity as in Chinese business ethics, however, there have been strident voices for a different posture with respect to *guanxi*. An early and important example is the Local Church (*difang jiaohui*) founded by Watchman Nee (*ni tuosheng*), the forerunner of the house churches with which roughly 80 percent of China's Christians are affiliated today.[55] This nonconformist movement began in the 1920s as a reaction to the heavy-hand-edness and imperialism of Western denominational missions in China. With the encouragement of a Plymouth Brethren missionary in China who had left one of the Western missions, Watchman Nee developed an indigenous Chinese theology which emphasized the priesthood of believers, elimination of ecclesiastical structures, withdrawal of Christians from corrupt mainstream (i.e. Western) Christianity, and the imminent second coming of Christ.[56] Lay preachers were to be the norm, while full-time ministers who preached across several Local Churches would be like the NT apostles in receiving support from love gifts rather than regular salaries.[57]

The result of this egalitarian polity is that the Chinese idea of *guanxi* has been mostly emptied of hierarchy while retaining its strong relationality, as reflected in how members of Local Churches eschew titles and address one another as "brothers and sisters" regardless of their role in the church, theo-logical training, or status in society.[58] This practice contrasts notably with the Confucian expectation even among Asian Christians that cultural hierarchies of age, status, and position be retained within the church.[59]

---

54. E.g. Werner Mischke, *The Global Gospel: Achieving Missional Impact in Our Multicultural World* (Scottsdale, AZ: Mission ONE, 2015), 122–40.

55. Daniel H. Bays notes that the Local Church (aka the Assembly Hall) is among several independent Chinese Christian groups which outnumber denominations with Western con-nections and are neglected by scholars of Chinese Christianity ("The Growth of Independent Christianity in China, 1900–1937," in *Christianity in China: From the Eighteenth Century to the Present* [Stanford, CA: Stanford University Press, 1996], 309–10).

56. See the description of the Local Church's teachings in Xi Lian, *Redeemed by Fire: The Rise of Popular Christianity in Modern China* (New Haven, CT: Yale University Press, 2010), 155–78.

57. These themes run throughout Watchman Nee, *Church Affairs* (Anaheim, CA: Living Stream Ministry, 1994).

58. Cf. Teresa Zimmerman-Liu, "The Reconfiguration of Guanxi in a Twentieth-Century Indigenous Chinese Protestant Group," *Review of Religion and Chinese Society* 4 (2017): 83.

59. Cf. Benjamin C. Shin and Sheryl Takagi Silzer, *Tapestry of Grace: Untangling the Cultural Complexities in Asian American Life and Ministry.* (Eugene, OR: Wipf and Stock, 2016), 138–50; Samuel D. Ling, *The "Chinese" Way of Doing Things: Perspectives on American-Born Chinese and the Chinese Church in North America* (San Gabriel, CA: China Horizon, 1999), 147–52.

The Local Church has not escaped criticism for its issues with sectarianism, fundamentalism, and anti-intellectualism. At the same time, its legacy in China's house churches as well as its influence among overseas Chinese Christian communities testify to the appeal of a non-hierarchical approach to *guanxi*. As Teresa Zimmerman-Liu summarizes the Local Church's relational orientation,

> The strain on one person of maintaining so many close *guanxi* relationships is alleviated in the Local Churches by defining the social debt as one to the congregation as a whole. Any "son of God" can receive from any other "son of God," and all he or she must do in return is to serve another "son of God" at some point in the future.[60]

According to this description of God's royal children who are nonetheless free from the endless reciprocity of patron-client dynamics, the Local Church in its best instances mirrors the OT's critical contextualization of law and covenant. Similarly and to the extent that divine-human covenant in the OT can be described as patronage, Yahweh is the stronger party who takes the first step toward his people, in contrast to Chinese *guanxi*'s expectation that the first act of indebtedness always comes from the weaker party's offer of gifts or services.[61]

The Philippines offers another illustration of Western scholars understanding patron-client dynamics in a manner that Filipinos themselves can find inappropriate.[62] This gap is indicative of a larger debate between Western and Filipino scholars on the cultural traits of the Philippines. As the "father of Filipino psychology" Virgilio Enriquez observes,

> The token use of Filipino concepts and the local language have led to the identification of some supposedly Filipino national values. Even Americans recognize *utang na loob* ["debt of gratitude, social obligation"], they just happen to prefer *kaliwaan* ["financial capital, hard cash"] or immediate pay-offs whenever possible. To argue that *utang na loob* is a Filipino value is therefore misleading, to say the least, and dangerous at best. *Utang na loob* would be covenient [sic] in perpetuating the colonial

---

60. Zimmerman-Liu, "Reconfiguration of Guanxi," 83.
61. Li, "Performing Bribery in China," 7.
62. Cf. Georges, *Ministering in Patronage Cultures*, 123–25; Barbara E. Bowe, "Reading the Bible through Filipino Eyes," *Missiology: An International Review* 26 (1998): 345–60.

status of the Filipino mind. For example, the Filipino should be grateful for "American aid" regardless of how much it is shown to be a form of imperialism.[63]

Enriquez is not denying the importance of *utang na loob*,[64] only pointing out how the concept has a colonialist history of inquiry in which (American) patrons/scholars dictated to (Filipino) clients/students how patron-client dynamics (should) work.[65] In addition, the common lament of Filipinos that the Philippines is both the only Christian nation in Asia as well as one of the world's most corrupt societies makes it doubly important to prioritize insiders' descriptions and critiques of *utang na loob*.

Filipinos often use English explanations such as "debt of gratitude,"[66] "debt of the inner self,"[67] or "repaying personal favors"[68] to render *utang na loob* for outsiders. However, reciprocity of this nature is better described as an experience than a concept:

> In the circle of Filipino relationships every Filipino has *utang na loob* to someone, while others have *utang na loob* to him. In effect, *utang na loob* binds a group together. A Filipino avoids as much as possible placing himself in such a debt to an outside group, especially a rival or opposing group. It would be disloyal to accept a favor from someone in an opposing group because *utang na loob* creates deep personal and emotional obligations. *The Westerner is best warned before entering this web of reciprocal obligations, as even Filipinos are careful about getting themselves in someone's debt.*[69]

---

63. Virgilio G. Enriquez, "Filipino Psychology in the Third World," *Philippine Journal of Psychology* 10 (1977): 5–6.

64. Lourdes R. Quisumbing, "Some Filipino (Cebuano) Social Values and Attitudes Viewed in Relation to Development (A Cebuano Looks at Utang-Na-Loob and Hiyâ)," in *Changing Identities in Modern Southeast Asia*, ed. David J. Banks (Berlin: De Gruyter, 1977), 257–68, for example, shows that Tagalog *utang na loob* has equivalents in the major Filipino languages.

65. Enriquez's article dates from 1977, placing its publication during the rule of the American-supported dictator Ferdinand Marcos.

66. E.g. Jozon A. Lorenzana, "Ethnic Moralities and Reciprocity: Towards an Ethic of South-South Relations," *Bandung: Journal of the Global South* 2 (5 Feb. 2015): 9.

67. Alfredo R. Roces and Grace Roces, *Culture Shock! Philippines: A Survival Guide to Customs and Etiquette* (Tarrytown, NY: Marshall Cavendish, 2009), 36.

68. E.g. Cristina Jayme Montiel, "Philippine Political Culture: A Conceptual Framework," *Philippine Journal of Psychology* 33 (2000): 114.

69. Roces and Roces, *Culture Shock!*, 37, italics added.

While expatriates in the Philippines can afford to function outside of *utang na loob*, escape from these cycles is not an option for Filipinos (whether in their home country or not), particularly in respect to one's family members.

Toward parents especially, the unspoken understanding in Filipino families is that children owe a special debt of *utang na loob*. This leads to potentially endless reciprocity since

> children must be everlastingly grateful to their parents not only for all that the latter have done for them in the process of raising them but more fundamentally for giving them life. . . . A child's *utang na loob* to its parents is immeasurable and eternal. Nothing he can do during his lifetime can make up for what they have done for him.[70]

The extension of this kinship understanding to one's relationship with God as heavenly Parent (as traditionally understood, rather than the OT's view as presented in this chapter) naturally makes the unpayable debt exponential and eternal in scope. Evelyn Miranda-Feliciano observes in this regard that

> an unquestioning form of *utang na loob* tends to create a patron-client relationship that is oppressive. It creates a kind of dependency and mendicancy detrimental to the formation of a truly free, self-respecting individual, or nation for that matter. How do we release *utang na loob* from its negative, oppressive element and make it as biblical as possible?[71]

In answering Miranda-Feliciano's question, it is significant that *utang na loob*'s inner compulsion to repay coupled with the inability to repay causes Filipino Christians to suffer from intense guilt (in contrast to the frequent depiction of the Philippines as a shame-based culture). God as Father becomes the cosmic creditor to whom Filipino Christians feel impossibly obligated most of all, thereby exacerbating the toxic qualities of the "Padrino system" of patronage in the Philippines.[72]

Deuteronomy 26 sets forth a covenant feast which contextualizes patronage and kinship ideas in a manner resonant with Filipino *utang na loob*.

---

70. Mary R. Hollnsteiner, "Reciprocity in the Lowland Philippines," *Philippine Studies* 9 (1961): 396–97.
71. Evelyn Miranda-Feliciano, *Filipino Values and Our Christian Faith* (Metro Manila: OMF Literature, 1990), 72.
72. I owe this suggestion to Aaron Michael Nimo, one of my Filipino students.

Gratitude toward God takes center stage in this chapter's conclusion to the law code (Deut 12–26). But this theme appears without succumbing to the so-called "debtor's ethic" which makes present and future obedience merely an obligatory response to past favor.[73] Instead, Deuteronomy's motivation for feasting contrasts particularly with the Filipino custom of the "blow-out" (*balato*) party in which a host is expected to celebrate his or her own milestone (e.g. birthday, promotion) by treating everyone else, sometimes even to the point of financial ruin. Failure to do so leads to the accusation of being *walang utang na loob* ("ungrateful"), forcing a Filipino into an impossible choice between a guilt trip for stinginess and endless reciprocity in giving.

Moses enjoins a different kind of gratitude from Western OT scholarship's fixation on covenant (un)conditionality as well as from the darker side to Filipino culture's well-deserved reputation for generous hospitality. Deuteronomy 26 begins by directing the same "you" addressed throughout the book to look ahead to Israel's settled life in Canaan. The faithful worshiper must bring the firstfruits of the land that Yahweh gave both to the "ancestors" and to "you" (vv. 1–3). Following the priest's acceptance of the offering (v. 4), Moses insists that Yahweh has been Israel's true *padrino* (Tagalog/Spanish for "patron") rather than any human ancestor: "You shall declare before the LORD your God, 'My father was a wandering Aramean, and he went down into Egypt with a few people and lived there and became a great nation, powerful and numerous'" (v. 5). Israel's ancestor is unworthy of patronage since he was helpless when Yahweh chose him as "a wandering Aramean" (v. 5) and delivered him from the oppressive patronage of Egypt (vv. 6–8). Because Yahweh continues to provide for his people in the land (v. 9), the freewill offering of "you" (i.e. an Israelite *paterfamilias*) is Yahweh's way of caring for the less fortunate in Israel (vv. 10, 12).

The critical difference, however, is that this lavish sharing by "you" does not incur any *utang na loob* by its recipients. The only obligation for the entire community is that "you and the Levites and the foreigners residing among you shall rejoice in all the good things the LORD your God has given to you and your household" (v. 11). Strikingly, the Israelite form of the "blow-out" is still a festive and abundant meal, but with Yahweh himself as the party-host – all of Deuteronomy 26's activities are prescribed "before Yahweh" (vv. 5, 10[2x],

---

73. John Piper, *The Purifying Power of Living by Faith in Future Grace* (Sisters, OR: Multnomah, 1995), 31–39; cf. Vitaliano R. Gorospe, "Christian Renewal of Filipino Values," *Philippine Studies* 14 (1966): 219–20.

13). Yahweh's special presence at this covenant feast means that satisfaction in him and his gifts is the only debt incurred by the unworthy participants.[74] When God is acknowledged as the patron and kin who hosts the "blow-out," the Filipino cultural value of *utang na loob* is set free to be joyful giving without the expectation of a return.[75]

CONCLUSION

The triumph of solidarity over reciprocity is not only good news for the Chinese and Filipino cultures. It represents a key to the OT's distinctive worldview that challenges Western scholarship's tendency to reduce the intricacies of covenantal relationships mainly into demands, whether in legal terms (as in OT scholarship) or in kinship terms (as in missiology). The next chapter will apply these insights about the OT's subtle contextualizations within its world to how scholars of "Mediterraneanism" have usually approached the cultural values of honor, shame, and guilt.

---

74. Writing from a Filipino perspective, Narry Santos finds a similar understanding at work in Mark's gospel: "As co-clients to the same [divine] Patron-Broker, we are to learn to be benevolent and gracious to other Christians and to have greater reciprocity among ourselves as equals. We now need to see that we are not competitors or combatants for God's honor, but colleagues and co-contributors to the honor of the gracious and generous Patron-Broker to whom we are to give our same allegiance" (*Shame into Honor*, 262).
75. Miranda-Feliciano, *Filipino Values*, 73.

CHAPTER 6

HONOR, SHAME, AND GUILT

Years ago, when I was a pastor at a Chinese church in California, an American Christian publisher released a children's curriculum called "Rickshaw Rally." It was supposedly set in Japan, but blended "Asian" cultural elements such as rickshaws, sumo wrestlers, and Chinese restaurant takeout boxes. The stereo-typed Asian music had lyrics such as "Grab your kimono/Come on let's go on an Asian challenge/Racing in a rickshaw/We'll be making friends all over the Japanese islands" and "Wax on wax off/get your rickshaw ready" (combining a reference to the 1984 film *The Karate Kid* with a colonialist symbol of Asian backwardness). Although the church had previously purchased curriculum from this publisher, the leadership wisely decided this time to reject "Rickshaw Rally" due to its use of racial stereotypes. A decade would pass, unfortunate-ly, before that Christian publisher recognized its mistake and apologized.[1] Interestingly, Asians sometimes become unwitting participants in reducing their cultures to a pan-Asian mix of martial arts and redeeming lost honor. Pat Morita, an American-born Japanese and native speaker of English, faked a "Japanese" accent to play the role of Mr. Miyagi in *The Karate Kid*. And in the 2010 remake of *The Karate Kid*, Jackie Chan (from Hong Kong) portrayed a teacher of karate (which originated in Japan) who helps an American kid bullied by street youths in China (the home of kung fu).

Given these common misunderstandings, a closer look at Japanese culture will supply us in this chapter with fresh lenses to examine honor, shame, and guilt in the Old Testament. Besides making extensive use of honorific titles and being the first to receive the label of "shame culture," Japan is a society whose ideas about honor, shame, and guilt have been carefully studied by both Japanese and Western social scientists. Biblical scholars and missiologists, on the other hand, tend unfortunately to overlook how anthropologists have come to realize that honor and shame are far from being the symmetrical

---

1. John Rutledge, "LifeWay Apologizes to Asian-Americans for Rickshaw Rally," *Baptist Standard*, 8 November 2013, https://www.baptiststandard.com/news/baptists/lifeway-apologizes-to-asian-americans-for-rickshaw-rally/.

pair of values that they were once thought to be.[2] The previous chapter noted how the application of a "Mediterranean model" which can be suitable for the NT runs into major problems when extended across centuries to the OT (by Western biblical scholars) or across both time and geography to the Majority World (by Western missiologists). These distortions in Western scholarship suggest that an understanding of Asian cultural diversity can provide checks and balances in studying OT passages which are thought to feature "Mediterranean" cultural values. At the same time, it would be simplistic to speak of "Eastern" or "Asian" honor and shame as if they were unitary concepts which stand opposed to a Western emphasis on guilt. Japan and Korea, for example, differ in how they conceptualize honor and shame despite having many cultural similarities which spring from a deeply intertwined history.[3] For this reason, we will employ Japanese lenses as one Asian perspective that can assist in reading the OT better. It will become apparent along the way that the contrasts frequently drawn between collectivist "honor-shame cultures" and individualist "guilt-innocence cultures" are less straightforward than Western biblical scholars and missiologists typically present.[4]

HONOR, SHAME, AND GUILT IN WESTERN SCHOLARSHIP

The modern study of honor, shame, and guilt began in the waning days of World War II. As the defeat of Japan loomed, the US government commissioned Ruth Benedict, an anthropologist at Columbia University, to produce a cultural profile of Japan that would facilitate postwar governance and reconstruction. Benedict employed the research methods of the culture-and-personality school of her mentor Franz Boas to publish *The Chrysanthemum and the Sword: Patterns of Japanese Culture* in 1946. This book went through many reprintings in both Japan and the US, making it one of the most influential studies on Japan ever written.

The Chrysanthemum and the Sword attached the famous label of "shame culture" to Japan. Ruth Benedict wrote,

> For in Japan the constant goal is honor. It is necessary to command respect. . . . True shame cultures rely on external sanctions

---

2. Unni Wikan, "Shame and Honour: A Contestable Pair," *Man* 19 (1984): 635–52.
3. Emi Furukawa, June Tangney, and Fumiko Higashibara, "Cross-Cultural Continuities and Discontinuities in Shame, Guilt, and Pride: A Study of Children Residing in Japan, Korea and the USA," *Self and Identity* 11 (2012): 90–113.
4. Johannes Merz, "The Culture Problem: How the Honor/Shame Issue Got the Wrong End of the Anthropological Stick," *Missiology: An International Review* 48 (2020): 127–41.

for good behavior, not as true guilt cultures do, or an internalized conviction of sin. Shame is a reaction to other people's criticism. A man is shamed either by being openly ridiculed and rejected or by fantasying to himself that he has been made ridiculous. In either case it is a potent sanction. But it requires an audience or at least a man's fantasy of an audience. Guilt does not.[5]

Julie Robertson observes that with sweeping and elegant descriptions such as these, "Benedict made getting to know Japan look too easy, and the Japan she profiled seemed all too knowable; once inscrutable, the Japanese were suddenly crystal clear."[6]

Despite the book's popularity across the decades, there has always been sharp opposition both in Japan and in the West to its broad labels.[7] This is due not only to Benedict's descriptions of guilt and shame which clearly favored the internalized moral conscience of the West. It is also because of her understated but no less bold claim to describe the essence of Japanese culture even though she never did fieldwork in Japan, did not speak any Japanese, and relied on interviews with expatriate Japanese whose experiences with their "home" culture were skewed by imperial propaganda. Benedict thus has a complicated legacy with all her major conclusions coming under serious criticism.[8] However, one aspect of her thinking has persisted to the present: the dubious association of shame with *external* sanction and guilt with *internal* sanction, thereby linking "shame cultures" with collectivism and "guilt cultures" with individualism.[9]

British anthropologists built on the work of Benedict and her associate Margaret Mead beginning in the 1960s. They drew attention to the

---

5. Ruth Benedict, *The Chrysanthemum and the Sword: Patterns of Japanese Culture* (Boston: Houghton Mifflin, 1946), 171, 223.

6. Jennifer Robertson, ed., "Introduction: Putting and Keeping Japan in Anthropology," in *A Companion to the Anthropology of Japan*, Blackwell Companions to Anthropology 5 (Malden, MA: Blackwell, 2005), 6.

7. E.g. Gerhart Piers and Milton Singer, *Shame and Guilt: A Psychoanalytic and a Cultural Study* (Springfield, IL: Thomas, 1953); Takie Sugiyama Lebra, "The Social Mechanism of Guilt and Shame: The Japanese Case," *Anthropological Quarterly* 44 (1971): 241–55; Keiichi Sakuta, "A Reconsideration of the Culture of Shame," trans. Kimiko Yagi and Meredith McKinney, *Review of Japanese Culture and Society* 1 (1986): 32–39.

8. Sonia Ryang, *Japan and National Anthropology: A Critique* (London: Routledge, 2006), 47–72; Judith Modell, "The Wall of Shame: Ruth Benedict's Accomplishment in *The Chrysanthemum and the Sword*," *Dialectical Anthropology* 24 (1999): 193–215. See also the defense of Benedict by Millie R. Creighton, "Revisiting Shame and Guilt Cultures: A Forty-Year Pilgrimage," *Ethos* 18 (Sep. 1990): 279–307.

9. E.g. Andy Crouch, "The Return of Shame," *Christianity Today*, 10 March 2015, https://www.christianitytoday.com/ct/2015/march/andy-crouch-gospel-in-age-of-public-shame.html.

Mediterranean as a region characterized by *honor* rather than guilt as the opposite of shame. As argued especially by John Peristiany and Julian Pitt-Rivers, honor and shame represent "the values of Mediterranean society"[10] because of "the unity of the Mediterranean."[11] Pitt-Rivers extrapolated from modern Mediterranean societies to ancient ones in arguing that "honour is the value of a person in *his* own eyes, but also in the eyes of *his* society."[12] Here the references to "his" are not accidental, for Pitt-Rivers argued that honor in Mediterranean society reflects a strongly traditional view of masculinity. Men need to be aggressive to defend their honor but are vulnerable to shame due to the need to defend female chastity and confront all challengers within a world of "limited good" (social, economic, sexual, or otherwise).

Yet from the outset, so-called "Mediterraneanism" has been plagued by the circularity of reasoning that

> there exists within the circum-Mediterranean region something which is both worthy of cross-cultural examination and yet somehow "less" characteristic of other areas. . . . Massive generalizations of "honour" and "shame" have become counterproductive; their continued use elevates what began as a genuine convenience for the readers of ethnographic essays to the level of a theoretical proposition.[13]

This realization has led anthropologists to correct earlier misunderstandings and overstatements about "cultural types" and "national personality."[14] In the previous chapter, we explored how the discipline of anthropology struggled with the reification of "Mediterraneanism" in respect to patronage and kinship ideas.

Ironically in the 1980s and 1990s, Bruce Malina and other biblical scholars from their so-called "Context Group" drew upon such generalizations

---

10. John George Peristiany, ed., *Honour and Shame: The Values of Mediterranean Society* (Chicago: University of Chicago Press, 1974).

11. David D. Gilmore, ed., *Honor and Shame and the Unity of the Mediterranean* (Washington DC: American Anthropological Association, 1987).

12. Julian Pitt-Rivers, "Honour and Social Status," in *Honour and Shame: The Values of Mediterranean Society*, ed. John George Peristiany (London: Weidenfeld & Nicolson, 1965), 21, italics added.

13. Michael Herzfeld, "Honour and Shame: Problems in the Comparative Analysis of Moral Systems," *Man* 59 (1980): 340, 349.

14. John G. Peristiany and Julian Alfred Pitt-Rivers, "Introduction," in *Honor and Grace in Anthropology*, ed. John G. Peristiany and Julian Alfred Pitt-Rivers, Cambridge Studies in Social and Cultural Anthropology 76 (Cambridge: Cambridge University Press, 2005), 5–7.

for the Mediterranean region just as anthropologists were abandoning them. In *Biblical Social Values and Their Meaning: A Handbook*, for instance, the opening sentence of the "Honor/Shame" entry is typical for seeing a timeless Mediterranean culture reflected in both Testaments: "These are the core values in the Mediterranean world in general and in the Bible as well."[15] The prominence of the Context Group peaked in a 1996 issue of the scholarly journal *Semeia* which contained numerous essays on "Mediterranean" honor and shame in a variety of biblical texts. Also included, however, were two invited articles by anthropologists who found the understanding of honor and shame used by biblical scholars in the journal to be problematic at best. One of them coyly observed, "The papers in this volume might give the unwary reader the impression that anthropologists are largely in agreement on the meaning and significance of honor and shame in Mediterranean contexts. This is most definitely not the case, however."[16]

Biblical scholarship on honor and shame continued to progress in the early 2000s, thanks to the work of NT scholars not affiliated with the Context Group, most notably David deSilva.[17] They were more careful to restrict their comparisons to Greco-Roman sources and avoid generalizations about "Mediterranean society" and non-Western cultures. The advent of psychological approaches in biblical scholarship has also supplied a more balanced perspective by showing that the entwining of guilt, shame, and honor requires both psychology and anthropology to understand adequately.[18] Writing in 2013, for example, a Context Group scholar like John Pilch came to accept that the term "Middle East-North Africa" (MENA) to denote this region in the modern era is more accurate than speaking of a timeless "Mediterranean society."[19]

15. Joseph Plevnik, "Honor/Shame," in *Biblical Social Values and Their Meaning: A Handbook*, ed. John J. Pilch and Bruce J. Malina (Peabody, MA: Hendrickson, 1993), 95.

16. John Chance, "The Anthropology of Honor and Shame: Culture, Values and Practice," *Semeia* 68 (1996): 140. The other anthropologist's essay in the journal is by Gideon Kressel.

17. E.g. David Arthur deSilva, *The Hope of Glory: Honor Discourse and New Testament Interpretation* (Eugene, OR: Wipf and Stock, 2009); *Honor, Patronage, Kinship and Purity: Unlocking New Testament Culture* (Downers Grove, IL: InterVarsity Press, 2000); *Despising Shame: Honor Discourse and Community Maintenance in the Epistle to the Hebrews*, SBL Dissertation Series 152 (Atlanta: Scholars Press, 1995).

18. E.g. Colin Patterson, "The World of Honor and Shame in the New Testament: Alien or Familiar?," *Biblical Theology Bulletin* 49 (Feb. 2019): 4–14; Johanna Stiebert, *The Construction of Shame in the Hebrew Bible: The Prophetic Contribution*, JSOT Supplement Series 346 (London: Sheffield Academic, 2002).

19. John J. Pilch, *The Cultural Life Setting of the Proverbs* (Minneapolis, MN: Fortress, 2016), xi.

But much like older NT scholarship, Western missiologists in the new millennium have often continued to rely on the Context Group's earlier work on Mediterranean society without attending to the necessary qualifications and developments in anthropology since then.[20] Missiology of recent years often repeats outdated generalizations about "honor-shame cultures" as uniformly collectivist, while clearly placing the Majority World in this catchall category.[21] To the debatable extent that cultural values in the modern MENA region are equivalent to those of ancient Mediterranean society, Western missiologists have gone even further by generalizing about honor and shame in East Asia as well, often citing Japan as a typical case.[22]

In the process there has been a neglect of social-scientific work that challenges the idea of a single "East Asian" understanding of honor, shame, and guilt. We will address the case of Japan in the next section, while it is worth mentioning here that anthropologists and psychologists who have studied honor and shame in both the "Mediterranean" (as broadly understood in the Context Group's work) and Japan conclude that their contours in these two places are rather different.[23] Such variations across time and geography underscore the need to allow both modern cultures and biblical texts to speak for themselves, rather than imposing a generalized contrast between honor and shame which does not apply uniformly across collectivist societies.[24] Closer attention to the shape of Japanese honor, shame, and guilt will thus be helpful for tracing how the OT exhibits a similar posture of critical engagement with "Mediterranean" cultural ideas.

---

20. Christopher L. Flanders, "There Is No Such Thing as 'Honor' or 'Honor Cultures,'" in *Devoted to Christ: Missiological Reflections in Honor of Sherwood G. Lingenfelter*, ed. Christopher L. Flanders (Eugene, OR: Pickwick, 2019), 155.
21. E.g. Jayson Georges, *The 3D Gospel: Ministry in Guilt, Shame, and Fear Cultures*, updated and rev. ed. ([N.p.]: Timē Press, 2016); Roland Müller, *Honor and Shame: Unlocking the Door* (Philadelphia: Xlibris Corp., 2000).
22. E.g. Jayson Georges and Mark D. Baker, *Ministering in Honor-Shame Cultures: Biblical Foundations and Practical Essentials* (Downers Grove, IL: IVP Academic, 2016), 47, 143–44.
23. Mariko Asano-Tamanoi, "Shame, Family, and State in Catalonia and Japan," in *Honor and Shame and the Unity of the Mediterranean*, ed. David D. Gilmore (Washington DC: American Anthropological Association, 1987), 104–20; Michael Boiger et al., "Defending Honour, Keeping Face: Interpersonal Affordances of Anger and Shame in Turkey and Japan," *Cognition and Emotion* 28 (2014): 1255–69.
24. Wikan, "Shame and Honour."

HONOR, SHAME, AND GUILT IN JAPANESE CULTURE

East Asia is frequently considered a single cultural bloc of honor and shame.[25] While there is some truth in this generalization, it is striking that countries in this region have stark conflicts in recounting their difficult, shared past in World War II. On the one hand, Japan is riven by divisions over whether and how to apologize for atrocities that its empire committed during the war. The conflict between honor-shame and guilt-innocence paradigms within Japan is particularly evident in politics and historiography. China and Korea, on the other hand, were victims of Japanese imperialism who regularly chide "shameless" Japan and demand that their wartime oppressor stop trying to save face. Globalization has hardly resolved the anti-Japanese sentiment that reappears throughout East Asia whenever Japanese politicians visit shrines to wartime dead, the claims of "comfort women" (i.e. sex slaves) in Japan's former colonies are dismissed, or Japanese school textbooks undergo revisions that downplay war crimes. Since the reluctance of Japan to accept guilt (in contrast to Germany) continues to be attributed to its being a "shame culture,"[26] it is important to revisit Ruth Benedict's work from both Japanese and non-Japanese perspectives. In showing how collectivism in Japan differs from that of "Mediterranean" societies, we will gain an intercultural perspective on honor, shame, and guilt which highlights the distinctive posture of the OT.

As noted earlier, Benedict's understandings of guilt and shame presumed a questionable contrast between internal and external sanction. Her definitions supposed that the sanction of guilt looks inwardly to the self for moral standards, while shame looks outwardly to the community for approval and disapproval. Because such a dichotomy was simplistic, the British anthropologist Mary Douglas pioneered the use of *Grid-Group Theory* to move beyond a strict contrast between individualism and collectivism in the analysis of cultures. Alongside the comparative axis of *Group* commitment to measure one's strength of affiliation with others, Douglas added the axis of *Grid* control to gauge how much behavior is governed by rules external to oneself.[27]

The use of Group and Grid axes leads to a 2×2 classification of worldviews: (1) Low Group, Low Grid (Individualism); (2) High Group, Low Grid (Egalitarianism); (3) High Group, High Grid (Hierarchy); and (4) Low Group,

---

25. E.g. Mischke, *Global Gospel*, 76–77.
26. E.g. Elazar Barkan, *The Guilt of Nations: Restitution and Negotiating Historical Injustices* (New York: Norton, 2000), 63.
27. Mary Douglas, *Natural Symbols: Explorations in Cosmology* (London: Barrie and Jenkins, 1973), 77–92.

High Grid (Fatalism). Each country or culture exhibits variability within itself and over time, but the empirical data collected over several decades by the World Values Survey shows that it remains meaningful to speak of overall tendencies.[28] For example, the worldview of the United States would generally be classified as Individualism, Scandinavian countries as Egalitarianism, Japan and greater China as Hierarchy, and the Middle East as Fatalism. The fourfold categories of Grid-Group Theory show why it is mistaken to dichotomize between Western cultures as individualist (i.e. merely Low Group) and non-Western cultures as collectivist (i.e. merely High Group). It is striking, for example, that individualism in a Western country like Denmark reflects a high degree of Group affiliation but a low degree of Grid control. This combination differs from the low Group character of American individualism due to Scandinavians' sense of shared commitment to hands-off living. Similarly, the collectivism of a Mediterranean country like Egypt is High Grid and Low Group, reflecting a combination of social forces that press against the individual and thus view the community as competitive more than supportive. As we will see below, the competitive dynamics of honor and shame are also the essence of certain societies in the Mediterranean region and their Public Court of Reputation.

This chapter's focus on honor, shame, and guilt in the OT makes it beyond our scope to compare these cultural values across all Grid-Group combinations. In the following section, we will focus on honor, shame, and guilt in the OT while employing both Mediterranean and Japanese conceptions of these cultural values. As the High Grid and Low Group orientation of the Mediterranean is shown to be inadequate on its own for understanding the OT, a Japanese model will help by supplying an alternative to the usual association of guilt with individualism and shame with collectivism. The High Group and High Grid orientation of Japanese culture means that its conceptions of honor, shame, and guilt stand closer in certain respects to the OT than the Mediterranean even though Japan is geographically more distant. Using a combination of Mediterranean and Japanese perspectives will also illuminate how the OT is ultimately distinct in its presentation of these social values.

---

28. For four decades, the World Values Survey has conducted longitudinal sampling across countries which broadly supports Grid-Group Theory (Sun-Ki Chai, Ming Liu, and Min-Sun Kim, "Cultural Comparisons of Beliefs and Values: Applying the Grid-Group Approach to the World Values Survey," *Beliefs and Values* 1 [2009]: 193–208).

THREE OT CASE STUDIES FROM THE
TIME OF KING HEZEKIAH

Three kinds of OT texts from the eighth century BC – prophecy, historiography, and wisdom – offer special potential for intercultural comparisons of honor, shame, and guilt. During that century of upheaval in the ANE, the impending collapse of the northern kingdom of Samaria led to a substantial literary output in both Israelite kingdoms about the true nature of power and status. The scribes of King Hezekiah in the south, which barely survived the Assyrian crisis which had consumed the north in 722 BC, came to play an important role as keepers of literary traditions for both kingdoms. In addition, the Assyrian Empire to which the kingdom of Samaria fell and the Egyptian kingdom which Samaria had hoped would come to its aid were both prolific in using texts and pictures as propaganda for their royal might. In fact, Assyria and Egypt could be said to represent a "Mediterranean" value system of honor and shame with which OT writings of the eighth century offer an intentional contrast.

Before exploring various OT texts connected to King Hezekiah, it is useful to summarize the nature of power politics around the Israelite kingdoms during this period. Due to space considerations, we will focus on the Assyrian Empire's rebirth after several centuries of weakness when Tiglath-Pileser III rose to power in 745 BC. This was around the same time that kings Jeroboam of Samaria and Uzziah of Judah each passed from the scene after peaceful, prosperous reigns of several decades. It is thus far from accidental that Isaiah 6's majestic vision of Yahweh as King in his heavenly temple opens in verse 1 with a chronological reference to "the year that King Uzziah died" (i.e. 740 BC) – the Israelite kingdoms of Samaria and Judah were both sinking under the weight of internal crisis just as Assyria and its terrifying war machine were rising (again). Even as Neo-Assyria under Tiglath-Pileser III became undeniably powerful, its ongoing quest to recover the lost glory of the Old Assyrian Empire led to a strongly revisionist agenda in Assyrian historiography. Baruch Halpern humorously comments on the insecure empire's tendency to exaggerate:

> In Assyrian royal inscriptions . . . the torching of a grain field is the conquest of a whole territory beyond it. A looting raid becomes a claim of perpetual sovereignty. . . . *Interpreting such literature demands only a simple rule, the Tiglath-Pileser principle. The question is, what is the minimum the king might have done to lay claim to the achievements he publishes?* Looting a town?

He shoplifted a toothbrush from the local drug store. Ravaging the countryside? Perhaps he trampled crops near a farmstead. Receiving submission from distant kings in lands one hasn't invaded? A delegation arrived to inaugurate diplomatic relations. *Each small mark of prestige becomes the evidence for a grand triumph.*[29]

In sum, the Neo-Assyrian Empire pioneered the use of propaganda to magnify its claims of imperial power in a way that anticipated Nazi Germany nearly three thousand years later. Its claims of glory were never completely false, but Assyria's royal scribes and historians would take a kernel of truth and use mass media to place the king's achievements in the best possible light. Since raw strength was thus synonymous with royal honor, the Assyrian monarchy came to view any expression of weakness as shameful and obstacles to its hegemony as a mortal threat. The fact that "the great king" was the favorite title of Assyrian rulers for themselves in their annalistic literature was the embodiment of a "Mediterranean" ideal of masculinity – strong and boastful, while also being sensitive to honor claims and intent on humiliating all opponents, not merely defeating them (cf. Jer 2:36; 2 Chr 32:21).

The Prophecy of Isaiah in Mediterranean and Japanese Perspective

The OT writings of the eighth century BC portray a counterculture to the imperialism reflected in the Assyrian annals. For this reason, Japanese cultural categories will supply a useful alternative to "Mediterraneanism" for examining the prophet Isaiah's exposition of honor, shame, and guilt. To summarize, Japanese social scientists have noted that triggers for guilt and shame responses in Japan are often reversed from the inner-outer distinction in anthropology which was popularized by Ruth Benedict. In this regard, the psychiatrist Takeo Doi identifies a complex emotion called *amae* that Japanese people experience when losing a connection with their desired group. Counterintuitively for non-Japanese, the presence of *amae* means that the Japanese sense of guilt is more others-directed since it comes from the sense of disappointing others, while shame is the self-directed feeling of loneliness and inadequacy: "The man who feels shame must suffer from the feeling of finding himself, his *amae*

---

29. Baruch Halpern, *David's Secret Demons: Messiah, Murderer, Traitor, King* (Grand Rapids, MI: Eerdmans, 2001), 126, italics added.

unsatisfied, exposed to the eyes of those about him when all he wants is to be wrapped warm in his surroundings."[30]

The Japanese emotion of *amae* shows that shaming can serve a positive function since it sensitizes members of the Group to the expectations of the Grid and awakens a desire for reconciliation with others.[31] In contrast to Mediterranean society and its somewhat whimsical Public Court of Reputation,[32] what counts as honor and shame in Japan has typically been internalized by each person in this High Group and High Grid society rather than being subject to the fickle and competitive nature of honor in a High Grid and Low Group environment. Guilt is thus experienced within the Group as the shame of failing to meet its well-defined Grid expectations. For these reasons, Japanese concepts of honor, shame, and guilt provide a better comparison for Isaiah's Torah-shaped perspective on these values than the more tensive relationship between High Grid and Low Group dynamics in Mediterranean societies.

Isaiah 2 in Mediterranean and Japanese Perspective

Isaiah 2 is a passage that benefits particularly from rethinking the approaches of Western OT scholarship as well as the anthropological categories of "Mediterraneanism." In this chapter, the prophet's vision "in the last days" (v. 2) portrays Zion/Jerusalem as an honored place which is "the highest of the mountains" and "exalted above the hills" (v. 2). Since this is a vision about Judah and Jerusalem (v. 1), it is surprising that the city of Yahweh's people will also be where "all nations" and "many peoples" go on pilgrimage and summon one another, "Come [*lĕkû*], let us go up to the mountain of the LORD [Yahweh], to the house of the God of Jacob" (v. 3b–c NRSV). Their goal is that "he [Yahweh] may teach us concerning his ways, so let us walk [*nēlkāh*] in his paths" (v. 3d–e).[33] The desire of non-Israelite nations to obey Yahweh means that "instruction [*tôrāh*] will go forth from Zion and the word of Yahweh

---

30. Takeo Doi, *The Anatomy of Dependence*, trans. John Bester (New York: Kodansha USA, 2014), 55.

31. Margaret S. Odell, "An Exploratory Study of Shame and Dependence in the Bible and Selected Near Eastern Parallels," in *The Biblical Canon in Comparative Perspective*, eds. K. Lawson Younger, William W. Hallo, and Bernard F. Batto, Scripture in Context 4 (Lewiston, NY: Edwin Mellen, 1991), 220.

32. Zeba Crook, "Honor, Shame, and Social Status Revisited," *Journal of Biblical Literature* 128 (2009): 610.

33. Author's translation.

from Jerusalem"[34] (v. 3f–g). Yahweh's kingship will result in fair judgments for all peoples and a cessation of war between nations (v. 4). The optimism and future orientation of these verses typically lead Isaiah commentators to classify them as a self-contained oracle about Zion which is separate from the woe oracle that follows.[35]

It is indeed true that the tone and topic of Isaiah 2 then change suddenly. Returning to the present, the prophet confronts the disobedience of Yahweh's own people: "Come, O house of Jacob, and let us walk in the light of Yahweh" (v. 5).[36] This verse's commands to "come" (*lĕkû*) and "let us walk" (*nēlkāh*) echo the nations exhorting themselves to "come" and "let us walk" (v. 3) in the ways of Yahweh. Despite this exact repetition, scholars trained in the habits of form criticism tend to divide the chapter into the disparate genres of Zion oracle (vv. 1–4) and woe oracle (vv. 5–22).[37] Salvation and judgment are thought to be theologically incompatible ideas which arose in different historical periods, so Western OT scholarship typically views their juxtaposition in prophetic literature as the later work of an editor or redactor.

However, the logical progression between Isaiah 2's positive and negative halves is easier to perceive from a Japanese perspective of High Group and High Grid. The fourfold repetition of the Hebrew root *hlk* supplies a grotesque mirror image: disobedient Judah is being shamed through a company of obedient nations who are more enthusiastic about Yahweh and his Torah than his own people are. The result of the nations' obedience to "come" as a Group and "walk" within the Grid of Yahweh's instruction will be lasting peace (vv. 1–4), but Judah faces the threat of Assyrian imperialism since its neglect of Yahweh's Torah has made it a stranger in its own honored place (cf. 1:2–17). This reversal of fortunes heightens the need for wayward Judah to "come" and "walk" in Yahweh's ways (v. 5).

In contrast to Western form criticism's difficulty in seeing theological coherence, Japanese cultural lenses highlight how shame has the positive aim of instilling a proper sense of guilt in Judah by singling it out from the larger

---

34. Author's translation.
35. E.g. H. G. M. Williamson, *A Critical and Exegetical Commentary on Isaiah 1–5*, International Critical Commentary (London: Bloomsbury, 2006), 189; James W. Watts, *Isaiah 1–33*, 2nd ed., Word Biblical Commentary 24 (Nashville, TN: Thomas Nelson, 1985), 26–29.
36. Author's translation.
37. E.g. Watts, *Isaiah 1–33*, 30–38. Sometimes v. 5 is considered part of the Zion oracle, with v. 6 marking the start of the woe oracle (e.g. Joseph Blenkinsopp, "Fragments of Ancient Exegesis in an Isaian Poem (Isaiah 2:6–22)," in *Essays on the Book of Isaiah*, Forschungen zum Alten Testament 128 [Tübingen: Mohr Siebeck, 2019], 135–41).

community of nations to which it wishes to belong.[38] The history of Japan similarly illustrates how the wheels of modernization began to turn after the American navy sailed into Edo Bay (later known as Tokyo Harbor) and jolted a feudal nation into realizing where it stood on the world stage relative to its stronger counterparts.

The woe oracle continues in Isaiah 2:6–22 with the picture of a people who are unaware of their guilt before Yahweh because of confusion about what truly constitutes honor and shame. From a Mediterranean perspective, it might appear at first that Isaiah is complimenting his people for being a powerful nation like Assyria: "Their land is full of silver and gold; there is no end to their treasures. Their land is full of horses; there is no end to their chariots. Their land is full of idols; they bow down to the work of their hands, to what their fingers have made" (vv. 7–8). Isaiah's description of Judah in thrall to Assyrian imperialism accords well with what Julian Pitt-Rivers observed about social status in the Mediterranean as superior power coupled with the ability to silence all challengers.[39] In the next verse, however, the prophet Isaiah offers the surprise that Judah's boastful extravagance will bring shame rather than honor: "So people will be brought low and everyone humbled" (v. 9a–b). The prophecy of Isaiah has reversed the Mediterranean's usual cause-and-effect relationship between honor and status: pride will be humbled instead of rewarded.[40]

By contrast, the condemnation of Judah's pride resonates with the Japanese cultural emphasis on immodesty as shameful. This is also true of the verdict that "the eyes of the arrogant will be humbled and human pride brought low" (v. 11a–b). At the same time, it is notable that Isaiah 2 does not grant the expected corollary of the Japanese cultural principle that modesty is itself a form of honor. Instead, the chapter repeatedly asserts that no human conduct can bring honor, since "[Yahweh] alone will be exalted in that day" (vv. 11, 17). Shame in Isaiah comes from neither a lack of status (as in the Mediterranean) nor a lack of modesty (as in Japan), but from the fact that Yahweh is the only source of honor who opposes every form of human pride (vv. 12–16). Despite this countercultural note, Isaiah 2 concludes by describing the same inclination to hide when shamed which characterizes Japanese culture. Not only will idols disappear in Yahweh's presence (vv. 18, 20), but all peoples (and not merely Judah) will conceal themselves in the presence of Yahweh's

---

38. E.g. Sakuta, "Culture of Shame," 33.
39. Pitt-Rivers, "Honour and Social Status."
40. Stiebert, *Construction of Shame*, 89.

incomparable glory (vv. 19, 21). The final outcome of such humiliation will not be fear, however, but joyful and carefree dependence on Yahweh (e.g. Isa 12:2; 26:4; 30:15–16) in a manner analogous to Japanese *amae*. All of this diverges from the Mediterranean model's idea of challenge-and-riposte which views deference, modesty, and dependence on others as liabilities in the Public Court of Reputation.[41]

In summary, the High Grid and High Group orientation of Japanese culture illuminates aspects of Isaiah 2 which are obscured in both Western OT scholarship as well as Western anthropology and missiology. Most significant among these is shame's formative role in convincing Judah that it stands outside both the Group of reverent nations and the Grid of Yahweh's righteous ways. However, honor in Isaiah ultimately comes not from the Japanese cultural modesty of "taking one's proper station"[42] with respect to a Group, but from a biblical understanding of humility which regards the Grid of Yahweh's character as the sole authority to impart honor to the obedient and shame to the disobedient. The reality of a "Divine Court of Reputation" in OT prophetic literature means that all human claims to honor in the Public Court of Reputation are relativized, including Mediterranean and Japanese ones.[43] The unique character of Yahwistic honor, shame, and guilt will come into sharper focus in the next section's exploration of royal storytelling and historiography in the face of an overwhelming enemy – a situation that characterizes both Samaria and Judah during the Assyrian threat of the eighth century BC and imperial Japan's defeat in World War II.

Second Kings 17–20 in Mediterranean and Japanese Perspective

Another look at honor and shame in intercultural perspective comes from the narrative in 2 Kings 17–20. This passage records the weak and tiny Israelite kingdoms reacting to the mighty Assyrian Empire arriving on their doorstep. Unexpectedly, guilt rather than power initially takes center stage as 2 Kings 17 explains that the fall of the northern kingdom of Samaria was due more to Samaria's sin than to Assyria's power. Poetic justice is well served when

---

41. Stiebert, 108.
42. As described by Benedict, *The Chrysanthemum and the Sword*, 43.
43. Te-Li Lau, *Defending Shame: Its Formative Power in Paul's Letters* (Grand Rapids, MI: Baker Academic, 2020), 85–86; Daniel Wu, *Honor, Shame, and Guilt: Social-Scientific Approaches to the Book of Ezekiel*, BBR Supplement Series 14 (Winona Lake, IN: Eisenbrauns, 2016).

Samaria's penchant for imitating the nations (17:8, 11, 15–17) is punished by the brutal hand of the nations (17:1–6, 20, 23).

This is not merely the homeopathic remedy of using evil against evil, for the guilt of Samaria is repeatedly described in 2 Kings 17 as a public matter of violating Yahweh's Torah which governs his land and the people who live in it (cf. Lev 18:24–30; Deut 12:1). The nations which Assyria brings in to replace Samaria are depicted as suffering the same consequences as Samaria for being ignorant about Yahweh as the God of the land who still rules it despite the deportation of its original inhabitants. In an ironic twist, Assyria is forced to call back one of Samaria's priests in exile to teach the new inhabitants of Samaria's land how to venerate Yahweh properly, lest the (disgraced?) God of Israel punish them severely (17:24–33).

In sum, the fall and exile of Samaria are portrayed as the High Group matter of international involvement in a High Grid matter – keeping Yahweh's commands which apply equally to non-Israelites and Israelites. This configuration of shame and guilt in 2 Kings 17 clashes with both the priority of shame over guilt in the High Grid and Low Group orientation of Mediterranean cultures, as well as the Low Grid orientation of Western cultures which devalues shame in favor of guilt as a private and individual matter. Later, we will comment on the High Group and High Grid similarities between the Israelite and Japanese cultures in their views of honor, shame, and guilt.

The Mediterranean model of honor and shame is still useful for the next section in 2 Kings 18–19, but more with respect to the Assyrian Empire than Judah. As the Assyrians besiege Jerusalem in the way they did Samaria, 2 Kings 18 narrates an envoy coming from the "the great king" of Assyria to taunt his Judahite counterparts with a series of honor claims: (1) Egypt and Pharaoh are useless allies (18:21, 24); (2) Yahweh cannot help since he is offended by Hezekiah's religious reforms (18:22; cf. 2 Chr 31:1); (3) Assyria could spare Judah two thousand horses to make the battle more even, but Judah would still lack the riders for them (18:23); (4) recent military history suggests that Yahweh is actually fighting against the Israelites (18:25);[44] (5) the inhabitants of Jerusalem will soon be consuming their own excrement and urine (18:27); and (6) neither Yahweh nor Hezekiah has the power to deliver Jerusalem since Assyria and its gods are clearly stronger than all others (18:31–35). Besides

---

44. To be precise, the envoy claims that Yahweh commanded Assyria to sack Judah, but this is likely an interpretation of Yahweh's disfavor toward the Israelites based on the fact that Samaria has already fallen to Assyria.

such bombast, the envoy's intention to publicly shame Yahweh, Hezekiah, and Jerusalem is also clear from how he shifts from addressing the official Judahite delegation in Aramaic (a trade language that ordinary Judahites would not know) to speak in Hebrew to Jerusalem's besieged inhabitants who are nervously eavesdropping from the city wall (18:26–28).

Second Kings 19 narrates various responses of Judah to the Assyrian envoy's psychological warfare of inflicting "Mediterranean" shame. The officials of King Hezekiah express to the prophet Isaiah their hope that Yahweh will respond to such shaming by vindicating his honor: "It may be that the LORD your God will hear all the words of the field commander, whom his master, the king of Assyria, has sent to ridicule the living God, and that he will rebuke him for the words the LORD your God has heard" (19:4). Speaking for Yahweh, Isaiah directs the officials to reassure Hezekiah, "Do not be afraid of what you have heard – those words with which the underlings of the king of Assyria have blasphemed me" (19:6). With Yahweh's promise that Assyria will turn back (19:7), the stage might seem set for a mighty show of power by Yahweh which reverses "Mediterranean" shame into "Mediterranean" honor.

Yet this chapter unfolds differently than one expects. Prior to a rather brief narrative of Yahweh striking Assyria's armies (cf. 19:35–37), the chapter devotes three extended scenes to Yahwism's unique understanding of how the apparent defeat of "Mediterranean" shaming is merely a precursor to true honor (19:8–34). First, the Assyrian envoy sends a mocking message that repeats his taunts (cf. 18:19–35), this time accenting how Assyria's defeat of other kings and their gods means that Hezekiah and Yahweh stand no chance against the king of "Ashur" (19:8–13) – conveniently the shared name of both the national god and his patron nation. This confrontation raises the stakes for the two lengthier scenes that follow.

Second, Hezekiah brings the letter of the envoy's taunts before Yahweh in the Jerusalem temple with an urgent prayer. Interestingly, the prayer of the Judahite king combines a recognition of Yahweh's power with an affirmation of Assyria's honor claims:

> Give ear, LORD, and hear; open your eyes, LORD, and see; listen to the words Sennacherib has sent to ridicule the living God.

> It is true, LORD, that the Assyrian kings have laid waste these nations and their lands. They have thrown their gods into the fire and destroyed them, for they were not gods but only wood and stone, fashioned by human hands. (19:16–18)

Assyria has done and spoken better than it knows, for it can indeed lay claim to vanquishing all other nations, kings, and gods. But Assyria's presumptive conclusion that Hezekiah, his nation, and his god are next in line does not follow. The success of "Mediterranean" shaming is just a penultimate step before Yahweh displays his supremacy over the greatest of human powers and proves that he alone deserves honor. Hezekiah therefore prays in the same way that David and Solomon before him did: "Now, LORD our God, deliver us from his hand, so that all the kingdoms of the earth may know that you alone, LORD, are God" (19:19; cf. 1 Sam 17:46–47; 1 Kgs 8:60).

Third and finally, Yahweh answers through the prophet Isaiah that he has indeed allowed Assyria to flourish briefly in its strategy of "Mediterranean" shaming (19:20–28). Yet the tables will soon turn when Assyria flees in defeat and Jerusalem mocks its hasty departure (19:21). The pride of past victories is only a temporary form of honor (19:22–23) since Yahweh is much more powerful for planning to use Assyria as an instrument to humble other nations (19:24–26) before finally turning its arrogance into the means of its humbling (19:27–28). By contrast, the remnant of Judah will experience restoration when Yahweh vindicates the honor that he shares with his people by defending Jerusalem "for my sake and for the sake of David my servant" (19:34).

Following these three scenes, the chapter's conclusion with the Assyrian army's miraculous defeat by the angel of Yahweh (19:32–34) and the fall of the Assyrian king (19:35–37) is rather anticlimactic since the empire's "honor" has already been turned inside out by Yahweh's speech through Isaiah. Along these lines and true to form, the Assyrian king Sennacherib described his *failed* siege against Jerusalem as the *successful* act of shutting up King Hezekiah "like a bird in a cage" so that "it [was] unthinkable for him to exit by the city gate."[45] Rather than admitting that he could not get into Jerusalem, Sennacherib insists that Hezekiah could not get out! This is as close as Assyrian historiography comes to admitting defeat in war.

Following the demise of Assyria's claim to "Mediterranean" honor in 2 Kings 18–19, 2 Kings 20 returns to a focus on guilt and shame which benefits from a Japanese perspective. This cryptic chapter, which concludes the Hezekiah narrative of 2 Kings, has puzzled Western interpreters for its non-linear sequence and unexpected characterization of Hezekiah. Though chapter

---

45. For this translation from the "Sennacherib Prism," see Michael D. Coogan, *A Reader of Ancient Near Eastern Texts: Sources for the Study of the Old Testament* (Oxford: Oxford University Press, 2013), 81.

20 comes after the narrative of Judah's deliverance from Assyria in chapter 19, it is clearly set in a time before the Assyrian crisis reached its height. Yahweh gives Hezekiah fifteen more years of life so that he will not die from his illness, but instead witness Jerusalem's deliverance from Assyria in 701 BC (2 Kgs 19:35–36). The narrative portrayal of Hezekiah is also disturbing since the faithful intercessor of the preceding chapters has become an exhibitionist who shows off Judah's splendor to Babylon (20:12–15). In addition, he is rather apathetic that his actions will be the first step toward Judah's exile to Babylon 150 years later (20:16–19). What is happening in this passage which clashes with the positive portrayal of Hezekiah in the previous chapters? Some modern interpreters, following John Calvin, try to harmonize 2 Kings 20 with the previous chapters by arguing that Hezekiah's response to Isaiah's oracle of judgment reflects an attitude of trust rather than selfishness: "The word of the Lord you have spoken is good. . . . Will there not be peace and security in my lifetime?" (20:19).[46]

Our discussion of Isaiah 2 illustrated the interpretive gains of examining a contested OT passage through the lenses of a High Group, High Grid society like Japan. Since 2 Kings 20 concerns the behavior of a king toward his people (both present and future), it is useful to supplement our earlier discussion with observations on how collectivism works when hierarchy comes into play. The Japanese anthropologist Takie Sugiyama Lebra has shown that guilt and shame play different functions within Japan's hierarchy of relationships rather than being strictly individualist or collective. Between Japanese of relatively similar status or rank, guilt is the more natural reaction than shame when the party in the wrong can rectify the situation by taking some action toward the wronged party. When it is difficult to return a favor or repay a debt, a Japanese person suffers from increased "guilt [which] hinges upon tension between the lost balance of reciprocity and the pressure to restore it."[47]

Shame, by contrast, is an emotion experienced by Japanese in asymmetric social situations when repayment or restoration is not possible. When a Japanese person engages in conduct that is mismatched with his or her social honor or reputation (i.e. "face"), shame is experienced individually by the

---

46. For a full history of positive interpretations of Hezekiah as well as a critique, see Sehoon Jang, "Is Hezekiah a Success or a Failure? The Literary Function of Isaiah's Prediction at the End of the Royal Narratives in the Book of Isaiah," *Journal for the Study of the Old Testament* 42 (Sep. 2017): 117–35.
47. Lebra, "Social Mechanism," 246.

exposed person as well as collectively by those who share the same status.[48] Guilt actually resembles shame among Japanese in having a collectivist dimension, except that the former cultural value views others as victims of one's conduct in contrast to the latter as the awareness of one's exposure to others.[49] Or to restate in Grid-Group terms, shame and guilt in Japan both have individual and collective elements which converge when violating one's Grid of shared social norms leads to a desire to hide from one's Group, while seeking to regain solidarity with the Group once its scrutiny has passed.[50] This differs both from Western understandings of shame and guilt as a public-private or collective-individual dichotomy, as well as from the Mediterranean tendency for shame and honor to be zero-sum entities which require confrontation in the Public Court of Reputation to resolve.

The cultural norms of guilt and shame in Japan suggest a potential explanation for why Hezekiah's speech and conduct have such dire consequences for reasons not explained in 2 Kings 20. On the one hand, Isaiah's warning that immodest Hezekiah has both exposed and squandered "all that is in your house, and all that your fathers have laid up in store to this day" (v. 17 NASB) represents a violation of the Grid norm of shame toward a hierarchy, in this case both his ancestors and his God who imparted Judah's heritage to him. On the other hand, Hezekiah's fixation on his own survival at the expense of his people defies the Grid norm of guilt toward those who are his victims, in this case his descendants and the nation to be deported to Babylon (v. 18). For in commenting to Isaiah that "the word of the LORD you have spoken is good" (v. 19), it is not only that Hezekiah has succumbed to pride, as scholars from Western individualist cultures rightly observe. He has also failed in his Grid obligations to exhibit the proper shame and guilt toward various communities within his Group. There is more here than Hezekiah acting like a typical ruler or patriarch in a Mediterranean society, and the severity of his offenses becomes apparent when Japanese categories are overlaid upon his similarly High Group and High Grid society.

Interestingly, the multifaceted characterization of Hezekiah in 2 Kings 18–20 anticipates the picture of Emperor Hirohito which has emerged of his involvement in World War II. Since his death in 1989, scholars of Japan have

48. Lebra, 251.
49. Takie Sugiyama Lebra, "Shame and Guilt: A Psychocultural View of the Japanese Self," *Ethos* 11 (1983): 203.
50. Sakuta, "Culture of Shame," 36.

shown that Hirohito played a much greater role in leading the nation toward war, defeat, and disaster than previously recognized or admitted by Japanese historians.[51] The fact that the official account of Hirohito's legacy could be re-examined only after his death stands in contrast to the official Israelite account which recorded both the good and the bad of Hezekiah's reign. Ironically, it has often been Ruth Benedict's descriptive labeling of Japan as "shame culture" that has come to play an unwitting prescriptive role in holding back Japan from fully reckoning with its imperial history.[52] The case of Hirohito highlights how unusual it is for royally sponsored historiography to tell the truth at its own expense, since the state-controlled media that emerged from Hezekiah's time evidently had shaming the state as part of its agenda. As Frederick Greenspan rightly notes, "Unlike other writings of its time, the Hebrew Bible is thoroughly critical of its own people."[53]

Proverbs in Mediterranean and Japanese Perspective

The third significant area of comparison between OT Israel and Japan lies in how moral hierarchy is conceived in terms of the High Group and High Grid cultural orientation that they share. Proverbs 25–29 is useful in such a comparison since it exhibits the royal stamp of "the men of Hezekiah" (Prov 25:1) who compiled Solomon's proverbs within a Mediterranean cultural context during the eighth century BC, the period of interest which has already been useful for our case studies. Similarly in Proverbs, the work of these royal sages frames honor, shame, and guilt in a manner that has points of contact with Japanese understandings of these cultural values but ultimately does not conform to them. This clash of cultures is even more pronounced with reference to Mediterranean values.

The theocentric vision of Proverbs 25–29 stands at odds with the Public Court of Reputation in Mediterranean societies since "fear of man will prove to be a snare, but whoever trusts in the LORD is kept safe" (29:25). Continually in these five chapters, the sages of Hezekiah emphasize the paradox that honor comes from humility before God rather than claiming honor in public (e.g.

51. E.g. John W. Dower, *Embracing Defeat: Japan in the Wake of World War II* (New York: Norton, 1999).
52. Elson Boles, "Ruth Benedict's Japan: The Benedictions of Imperialism," *Dialectical Anthropology* 1–2 (2006): 27–70; John Lie, "Ruth Benedict's Legacy of Shame: Orientalism and Occidentalism in the Study of Japan," *Asian Journal of Social Science* 29 (2000): 249–61.
53. Frederick E. Greenspahn, "Syncretism and Idolatry in the Bible," *Vetus Testamentum* 44 (2004): 480.

25:6–7; 28:25). The nature of honor is fundamentally different from the Public Court of Reputation since "seeking one's own glory is not glory"[54] (25:27; cf. 29:23) and recognition from one's peers can be the most dangerous test of character (27:21; cf. vv. 1–2). Similarly, impulsiveness in public (29:20) is unwise since one risks humiliation (25:8–10) or escalation of conflict (29:8–9, 11). It is better to choose one's words slowly and wisely (29:11, 20), especially when one is in the presence of the powerful (25:11–15). The Mediterranean dynamic of challenge-and-riposte is inferior in God's eyes to helping one's enemy and winning them over (25:21–22). This is not to say that every public confrontation is unwise, since the presence of wisdom makes any rebuke an occasion for growth (25:12; 29:15, 17; cf. 29:1), especially when the parties involved are not overly concerned about shaming (27:5; 28:2).

The unreliability of the Public Court of Reputation (e.g. 26:17–28) makes it natural that honor and shame are redefined from the social and gender hierarchy of the Mediterranean into the moral terms of wisdom and folly which characterize OT wisdom literature.[55] It is natural, for example, that Proverbs 25–29 condemns the pursuit of status in the eyes of the community, especially through seeking to become rich (28:20, 22; cf. v. 11). The virtues of wisdom are available to all instead of depending on approval from others, as in the saying that "honor is not fitting for a fool" (26:1b) which opens an extended section about the various traits of folly (vv. 1–12). The foolish are those who need correction from others but often refuse it (vv. 3–5), are untrustworthy with their words (vv. 6–7, 9), disappoint those who give them honor that they are unable to handle (vv. 8, 10), tend to repeat their mistakes rather than learning from them (v. 11), and are wise in their own eyes (v. 12).

The stark contrasts between righteous/wise and wicked/foolish means that honor and shame in Proverbs 25–29 function rather differently from the strongly gendered norms of "Mediterranean" societies. David Gilmore memorably said that

> in the Mediterranean lands, masculine rivalries seem to be in-
> tensified by an erotic dimension, which . . . triangulates the
> sexual relationship, bringing into play an essentially homoerotic
> aim along with a heterosexual object. . . . So, male dishonor im-
> plies more than loss of social prestige; it also implies loss of male

---

54. Author's translation.
55. W. R. Domeris, "Shame and Honour in Proverbs: Wise Women and Foolish Men," *Old Testament Essays* 8 (1995): 86–102.

social identity, of masculinity. Mediterranean honor, then, is a "libidinized" social reputation; and it is this eroticized aspect of honor – albeit unconscious or implicit – that seems to make the Mediterranean variant distinctive.[56]

In the same volume, Mariko Asano-Tamanoi, a Japanese anthropologist who did fieldwork in both Spain and Japan, observes that these two countries differ since honor and shame in Japan focus on one's role in society, in contrast to the emphasis on sexual potency for men and sexual purity for women which typifies the Mediterranean.[57]

However, Proverbs 25–29 exhibits a different kind of clash with Japanese culture due to its disregard for social hierarchy. The authority of God's law means that his standards are the ultimate arbiter of righteousness and guilt for every individual (28:1–5, 7, 9, 18; 29:18). For this reason, the wise and righteous have a duty to resist the wicked even when this means defying the crowd (25:26). The primacy of holiness over fulfilling one's expected role can also be seen in how Proverbs 25–29 praises the poor and weak who are righteous (e.g. 28:6, 11), but criticizes the strong and rich who are wicked (e.g. 28:8, 15–16, 22; 29:2) or arrogant (e.g. 28:11). While the themes of modesty (25:6–7) and minding one's own business (25:17; 27:14) resonate with Japanese culture's emphasis on staying within one's class, the moral vision of Proverbs 25–29 is ultimately at odds with Japan's characteristic emphasis on the rank ascribed to each individual within a hierarchy.[58] In other words, the Torah-shaped Grid orientation of OT wisdom literature entails an individual moral duty to defy the collective norms of the Group when God's requirements demand it. This is still not the individualism of Western culture nor the penchant for confrontation in Mediterranean culture, for Japan's combination of High Group and High Grid elements still makes interdependence of greater value than competing with one another.[59]

CONCLUSION

The Japanese balance between collective identity and individual responsibility offers the potential for bringing together honor, shame, and guilt in a

---

56. David D. Gilmore, "Introduction," in *Honor and Shame and the Unity of the Mediterranean*, ed. David D. Gilmore (Washington DC: American Anthropological Association, 1987), 10–11.
57. Asano-Tamanoi, "Shame, Family, and State," 116–17.
58. As influentially described by Chie Nakane, *Japanese Society* (Berkeley, CA: University of California Press, 1970).
59. Sakuta, "Culture of Shame," 38.

more holistic way than both Western and Mediterranean models. Despite Ruth Benedict's influential label of Japan as a "shame culture" which finds it difficult to accept guilt, it is notable that the combination of High Grid and High Group orientations means that Japanese can deviate from their culture's dominant norms whenever a Japanese counterculture possesses a sufficiently robust Grid orientation. This is precisely what has happened when Japanese Christians, shaped by biblical values, have taken the lead in apologizing for the atrocities of their wartime empire.

Two recent examples will suffice to illustrate how Japanese Christians have sought to atone for imperial Japan's sins in a manner that their own government and people have often struggled to do. Dr. Takamitsu Muraoka, one of the world's preeminent Hebrew scholars, has tithed his time since retirement from the University of Leiden to visit and teach in Asian countries which suffered under Japanese imperialism, all at his own expense. Besides offering his services as an OT scholar, he has also made it a practice to meet with elderly victims of the Japanese soldiers on these visits to ask for their forgiveness. Muraoka's memoirs contain his poignant reflections on these trips that are motivated both by biblical teaching and Japan's lack of full reckoning for its actions during World War II.[60]

Similarly, Japanese Christians sought out Christians in northeastern India to make amends for atrocities committed during the fierce Battles of Kohima and Imphal in 1944. These efforts culminated in November 2015, when Naga Christians hosted Japanese Christians at a reconciliation summit held in Kohima, the capital of the Indian state of Nagaland where the fiercest fighting had taken place between the Japanese and the British colonial army.[61] Rev. Jun Takimoto, a Japanese pastor and leader of his country's delegation, addressed the Naga attenders at the summit: "We want to express to you our heartfelt apologies that the Japanese really caused a lot of trouble, anxiety and problem [sic] to you. . . . We actually should have come here much sooner because the actual battle happened 71 years ago."[62] Naga Christian leaders also called upon their own people to forgive the Japanese in Christ's name and seek

---

60. Takamitsu Muraoka, *My Via Dolorosa: Along the Trails of the Japanese Imperialism in Asia* (Bloomington, IN: AuthorHouse, 2016).
61. Video excerpts of the Japan-Naga Christian Reconciliation Summit in 2015 have been compiled at "Japan-Naga Christian Reconciliation Summit," YouTube, 12 November 2019, https://www.youtube.com/watch?v=iKeNUeloKEo&.
62. As reported by Alice Yhoshu, "Healing WWII Wounds after 70 Years: Japan-Naga Reconciliation Summit Underway," *Eastern Mirror Nagaland*, updated 29 November 2015, https://easternmirrornagaland.com/healing-wwii-wounds-after-70-years-japan-naga-reconciliation-summit-underway/.

amends for their own cruelty toward the Japanese in the course of the battle. These two Asian cultures would typically be classified as "shame cultures" by missiologists, making it noteworthy how sincerely the participants in the reconciliation summit acknowledged their guilt for actions that they had not personally committed.

In sum, it is precisely the High Grid and High Group orientation of Japanese culture which has empowered Japanese Christians to defy their culture's usual expectations of honor, shame, and guilt. This ability to hold biblical understandings of these values mirrors how High Grid, High Group Israel also became a counterculture within its context which defied the usual ways of representing power. The next chapter will explore how Israel's worship exhibited the same posture of critical engagement toward ancient Near Eastern ideas of iconography for representing deity in visible and propagandistic ways. The "sacred emptiness" of Israel's aniconism was not merely a matter of religion and philosophy, since the reality of royal sponsorship in maintaining sacred space and divine images always involved economics and politics as well.

CHAPTER 7

ANICONISM AND ICONOGRAPHY

The Roman Catholic Church has traditionally emphasized the use of images, rituals, and liturgy in worship. These were also frequently the vehicle by which late-medieval Catholicism became corrupt. It is thus understandable that the Reformers were suspicious of all things visual and ritual as signs of empty religion. Such outward expressions in worship were often vilified by Martin Luther as "papist" or "Romish." He also attached the pejorative label of "Judaizers" to advocates of such practices, making the Old Testament somewhat guilty by association. The legacy of Lutheranism's characteristic division between law and gospel has frequently been a contrast between Jewish legalism as supposedly found in the Torah on the one hand, and the anti-ritual bent of the Christian gospel on the other. John Calvin's view of the OT was more positive than Luther's overall, but he concurred that the preaching and hearing of the word of God took precedence over anything in the visual realm of worship. With Luther and Calvin leading the way, one unintended result of the Reformation has been five centuries of Protestant unease about the suitability of *beauty* as a category for doing theology.[1]

The Western emphasis on theology in the abstract has sometimes left Asian Christians without concrete expressions of faith. This gap can open the door to the "split-level Christianity" and folk religion mentioned in earlier chapters. In the Philippines, for example, Christians face the constant challenge of reconciling a native emphasis on icons of various kinds (whether from pre-Hispanic cultures or Spanish Catholic influences) with Reformation theology's move away from icons and images due to strong cultural associations with Catholicism.[2] It may thus come as a surprise to Asian Christians that the OT does not altogether endorse the view of the Reformers that "the prime symbol of true belief is the word, invisible and heard; the prime symbol of false

---

1. Cf. Jonathan King, *The Beauty of the Lord: Theology as Aesthetics*, Studies in Historical and Systematic Theology (Bellingham, WA: Lexham Press, 2018).
2. M. Padilla Maggay, "Art and Aesthetics," in *Global Dictionary of Theology: A Resource for the Worldwide Church*, eds. William A. Dyrness and Veli-Matti Kärkkäinen (Downers Grove, IL: IVP Academic, 2008) 64–66.

belief is the image, visible and seen."[3] Authentic biblical faith and worship are certainly inclusive of the abstract, individual, interior, and spiritual realms. However, it tends to be Western understandings of icons and iconography in the OT that, with a major assist from certain streams of Greek philosophy, have caused Protestant Christianity to place materiality and spirituality in a contrastive relationship.[4]

For these reasons, the present chapter will begin by reassessing Western approaches to visual imagination through an examination of *aniconism* and *anthropomorphism* in Exodus and Ezekiel. These are two books whose physical and concrete depictions of God's presence are usually downplayed by Christian theologians and OT scholars in favor of spiritual and abstract categories. It is no small irony that the success of the Protestant Reformation means that Western Christian readers of the OT typically do not experience discomfort or cultural dissonance when the OT militates against the making of images, as in the parodies of idol-making in Isaiah, Jeremiah, Habakkuk, and certain psalms. Thus, I will use a case study of Thailand and its ubiquity of religious images to provide a better comparison for the OT's teaching on icons and iconography than the Western cultural lenses through which "a graven image is indeed an exotic phenomenon!"[5] Unlike for Western Christians, Thai Christians would find the image-making ceremonies described in the OT prophets to be familiar from their own experiences in a Buddhist and iconographic culture.

A HISTORY OF VISUAL IMAGINATION IN WESTERN CHRISTIANITY

Any consideration of visual imagination in Western Christianity must begin not with the Reformation, but with St. Augustine a millennium prior. This church father of the Latin tradition is claimed in different ways by Catholic, Protestant, and Orthodox Christians alike. In fact, Augustine's writings have been foundational for both Christian theology as well as Western civilization more broadly, especially through his *Confessions* and *City of God*. In these and other works, Augustine drew on the thought of Plotinus, a Neoplatonist philosopher, to conceive of God as the highest good who invites people to

---

3. Charles Garside, *Zwingli and the Arts* (New Haven, CT: Yale University Press, 1966), 175, quoted in William A. Dyrness, *Visual Faith: Art, Theology, and Worship in Dialogue*, Engaging Culture (Grand Rapids, MI: Baker Academic, 2001), 54–55.
4. Gottwald, *Tribes of Yahweh*, xxv.
5. Kari Storstein Haug and Knut Holter, "No Graven Image? Reading the Second Commandment in a Thai Context," *Asia Journal of Theology* 14 (2000): 20.

pursue him in inward, upward, and invisible ways.[6] Book VII of *Confessions* recounts Augustine's turn away from materiality and toward immateriality as he yearned for God's presence:

> With all my heart I believed you to be incorruptible, immune from injury, and unchangeable. Although I did not know why and how, it was clear to me and certain that what is corruptible is inferior to that which cannot be corrupted; what is immune from injury I unhesitatingly put above that which is not immune; what suffers no change is better than that which can change. *My heart vehemently protested against all the physical images in my mind, and by this single blow I attempted to expel from my mind's eye the swarm of unpurified notions flying about there.*[7]

Later in the same part of *Confessions*, Augustine explicitly draws on (Neo-) Platonism to add inward and upward dimensions to the immaterial direction of his journey:

> By the Platonic books I was admonished to return into myself. With you as my guide I entered into my innermost citadel. . . . I entered and with my soul's eye . . . saw above that same eye of my soul the immutable light higher than my mind. . . . When I first came to know you, you raised me up to make me see that what I saw is Being, and that I who saw am not yet Being. And you gave a shock to the weakness of my sight by the strong radiance of your rays, and I trembled with love and awe.[8]

Augustine uses the physical phenomenon of light to describe his newfound knowledge. But he is unmistakably speaking of a nonphysical kind of epiphany. In his own words, insight from God is "not the light of every day, obvious to anyone, nor a larger version of the same kind . . . but a different thing, utterly different from our kinds of light."[9]

---

6. Scott MacDonald, "The Divine Nature: Being and Goodness," in *The Cambridge Companion to Augustine*, ed. David Vincent Meconi and Eleonore Stump, 2nd ed. (Cambridge: Cambridge University Press, 2014), 17–36.

7. Saint Augustine, *Confessions*, trans. Henry Chadwick, Oxford World's Classics (Oxford: Oxford University Press, 2008), VII.1 (111), italics added.

8. Augustine, *Confessions*, VII.10 (123).

9. Augustine, VII.10 (123). It would go too far, though, to say that Augustine uniformly denigrated the value of creation or physical beauty. Some passages in Augustine's writings can be interpreted in this manner, but his mature thought viewed their role as contingent in pointing

In a similar fashion, *The City of God* was Augustine's tractate about the theological catastrophe of his day: how could the seemingly invincible city of Rome be overrun by Goth barbarians in AD 410? His answer was that the physical "City of Man" on earth below could never be equated with the spiritual "City of God" in heaven above, though inhabitants of the latter could be found dwelling in the former. The logical connections that Augustine made between several kinds of conceptual dualities – substance (physical vs. spiritual), spatial (heavenly vs. earthly), and moral (good vs. evil) – have had a profound influence on all Christian theology after him.[10] This is not to say that the so-called "Hellenization thesis" and its sharp contrast between Hebrew and Greek ways of thinking is correct,[11] only that Augustine's polarities have become second nature for many Protestant Christians today. They are intuitively thought to be biblical and universal even when they represent a particular contextualization of Christian faith for Greco-Roman culture in the fifth century AD.[12]

Let us move from Augustine to three examples of Protestant Christian theology which each owe a clear debt to him. The first is *The Pilgrim's Progress*, John Bunyan's beloved allegory of the believer's plodding but steady journey from the City of Destruction to the Celestial City. This contrast between cities echoes motifs from Augustine's *City of God* (as well as Revelation 21–22). It is ambiguous at times whether Bunyan's Celestial City is physical or not, but it is clear that the pilgrimage of "Christian" (the main character) involves leaving behind the present corrupt world rather than living redemptively within it.

The eminent Dutch Reformed theologian Herman Bavinck furnishes another example of prioritizing the immaterial realm as timeless and trustworthy over the material realm as fleeting and deceptive. In the second volume of

---

fallen humanity to the highest Source of beauty (Carol Harrison, *Beauty and Revelation in the Thought of Saint Augustine*, Oxford Theological Monographs [Oxford: Oxford University Press, 1992], 53). I am indebted to Steve Pardue for drawing my attention to Harrison's book.
10. The usual term "dualism" is too loaded to be helpful. Of these polarities, it is particularly important to note that the antimony of good and evil is not between equal spiritual powers. Such a view would revert to the Manicheanism with which Augustine dallied before his conversion.
11. As championed especially by Adolf von Harnack (1851–1930), the German theologian and church historian, in *What Is Christianity? Sixteen Lectures Delivered in the University of Berlin 1899–1900*, repr. ed. (San Diego, CA: Book Tree, 2006). For a critique of the Hellenization thesis and Augustine's supposed role in bringing Greek philosophy into Christianity, see Michael Allen, "Exodus 3 after the Hellenization Thesis," *Journal of Theological Interpretation* 3 (2009): 179–96.
12. J. Richard Middleton, *A New Heaven and a New Earth: Reclaiming Biblical Eschatology* (Grand Rapids, MI: Baker Academic, 2014), 33–34.

his *Reformed Dogmatics*, Bavinck explains God's attribute of invisibility in a manner reminiscent of the above passages from Augustine's *Confessions*:

> Scripture clearly teaches the spirituality and invisibility of God. . . . Also, when Scripture speaks of God's face, glory, and majesty, it uses figurative language. Like all God's perfections, so also that of God's glory is reflected in his creatures. . . . Just as the contemplation of God's creatures directs our attention upward and prompts us to speak of God's eternity and omnipresence, his righteousness and grace, so it also gives us a glimpse of God's glory. What we have here, however, is analogy, not identity. This already comes out in our language. Speaking of creatures, we call them pretty, beautiful, or splendid: but for the beauty of God Scripture has a special word: glory. *For that reason it is not advisable to speak – with the church fathers, scholastics, and Catholic theologians – of God's beauty.*[13]

It is revealing that Bavinck offers a choice between literal and figurative understandings of God's "glory," while evidently favoring the latter due to the mixed connotations of the term "beauty" and its rootedness in the physical world.[14] As we will see, however, Exodus and Ezekiel conceive of the divine presence as both the concrete "glory" of his physical presence as well as the abstract "name" of his essence and reputation. A biblical understanding of aniconism and iconography thus does not require Hellenistic philosophy's dichotomy between the immaterial and material and its value system that favors the first over the second. Instead, the OT depicts God more as physically *in-visible* (i.e. unseeable) than spiritually *invisible*. This contrasts notably with Bavinck's uses of the terms "spirituality" and "invisibility" synonymously to denote immateriality,[15] even though the NT Greek term *aoratos* that English Bibles render "invisible" (e.g. Col 1:15; 1 Tim 1:17) is less about nonphysical, spiritual, or abstract existence than the visual reality of "pertaining to that which people cannot see."[16]

---

13. Herman Bavinck, *Reformed Dogmatics*, ed. John Bolt, trans. John Vriend, 4 vols. (Grand Rapids, MI: Baker Academic, 2003), 2:253–54, italics added.
14. Interestingly in this same passage (n. 13), Bavinck distances himself from Augustine, to whom he attributes the Neoplatonist view that ultimate beauty is found in God. But as noted above (n. 9), Augustine's thought contains both world-denying and world-affirming elements when it comes to physical beauty.
15. See also Bavinck, *Reformed Dogmatics*, 2:187.
16. L&N §24.3–4.

The third and final example of Christian theology in the tradition of Augustine comes from Wayne Grudem. In his *Systematic Theology*, a textbook widely used in evangelical seminaries, Grudem explores the OT phenomenon of *theophany* (e.g. Exod 24:9–11) somewhat differently from Augustine, Bunyan, or Bavinck. He observes that the usual categories of physical and spiritual fail to do justice to the majesty of God's presence:

> God does not have a physical body, nor is he made of any kind of matter like much of the rest of creation. . . . God's being is not even exactly like our own spirits, for these are created things that apparently are able to exist only in one place in one time. Instead of all these ideas of God, we must say that God is *spirit*. Whatever this means, it is a kind of existence that is unlike anything else in creation.[17]

Grudem's formulation is helpful for understanding God's presence as "spiritual" in the broader terms of an uncontainable mystery rather than as the strict and limited opposite of "physical." At the same time, a hint of Hellenistic categories reappears in his next statement about God's presence: "It is a kind of existence that is far superior to all our material existence."[18] Although some NT passages speak of the inferiority and futility of this-worldly pursuits (e.g. 2 Cor 4:16–5:4; Heb 11:13–16), chapter 4 of this book has already explored how the Hebrew Bible fills out this picture by balancing the material and immaterial dimensions of life with each other. However, the implications of this holistically balanced worldview have not always been reproduced in Western OT scholarship about God's presence, as we will now see.

ANICONISM AND ANTHROPOMORPHISM IN WESTERN OT SCHOLARSHIP

The approaches and conclusions of Christian theology across two millennia run parallel to those of OT scholarship during the last two centuries. Not unlike how Augustine "vehemently protested all the physical images of my mind," OT scholarship has often set the written Scriptures at odds with the visual,

---

17. Wayne A. Grudem, *Systematic Theology: An Introduction to Biblical Doctrine* (Grand Rapids, MI: Zondervan Academic, 1995), 188.
18. Grudem, *Systematic Theology*, 188. Later on the same page, Grudem asserts: "Why is God spirit? All that we can say is that this is the greatest, most excellent way to be! This is a form of existence far superior to anything we know." This conclusion only follows within a philosophical framework that has already assumed that spiritual and immaterial existence is superior to physical and material existence.

material, and physical realities from which they came. The conclusion of Swiss OT scholars Othmar Keel and Christoph Uehlinger, in their standard work on divine iconography in ancient Israel, is worth quoting in full:

> It is a crass anachronism to continue to assert, as do those schol-
> ars who put no stock in images, that pictures are meaningless
> decoration. The idea that pictures and their production were
> important only if they measured up to some primarily or even
> exclusively formal and aesthetic standard is a viewpoint that
> is no older than the nineteenth century and is typical of so-
> called "enlightened," western civilization. Only modern west-
> ern-thinking individuals hold such a view. . . . The world of
> Canaanite-Israelite religion is foreign to us. A deaf-mute from
> the western world, suddenly transported to ancient Palestine,
> would find it easier to adjust than would a blind person similarly
> transported. . . . Many biblical scholars work their way through
> ancient Palestine like the blind, having learned the idiom or id-
> ioms of that world with much difficulty. . . . This approach to
> the biblical texts is based on a one-sided view of the Bible as the
> *Word* of God.[19]

As hinted earlier, Western Protestantism's cultural bias against images is most evident in OT scholarship's tendency to interpret the prohibition on making images or likenesses of God – the concept of *aniconism* – in terms of the spirituality or invisibility of God. This understanding is held to be incompatible with other OT passages with physical manifestations or hu-man-like descriptions of God – the concepts of *theophany* and *anthropomor-phism*.[20] Accordingly in Julius Wellhausen's *Prolegomena to the History of Israel*, he assigned the Genesis narratives with theophanic appearances of Yahweh

---

19. Othmar Keel and Christoph Uehlinger, *Gods, Goddesses, and Images of God in Ancient Israel*, trans. Thomas H. Trapp (Minneapolis, MN: Fortress, 1998), 395, italics original. Interestingly, the neglect of archaeology in OT scholarship sometimes overcorrects to the opposite extreme. Critical scholars can prioritize material remains over the OT text to such an extent that the lack of explicit evidence for aniconism is taken as evidence for iconism in Israel. But as Richard S. Hess rightly notes (*Israelite Religions*, 165–66), how much material evidence could ever be found for the absence of something? This is the *fallacy of negative evidence*.

20. See the overview of Western OT scholarship on aniconism in Mettinger, *No Graven Image?*, 16–27.

to the Yahwist source (J) in the tenth century BC, while the aniconism of the Decalogue belonged to the Elohist source (E) in the ninth century BC.[21]

Gerhard von Rad used a different critical method but worked with similar presuppositions about competing modes of divine presence. In an influential study, von Rad proposed that Deuteronomy's abstract theology of Yahweh's "name" relegated the divine presence to heaven, while the Priestly source's concrete theology of the "glory" envisions the divine presence on earth, especially through the ark and tabernacle.[22] The ark of the covenant in Deuteronomy, by contrast, was thought by von Rad to be a demythologized box without any sacral power that served merely as a container for the Decalogue tablets.

Running through both the source criticism of Wellhausen and the tradition criticism of von Rad, however, is an unstated *either-or* assumption with roots in Neoplatonism. The divine presence must be *either* abstract, spiritual, and heavenly, *or* concrete, physical, and earthly. The result is that OT passages in which these supposedly contradictory conceptions appear side by side are composite texts that come from different periods in Israel's history. While each pole of Western scholarship's forced choice between notions of divine presence can claim some biblical support, there remains the challenge of how to conceptualize the abstract/spiritual/heavenly and concrete/physical/earthly poles in a *both-and* manner that accounts for the entirety of the biblical material in a coherent way.[23] If they were really contradictory, as Wellhausen and von Rad assert, then why would they be juxtaposed in the canonical form of the text as if the OT's final editors were blind to (supposedly) obvious inconsistencies?[24]

Especially significant in this regard are the OT's references to the "face" (*pānîm*) of Yahweh. This is an anthropomorphism that joins the OT's transcendent and immanent conceptions of the divine presence and joins the polarities

---

21. In Julius Wellhausen's reconstruction, the J and E sources were joined at an early date, enabling a passage like Exodus 20 to contain both references to "Yahweh" (from J) and the Decalogue's prohibition on images (from E).

22. Gerhard von Rad, "Deuteronomy's 'Name' Theology and the Priestly Document's 'Kabod' Theology," in *Studies in Deuteronomy*, Studies in Biblical Theology (London: SCM, 1953), 37–44.

23. Howard Schwartz, "Does God Have a Body? The Problem of Metaphor and Literal Language in Biblical Interpretation," in *Bodies, Embodiment, and Theology of the Hebrew Bible*, eds. S. Tamar Kamionkowski and Wonil Kim, Library of Hebrew Bible/Old Testament Studies 465 (New York: T&T Clark, 2010), 220.

24. As R. N. Whybray famously noted, "thus the [documentary] hypothesis can only be maintained on the assumption that, while consistency was the hallmark of the various documents, inconsistency was the hallmark of the redactors" (*The Making of the Pentateuch: A Methodological Study*, JSOT Supplement Series 168 [Sheffield: JSOT Press, 1994], 49).

that both Christian theologians and Western OT scholars have usually worked with.[25] Particularly in Exodus 33, the numerous references to the *pānîm* of Yahweh defy attempts to divide them simply into literal "face" and figurative "presence."[26] This chapter is notable for two statements in the same context about the *pānîm* of Yahweh that appear contradictory:

> Narrator: "[Yahweh] would speak to Moses face to face [*pānîm 'el-pānîm*], as one speaks to a friend." (33:11)

> Yahweh: "You [Moses] cannot see my face [*pānîm*], for no one may see [my face] and live." (33:20)

Besides these and other references to the divine *pānîm* (vv. 14, 15), the OT's other terms for divine presence that von Rad saw as competing – *kābôd* ("glory") and *šēm* ("name") – both appear as well. As Gordon McConville observes, this chapter's confluence of terms and concepts means that the divine *pānîm* is simultaneously transcendent and far as Yahweh's *kābôd*, while also being immanent and near as Yahweh's *šēm*: "The glory of God is unapproachable and dangerous and may not be seen by the people, or even by Moses. The name of God, on the other hand, is something with which his worshippers are permitted to become familiar."[27] In other words, the conditions that must be met for a holy God to remain among his sinful people (cf. vv. 12–13) are that he is simultaneously present "face to face" (v. 11) as well as absent so that "no one can see my face" (v. 20) – both *deus revelatus* and *deus absconditus*, in Luther's famous terms. Against OT scholarship's attempts to unravel them into tradition layers or otherwise regard them as inconsistent,[28] these polarities are the mystery of the divine presence that holds Exodus 33's narrative together.[29]

A similar tendency to pit concrete and abstract ideas of divine presence against one another can be seen in Western interpretations of *anthropomorphism* in Ezekiel. This book is one of the OT's most strident in denouncing the

---

25. C.-L. Seow, "Face," *DDD*, 322, notes the pivotal role of Hebrew *pānîm* by which "the ancient Israelites were able to speak of the deity's simultaneous transcendence and immanence."
26. James Barr, "Theophany and Anthropomorphism in the Old Testament," in *Congress Volume Oxford 1959*, eds. G. W. Anderson et al., Supplements to Vetus Testamentum 7 (Leiden: Brill, 1960), 35.
27. J. G. McConville, "God's 'Name' and God's 'Glory,'" *Tyndale Bulletin* 30 (1979): 156.
28. E.g. Samuel L. Terrien, *The Elusive Presence: Toward a New Biblical Theology* (Eugene, OR: Wipf and Stock, 2000), 138–52, who still attributes the finely balanced theology of presence in the Sinai theophanies to the work of different tradents.
29. R. W. L. Moberly, *At the Mountain of God: Story and Theology in Exodus 32–34*, JSOT Supplement Series 22 (Sheffield: JSOT Press, 1983), 65–66.

idols of Judah in the sixth century BC. In the service of this polemic, however, Ezekiel is also the most creative of the OT prophets in using visual imagination from the human and animal realms to depict sacred space. Simply put, the way in which Ezekiel attacks idolatry differs greatly from the more Western emphasis on an abstract, invisible, spiritual, or heavenly notion of divine presence. Ezekiel instead adopts a contextual and contextualizing posture by appropriating ancient Near Eastern iconography in its opening vision of "the appearance of the likeness of the glory of the LORD" (Ezek 1:28). Like the theophanies of Genesis, the divine presence in Ezekiel is a concrete manifestation within sacred space that simultaneously reveals and conceals. It is more than visible and physical but certainly not less than these, for Ezekiel represents the presence of Yahweh using physical phenomena that are amorphous and suggestive of transcendence (e.g. fire, rainbow) rather than being spatially bound.[30] And as in Exodus, the divine presence in Ezekiel assumes a holistic character that shows how aniconism and anthropomorphism are less at odds with one another than Western Christians might expect.

Modern readers of Ezekiel often find his description of icons to be bizarre and otherworldly. In the throne vision of chapter 1, the prophet sees four "living creatures" that are animal-human hybrids. Each has four wings, legs of calves, human hands, and faces that are a combination of human and eagle faces as well as the face of another animal such as a lion or bull (Ezek 1:5–11). *Anthropomorphism* (i.e. depiction using human features) thus goes hand in hand in Ezekiel with *theriomorphism* (i.e. depiction using animal features). Artistic depictions of these grotesque creatures struggle to depict these combinations and inevitably look like monstrosities from a comic book. Despite the unfamiliarity of these creatures to modern audiences, it was precisely their rootedness in Mesopotamian iconography that would have been powerfully evocative to Ezekiel's original audience of exiles who were refugees in Babylon. The prophet's vision drew upon a long history of visual imagination in Assyria and Babylon which mixed human and animal forms in mythical icons that were either deities themselves or served as gatekeepers to the presence of the gods.

The hybrid character of these icons can be seen in several specimens that archaeologists excavated from Iraq and which are now kept in the British

---

30. Jill Middlemas, "Exclusively Yahweh: Aniconism and Anthropomorphism in Ezekiel," in *Prophecy and the Prophets in Ancient Israel: Proceedings of the Oxford Old Testament Seminar*, Library of Hebrew Bible/Old Testament Studies 531 (London: T&T Clark, 2010), 319–20.

Museum. The first is a pair of winged statues, one a human-headed lion and the other a human-headed bull with birds' wings, that was found in the ninth-century BC Assyrian palace at Nimrud (see left photograph of the lion-bodied statue). The second, from about a century later, is a pair of winged bulls with human heads from the palace of Sargon II at Khorsabad (see right photograph of one of the pair). Each of these imposing statues (called a *lamassu* or *shedu* in Akkadian) weighs 10–20 tons. As propaganda, their purpose is to project Mesopotamian royal ideology in a visual, tangible way that instills reverence toward the empire among both native and captive peoples.

(photos by the author)

The clear similarities between Ezekiel's odd vision and Mesopotamian iconography raise the question of why the caretakers of Yahweh's presence would be portrayed using motifs that are at home in the sixth century BC. It is surprising that hybrid creatures that evoke Babylon's deities should appear alongside Yahweh's presence (Ezek 1:22–28) in a book that is so fervent in its aniconism. Indeed, John Kutsko has noted that Ezekiel uses a vocabulary palette to condemn idolatry which is unparalleled in the rest of the OT for its colorfulness.[31] The frequent use of *gillûlîm* ("[dung] circles/pellets"; 39x in the book) is particularly biting as a scatological term that derides the worthlessness of Israel's idols (e.g. 6:4–6; 14:3–7; 20:7–8). One might therefore expect Ezekiel, as the OT's most scathing prophet of aniconism and a frequent communicator of prophetic sign-acts, to engage in some form of ritual desecration of *lamassu* sculptures.[32]

However, Ezekiel takes the surprising route of using Mesopotamian iconography to denounce Israel's idolatry. Brian Neil Petersen shows that, far from avoiding icons entirely for the sake of aniconism,

> Ezekiel incorporated these symbols representative of the Babylonian gods into his vision, but lowered their stature to the level of mere attendants to the greater deity, Yahweh. . . . The use of real-life iconography adapted to an aural and/or literary setting seems to be a possibility when "educating" the [likely illiterate] exilic community about the nature of their offended God, especially if the vision/prophecy was read aloud in a public place. . . . The symbolism behind the creatures is striking when one looks at what they stood for in Babylon. Ezekiel here is divesting them of their role as "gods" . . . while keeping aspects of their representative status intact.[33]

In summary, the prophet uses a contextualization strategy that resonates with the Asian cultural practice of *homeopathy*. Ezekiel is beating Mesopotamian icons at their own game.

The "living creatures" are no longer the fearsome sentinels or divine symbols that such iconography would represent in the culture of Babylon. They merely serve to hold up Yahweh's mobile throne that both appears to the exiles in Babylon (ch. 1) as well as transports the prophet in a vision to Judah (chs. 8, 10). While the OT declares that Yahweh's presence is ultimately incomparable and beyond description (e.g. 1 Kgs 8:27; Ps 89:6–8), Ezekiel illustrates this

---

31. John F. Kutsko, *Between Heaven and Earth: Divine Presence and Absence in the Book of Ezekiel*, Biblical and Judaic Studies 7 (Winona Lake, IN: Eisenbrauns, 2000), 28–35.
32. This is precisely what happened to the *lamassu* sculptures that remained at the archaeological site of Nimrud. When the Islamic State of Iraq and Levant (ISIL) briefly overran parts of northern Iraq in 2014 and 2015, its fighters destroyed 90 percent of the site, defacing the *lamassu* since these pre-Islamic sculptures were considered idolatrous.
33. Brian Neil Peterson, *Ezekiel in Context: Ezekiel's Message Understood in Its Historical Setting of Covenant Curses and Ancient Near Eastern Mythological Motifs*, Princeton Theological Monograph Series 182 (Eugene, OR: Pickwick, 2012), 120–21.

timeless message using cultural forms that were familiar to his people in the sixth century BC.[34] Those who remained in Jerusalem apparently misunderstood the combination of Babylon's victory and the aniconism of the Jerusalem temple to mean that Yahweh was no longer present among them. Ironically, it is the mobile "glory of Yahweh" (1:28; 8:4; 9:3) that brings Ezekiel back to Jerusalem for him to overhear the people saying, "The LORD does not see us; the LORD has forsaken the land" (8:12; cf. 9:9). Idolatry within the temple precincts means that the people's complaint about Yahweh's apparent absence becomes a self-fulfilling prophecy: Yahweh's glory and the living creatures, now explicitly identified as Israelite "cherubim" and not merely as plays on Mesopotamian icons, take their leave of Jerusalem (10:4–19).

ANICONISM AND ANTHROPOMORPHISM IN THE MODERN WEST'S ENCOUNTER WITH ASIA

Misunderstandings about aniconism and anthropomorphism are not limited to ancient Israel. The modern West has fallen into two kinds of similar errors, both of which involve how the OT prophets satirize the idol-making ceremonies of the nations. The first comes in the modern West's encounter with the robust iconography of the non-Western world. Particularly in the nineteenth century, Western missionaries in Asia tended to envision themselves in the role of the OT prophets by railing against the horrifying idols that lay before their eyes. The icons of ancient Mesopotamia became superimposed upon the icons of nineteenth-century Asia. This is evident in how British missionaries regarded "India, with its temples still thriving and alive with ritual activity . . . [as] a manifestation of an idolatry as pervasive as any in the ancient world. . . . India, although the jewel of the Empire, became the most glaring illustration of the nineteenth-century's definition of 'idolatry.'"[35] The next chapter will address the clash of worldviews between the West and India.

Similarly in Thailand (then called Siam), an American missionary account from the same period used biblical language to condemn the Theravada Buddhist use of visual icons: "They raise the gods of silver and gold, of brass, iron, wood and stone, which see not, nor hear, nor know: and the God in

---

34. Daniel I. Block, *The Book of Ezekiel, Chapters 1–24*, New International Commentary on the Old Testament (Grand Rapids, MI: Eerdmans, 1997), 108.
35. Joanne Punzo Waghorne, "The Divine Image in Contemporary South India: The Renaissance of a Once Maligned Tradition," in *Born in Heaven, Made on Earth: The Making of the Cult Image in the Ancient Near East*, ed. Michael B. Dick (Winona Lake, IN: Eisenbrauns, 1999), 213, 215.

whose hand their breath is, and whose are all their ways, they have not glorified."[36] It is indisputable that these Western missionaries were motivated by a genuine sense of call in sharing the gospel with the Indian and Thai people. At the same time, there was a strong undercurrent of Orientalism in their misapplication of the OT's image-making parodies to the (heathen) "other" rather than the (Israelite) "self." The common interpretive error of excusing oneself from prophetic critique will be examined below in the parody passages of Isaiah 44 and Jeremiah 10.

The second and more recent error is of twentieth-century vintage. It comes from the dim view that scholars have generally come to hold of the OT idol parodies in the prophetic books. Their verdict is that the prophets of Israel were ignorant about the nature of Mesopotamian icon-making in ridiculing it as an empty exercise in craftsmanship. Supposedly, OT prophetic mockery of divine icons as merely the work of human hands is a distortion of Mesopotamian cultic practices such as the *mis pi* ritual. Also known as the "opening of the mouth," this is the step-by-step process that enables a theological paradox: the divine image is both "born in heaven" as well as "made on earth." The dismissiveness of Robert Carroll toward OT idol parodies is typical:

> The polemics are all good clean abuse and no doubt stimulated the piety of the Yahwistic devotees. But they are also singularly lacking in penetrative argument. A comparable analogy to their argument would be to abuse the Bible by describing how forests are cut down, taken to the pulp mills, turned into wood pulp, then taken to paper-making factories and processed into reams of paper. At this juncture details might be given about the printing processes and the mechanics of the publishing trade. After which the printing and distributing of Bibles might be described and the polemic end with a dismissal of the semantic significance of the finished product on the grounds that it merely amounts to an amalgam of wood pulp, ink, and binding. Now such an argument would be dismissed out of hand as a ludicrous example of sheer reductionism of the grossest materialistic type.

---

36. Cited in Kam-wah (Joseph) Siu, "American Missionary Views on Siamese Culture and Their Evangelical and Social Works in Siam between the Mid-19th Century and the Early 20th Century," paper, Chinese University of Hong Kong, 30 March 2019, 32, https://www.harvard-yenching.org/wp-content/uploads/legacy_files/featurefiles/SIU%20Kam%20Wah_American%20Missionary%20Views%20on%20Siamese%20Culture.pdf.

In many ways it would represent a failure to see the wood for the trees! But it is equally ludicrous to see any more substance in the Old Testament polemics against idols and idol makers.[37]

Alternatively, a scholar like Thorkild Jakobsen can distance himself from ANE image consecration as well as the OT prophets who mock it by relegating both to the realms of superstition and magic:

> Truly, a weird and extraordinary performance! The central rite in which the image is engendered and born of water and wood is as primitive and crude as one could find anywhere – almost fetishistic – and it is not difficult to focus on that and dismiss, as just a lot of hocus-pocus, the various incantations with which this primitive rite is hedged around and explained as being other than what it patently is. That, apparently, is more or less what the prophets did. To them, the image was exactly what it was in the primitive rite, "a block of wood," and it remained that – and only that.[38]

Both Carroll and Jakobsen purport to assess ANE rituals (whether Mesopotamian or Israelite) from a critical distance. However, their presupposition is clearly that modern scholars are more informed about the ancient Near East than the Israelite prophets were. This tendency to denigrate the "other" as strange and uncivilized shows that Orientalism toward ancient West Asia remains just as present in the OT scholarship of late modernity as it was toward the modern Far East during the height of colonialism and Christendom. The academic dress of such condescension should not obscure the fact that these Western OT scholars regard themselves as privileged observers in a subject-object relationship with practices that they find backwards.

What would happen, though, if one were to read the OT idol parodies with provisional sympathy and without the cultural snobbery that regards icons and iconography as primitive? The strangeness of the rituals mocked by the OT prophets (and the impossibility of their logic, by extension) has often led Western readers of these texts to align themselves instinctively with the Israelite side of the polemic in misunderstanding it as a Neoplatonic contrast

---

37. Robert P. Carroll, "The Aniconic God and the Cult of Images," *Studia Theologica: Nordic Journal of Theology* 31 (1977): 52–53.
38. Thorkild Jakobsen, "The Graven Image," in *Ancient Israelite Religion: Essays in Honor of Frank Moore Cross*, eds. Patrick D. Miller, Paul D. Hanson, and S. Dean McBride (Philadelphia: Fortress, 1987), 28.

between a single aniconic/spiritual/invisible deity and multiple iconic/material/visible deities.

The dominance of this cultural perspective with Protestant roots can be seen in the puzzling logic of OT scholar Michael Dick. Despite being a practicing Catholic,[39] Dick links aniconism and monotheism to each other in a characteristically Protestant manner: "The theological stresses of 586 BC [i.e. the Babylonian exile] assured both the triumph of Yahwistic monotheism and of aniconic worship: Yahweh's cult had probably always been aniconic, *but now there were no gods but Yahweh, so there was utterly no room for any cult image!*"[40] Dick seems to regard this theological conclusion as self-evident, but it is unclear why polytheism and iconography are interdependent, as if a transition toward monotheism (i.e. a reduction in the number of gods) requires a corresponding move toward aniconism (i.e. an elimination of images). Hinduism, for example, is known for its plethora of icons that are found in a vast number of competing sects that can be atheistic, monotheistic, or polytheistic.

REEXAMINING THE OT IDOL PARODIES FROM AN ASIAN PERSPECTIVE

Cultural snobbery toward the "otherness" of the OT in its world can be mitigated by adopting interpretive lenses that are closer to the OT's own. As suggested earlier, a Thai perspective is helpful for a better understanding of OT idol parodies in their world since it contrasts with a Western perspective in which "a graven image is indeed an exotic phenomenon!"[41] Two aspects of the Thai worldview are pertinent for the reexamination of OT idol parodies in Isaiah 44 and Jeremiah 10 that will follow.

First and as explained by Kirti Bunchua, a leading Thai philosopher, "the Westerner likes to *define*, the Thai likes to *narrate*. The Thai are unlike the Westerner in that they do not find a need to define what they see or experience. . . . Their interest would lie more in the area of what something *does* and how it may affect one."[42] Second and specifically with regard to

---

39. Christopher Walker and Michael B. Dick, "The Induction of the Cult Image in Ancient Mesopotamia: The Mesopotamian Mis Pî Ritual," in *Born in Heaven, Made on Earth: The Making of the Cult Image in the Ancient Near East*, ed. Michael B. Dick (Winona Lake, IN: Eisenbrauns, 1999), 57, n. 2.

40. Michael B. Dick, "Prophetic Parodies of Making the Cult Image," in *Born in Heaven, Made on Earth*, 2, italics added.

41. Haug and Holter, "No Graven Image?," 20 (as mentioned in n. 5).

42. As summarized by Steve Taylor, "A Prolegomena for the Thai Context: A Starting Point for Thai Theology," *Evangelical Review of Theology* 29 (2005): 39, in an interview with Bunchua,

image-consecration rituals, the Thai have a supernaturalist worldview that reflects the concept of *amphicosmic ontology*, a traditional belief system about icons that "views the statue as an object that stands at the boundary between the world of the human and the visible, and the world of the invisible – a world of gods, ghosts, and the dead . . . *an existence that places the statue on the boundary between two dimensions.*"[43] This contrasts with the anti-supernatural lenses of the Enlightenment which, ironically, have often found theological justification in Western Christianity due to the Reformation's understanding of aniconism. A Thai person, however, will tend to assess truth claims about a given deity's reality by the external criterion of power rather than the internal category of essence.[44] Such an emphasis on function more than ontology is characteristic not only of the Thai, but also of the Old Testament: monotheism in biblical perspective is primarily the matter of Yahweh's incomparable power vis-à-vis other deities and only secondarily the question of how many deities exist.[45]

A closer look at Isaiah 44 and Jeremiah 10 shows greater affinity with the Thai outlook's emphasis on concrete and efficacious function than with the West's inclination toward an ontological contrast between material and spiritual realms. In comparing Israelite and Mesopotamian concepts of divinity, both prophetic passages highlight the uselessness of the images rather than their nonexistence as real beings or the spirituality of the true God. Drawing on material categories, Isaiah 44 asserts that both image-makers and their work are "futile/vapor/vanity" (Heb. *hebel,* v. 9; cf. 38x in Eccl) and "of no profit" (vv. 9, 10 NASB). And jumping to the social realm, the trait of uselessness is also reflected in how witnesses of the image-making process will find the work lacking, thereby causing the artisan to be "put to shame" (v. 11). The intuitive logic of uselessness in these verses has sometimes eluded Western OT scholars who are expecting a more linear or didactic form of argument.[46] But it accords

---

italics original.
43. Nijay K. Gupta, "'They Are Not Gods!' Jewish and Christian Idol Polemic and Greco-Roman Use of Cult Statues," *Catholic Biblical Quarterly* 76 (2014): 709, italics original.
44. Erik Cohen, "Christianity and Buddhism in Thailand: The 'Battle of the Axes' and the 'Contest of Power,'" *Social Compass* 38 (1991): 115–40.
45. See ch. 4 for further discussion.
46. E.g. R. N. Whybray, *Isaiah 40–66*, New Century Bible Commentary (London: Marshall, Morgan & Scott, 1975), 99–100; Claus Westermann, *Isaiah 40–66: A Commentary*, trans. David M. G. Stalker, The Old Testament Library (London: SCM, 1969), 148–49; cf. Marvin A. Sweeney, *Isaiah 40–66*, The Forms of the Old Testament Literature 19 (Grand Rapids, MI: Eerdmans, 2016), 99.

well with what a Thai philosopher calls "the Thai move from *particular* to *particular* without working back to the source principle."[47]

Jeremiah 10 similarly comments that the cost and skill that go into making divine images (vv. 3–4) belie the fact of their impotence: "Like a scarecrow in a cucumber field, their idols cannot speak; they must be carried because they cannot walk. Do not fear them; they can do no harm nor can they do any good" (v. 5). Human leaders who are supposedly mighty are similarly diminished by venerating such dumb objects: "They are all senseless and foolish; they are taught by worthless wooden idols" (v. 8; cf. Pss 115; 135). The functional worldview that the OT shares with Thai culture is reflected in how Yahweh is distinguished from idols, not by virtue of a spiritual or invisible *essence* but because his physical *strength* surpasses theirs: "No one is like you, LORD; you are great, and your name is mighty in power. . . . When he is angry, the earth trembles; the nations cannot endure his wrath" (Jer 10:6, 10). Most provocatively, Jeremiah's polemic briefly switches into Aramaic for a single verse so that the nations are confronted in their own language and categories about the uselessness of their deities: "'Tell them this: [switch to Aramaic] "These gods, who did not make the heavens and the earth, will perish from the earth and from under the heavens."' [revert to Hebrew] But God made the earth by his power; he founded the world by his wisdom and stretched out the heavens by his understanding" (vv. 11–12).

Yahweh's uniqueness among the gods is also found in being the true Artisan who is not himself "formed" (Isa 43:10). Instead, he is the one who "forms" (*yṣr*) his people as a potter does (Isa 43:1, 7, 21; 44:2; cf. 45:9; 64:8; Jer 18:1–6). This indicates that the main contrast at hand in the OT idol parodies is between Yahweh and the image-makers rather than between Yahweh and the images that they make. As Nathan MacDonald observes, "The idol-fabricators take a tree and form a dead idol that cannot see or hear; YHWH takes dead Israel, who cannot see or hear, and forms new life."[48] The party under censure is not a heathen "other" but Israel as a nation that is just as deaf, blind, and clueless as the idols that it venerates (Isa 6:9–10; 42:16–20; 43:8; 44:9).[49] The rhetorical surprise of the idol parodies can be summarized as follows: "The authors of Israelite icon parodies attacked the cult images of Babylon, but

---

47. Kirti Bunchua, quoted in Taylor, "Prolegomena for the Thai Context," 40, italics original.
48. Nathan MacDonald, "Aniconism in the Old Testament," in *The God of Israel*, ed. Robert P. Gordon, University of Cambridge Oriental Publications 64 (Cambridge: Cambridge University Press, 2007), 31.
49. MacDonald, "Aniconism in the Old Testament," 30.

their true target was Israel and the cult of Yahweh."[50] Unfortunately, the failure
in OT scholarship to detect the self-directed nature of the polemic mirrors
Orientalism's mistake of deploying the idol parodies as attacks on other cultures. It is therefore crucial to emphasize that the ultimate purpose of these
polemical passages is to remind Yahweh's own forgetful people of their special
birth and calling: "Remember these things, O Jacob, and Israel, for you are my
servant; I formed you; you are my servant; O Israel, you will not be forgotten
by me" (44:21 NRSV). Only when Israel has been chastened and revived can
it resume its missional calling to serve among the nations as a true rather than
false "witness" of Yahweh's mighty acts (Isa 43:9, 10, 12; 44:8; cf. Acts 1:8).

The arguments made in OT idol parodies have special relevance for *amphicosmic ontology* in which "the statue becomes a portal to another realm,
such as the world of the gods"[51] – precisely the understanding of icons in
the Thai Buddhist context. Donald Swearer, a foremost scholar of Buddhism
in Southeast Asia, notes in passing that the Mesopotamian *mis pi* ritual of
opening the image's mouth has striking similarities to the daylong consecration ceremony of opening the eyes of Buddha images in northern Thailand.[52]
As reconstructed from several fragmentary texts by Assyriologists, the steps
involved in consecrating a Mesopotamian image each have a close analogue
in Thai Buddhist rituals: (1) determining the opportune time and place to
consecrate the image; (2) reciting hymns to the deity represented by the image,
thereby connecting it to the ultimate reality to which it points; (3) purifying
the image whose mouth has not yet been ritually opened in a ceremony with
consecrated water; (4) reciting incantations that open the image's mouth by
affirming its origin in heaven rather than on earth; (5) waiting for the dawn's
arrival to fully enliven the image; and (6) dismantling the instruments and
space used for consecration of its final resting place. This is not to say that the
Mesopotamian "opening of the mouth" ritual is always fixed in the sequence
given here (different versions of the texts exist across times and places), nor to
argue that it corresponds in every detail to the "opening of the eyes" for Thai
Buddhist images. Among other differences, the Mesopotamian ritual invokes
an entire pantheon of gods to witness the ritual, while the Thai ritual focuses

---

50. Nathaniel B. Levtow, *Images of Others: Iconic Politics in Ancient Israel*, Biblical and Judaic
Studies from the University of California, San Diego 11 (Winona Lake, IN: Eisenbrauns, 2008),
18.
51. Gupta, "'They Are Not Gods!,'" 708.
52. Donald K. Swearer, "Hypostasizing the Buddha: Buddha Image Consecration in Northern
Thailand," *History of Religions* 34 (Feb. 1995): 263.

on the Buddha while mentioning deities only in passing.[53] The commonalities between the rituals are nonetheless unmistakable due to their shared purpose: infusing the everyday and profane with the numinous and sacred by ushering worshipers along the image's own journey of enlightenment from the absence of the deity/Buddha to its powerful presence.

Read against a Thai background, then, the OT idol parodies draw vividly upon practices that are common rather than strange. And just as provocatively for Israelites as for Thai Christians, the people of Yahweh are supposed to realize that the idol parodies are intended for *them* as a special and missional people. Thai Christians resemble Israelites in this regard for wondering what their minority status says about their God's ability to solve real problems as compared with the deities of their majority culture. Isaiah 40–48 portrays Yahweh as the ultimate answer to the kinds of empirical questions posed by OT Israelites, Thai Christians, and Thai Buddhists alike: he alone is the *Creator* who can truly give water (41:17; 43:20; 44:3), he is the real *Diviner* who both explains the past (41:26–29) and predicts the future (41:21–24; 42:9), and he is the only *Savior* who is certain to deliver those who trust in him (43:8–13; 44:25). Other deities may appear imposing to Yahweh's people due to their weighty and valuable images, but he is the only deity worthy of veneration since he carries his people rather than needing to be carried by them (46:1–3). No images of Yahweh are necessary because his people are where his presence actually dwells, whether at home in the land or scattered in exile.[54]

In sum, OT idol polemics use countercultural ideas to portray hidden Yahweh as far more alive, powerful, and glorious than his rivals in the divine realm. The latter are challenged to speak as if they are real entities (in contrast to Western idol polemics about the *existence* of deity), but are helpless to do so rather than being dead (in keeping with a non-Western emphasis on the *function* of deity).[55] It is for this reason that Thai Christians today have developed a distinctive theology from their lived experiences that joins the universality of the God of the Bible with the local supernaturalism of Thai

---

53. While the elements in each ritual are respectively listed by Walker and Dick ("Mesopotamian Mis Pî Ritual") and Swearer ("Buddha Image Consecration"), the comparison here between them is my own.
54. MacDonald, "Aniconism in the Old Testament," 34.
55. Kelly Michael Hilderbrand and Sutheera Sritrakool, "Developing a Thai Theological and Biblical Understanding of the World: Rethinking Thai Cosmology in Light of Divine Council Theology," *Transformation: An International Journal of Holistic Mission Studies* 38 (Jan. 2021): 63–77.

Buddhism.[56] At the same time, constructive work remains to be done by Thai Christians in incorporating their culture's highly developed sense of aesthetics into a theology of divine presence that embraces visual and ritual dimensions.[57]

CONCLUSION

The untapped potential of Thai theology illustrates how abstract and concrete ideas of God's presence are complementary in theologically generative ways which can overcome Western conceptual dichotomies and maintain a biblical balance.[58] Since unseen Yahweh both speaks and acts in a manner that other deities with visible images cannot, it is apparent that the word of God's power and the power of God's word go closely together. In practice, however, Thai Christians have often found it difficult to maintain the theological juggling act between power encounter and truth encounter. They are situated in a strongly supernaturalist culture that views people as part of a much larger system of cause and effect with other powers.

It will thus be necessary for the next chapter to explore the more foundational matter of how Yahweh is the creator and sustainer of the universe. India will provide a useful case study in this regard due to its role as the meeting ground for three disparate worldviews: Western modernism's demythologization of an impersonal *nature*, Hinduism's conception of the physical and spiritual worlds as a single and sacred *monad*, and the OT's distinctive account of *creation* as fully alive and personal (for creatures both animate and inanimate) but still subject to a transcendent Creator. On this note, the theological rationale of the monotheism/polytheism distinction that was sometimes employed for colonialism in British India, as observed earlier for OT idol polemics, serves as a reminder that aniconism is never only a religious idea but one that also has social, economic, and political consequences. This reality is just as true in ancient Israel's discourses about power as it is in modern societies.[59]

---

56. Kosuke Koyama, *Water Buffalo Theology*, 25th Anniversary Ed. (Maryknoll, NY: Orbis, 1999), 56–63; Edwin Zehner, "Thai Protestants and Local Supernaturalism: Changing Configuration," *Journal of Southeast Asian Studies* 27 (1996): 293–319.
57. I owe this suggestion to Samuel Lim, one of my students who has served extensively as a missionary and missiologist in Thailand.
58. Cf. Cohen, "Christianity and Buddhism." In missiological terms, the usual (and false) dichotomy between "truth encounter" (i.e. abstract presence) and "power encounter" (i.e. concrete divine presence) is discussed by David J. Hesselgrave, *Paradigms in Conflict: 10 Key Questions in Christian Missions Today* (Grand Rapids, MI: Kregel, 2005), 167–203.
59. Levtow, *Images of Others*.

CHAPTER 8

CREATION AND PANTHEISM

The retail store called BritishIndia is a common sight in the malls of Southeast Asia. The company's website used to state, "Created for the tropics and inspired by the grand romance of the Colonial era, our stores offer timeless designs created with the philosophy of comfort and effortless dressing for both men and women in mind. Our customers are well travelled, socially active, and culturally aware."[1] Nostalgia for this sort of colonialism has been influential in both Asia and Western countries (as attested in films/musicals such as *The King and I, Miss Saigon*, and *Indochine*). On the one hand, the safari vibes of the BritishIndia brand evoke a common association between imperialism and cultural sophistication for the colonizer. On the other, empire is portrayed as a benevolent force that elevates the backwardness of the colonized.

Such romanticization of imperialism clashes with the ungenteel reality that European powers used the people and resources of their colonies to fund their various endeavors. As one example, the Indian economist Utsa Panaik calculated that the British colonial government of India drained the equivalent of US $44.6 trillion in goods between 1765 and 1938.[2] When adjusted for inflation and exchange rates, this figure is exponentially greater than the UK's annual GDP (e.g. US $2.9 trillion in 2019). Patnaik added on a summary note in an interview:

> Not only Britain, but the whole of today's advanced capitalist world flourished on the drain from India and other colonies. Britain was too small to absorb the entire drain from colonial India. So it became the world's largest capital exporter, which aided the industrial development of Continental Europe, the

---

1. http://britishindia.com.my/about-us/. Accessed 24 May 2021 (though the company's web domain has apparently expired as of this writing).
2. Utsa Patnaik, "Revisiting the 'Drain,' or Transfer from India to Britain in the Context of Global Diffusion of Capitalism," in *Agrarian and Other Histories: Essays for Binay Bhushan Chaudhuri*, eds. B. B. Chaudhuri, Shubhra Chakrabarti, and Utsa Patnaik, 1st ed. (New Delhi: Tulika Books, 2017), 277–317.

US, and even Russia. The infrastructure boom in these countries would not have been possible otherwise.[3]

This is not to say that Western empires acted uniformly in plundering their colonies. Nor is it the case that nothing good came out of the British Raj's tenure in India. But the hard figures provided by Patnaik show that the two centuries of "British India" were of substantially greater benefit to the empire than to its "Jewel in the Crown."[4] Jason Hickel, an economic anthropologist at the University of London, concludes that the West's frequent cultural myth of imperialism-as-progress has collapsed: "Britain didn't develop India. Quite the contrary – as Patnaik's work makes clear – India developed Britain."[5]

The nominally Christian stance of the British Raj might appear to support Lynn White's famous claim:

> Especially in its Western form, Christianity is the most anthro-pocentric religion the world has ever seen. . . . Christianity, in absolute contrast to ancient paganism and Asia's religions (except, perhaps, Zoroastrianism), not only established a dualism of man and nature but also insisted that it is God's will that man exploit nature for his proper ends.[6]

The subject-object relationship that the Bible supposedly envisions between humanity and the rest of creation stands in contrast with the pantheism of an Eastern religion like Hinduism which regards the entire natural order as divine and sacred. For this reason, it has not been uncommon for evangelical Christians to suspect that the theology of *creation care* is a covert form of New

---

3. In her most recent figures, Patnaik recalculates the drain on the basis of accrued interest and arrives at the higher figure of US $64.8 trillion (Utsa Patnaik and Prabhat Patnaik, "The Drain of Wealth: Colonialism before the First World War," *Monthly Review*, 1 February 2021, https://monthlyreview.org/2021/02/01/the-drain-of-wealth/).
4. It bears mentioning that Patnaik identifies herself as a Marxist economist. Interestingly, critics of her work tend to attack her Marxist economics but do not quarrel with her figures. One need not agree with Patnaik's socialistic framework or advocacy of reparations by Western empires to recognize imperialism's one-sidedness as exposed by her calculations.
5. Jason Hickel, "How Britain Stole $45 Trillion from India: And Lied about It," Al Jazeera, 19 December 2018, https://www.aljazeera.com/opinions/2018/12/19/how-britain-stole-45-trillion-from-india. For a broader argument along these lines by an evangelical scholar, see Vinoth Ramachandra, *Subverting Global Myths: Theology and the Public Issues Shaping Our World* (Downers Grove, IL: IVP Academic, 2008), 216–28.
6. Lynn White, Jr., "The Historical Roots of Our Ecologic Crisis," *Science* 155 (10 March 1967): 1205.

Age philosophy or Eastern mysticism which has infiltrated the church.[7] Indeed, the aftermath of Lynn White's controversial article in 1967 saw numerous proposals that Eastern pantheism would provide a better starting point for ecology than Christian theism ever did.[8] Since these controversies continue to the present day, it is important to ask: What is the Bible's own account of the relationship between humanity and (the rest of) the created order? Such a way of phrasing the question, with "the rest of" in parentheses, highlights the central controversy of whether Christian theology has uncritically followed Enlightenment dualism by setting humanity over and against the created order rather than being part of it.

The present chapter will examine the OT's teaching on creation between the contrasts represented by the West's tendency to demythologize creation into impersonal "nature" and Hinduism's blending of physical and spiritual dimensions into the singular living reality of "Brahman." We will use two case studies on the OT to trace a middle course between these worldviews: (1) the OT's personification of creation, a common feature of the poetic and prophetic books which is readily taken as figurative since literal interpretations feel pantheistic; (2) the OT's conception of time which is often thought to support Western understandings of time as linear rather than non-Western understandings as cyclical (such as Hinduism). To preview our conclusion, the OT offers a surprising perspective that is neither Western dualism nor Eastern monism with respect to space and time.[9] The uniqueness of the OT's philosophy of religion represents a non-Western set of assumptions and answers in approaching classic questions such as that of how evil originated in

---

7. Sabrina Danielsen, "Fracturing over Creation Care? Shifting Environmental Beliefs among Evangelicals, 1984–2010," *Journal for the Scientific Study of Religion* 52 (2013): 198–215.
8. As documented by Francis A. Schaeffer, *Pollution and the Death of Man: The Christian View of Ecology* (London: Hodder & Stoughton, 1970), 13–27.
9. Charles A. Moore challenges the typical characterization of Indian philosophy as *monism* ("Introduction: The Comprehensive Indian Mind," in *The Indian Mind: Essentials of Indian Philosophy and Culture*, ed. Charles A. Moore, An East-West Center Book [Honolulu: University Press of Hawaii, 1978], 13). In the rest of the book of which Moore is editor, however, the Indian contributors affirm that "all schools of Indian thought, including the Buddhists and Jainas, have a moral conception of nature" (Dhirendra Mohan Datta, "Indian Political, Legal, and Economic Thought," 267–68) and that "the ultimate reality is one ineffable Absolute (called Brahman)" (Kalidas Bhattacharyya, "The Status of the Individual in Indian Metaphysics," 299). Since Hindus of different stripes concur in regarding the universe as a single moral reality despite its multiplicity of forms, it still seems proper to describe Indian philosophy in terms of monism (H. M. Vroom, *No Other Gods: Christian Belief in Dialogue with Buddhism, Hinduism, and Islam* [Grand Rapids, MI: Eerdmans, 1996], 54, 70).

the universe and the holistic way in which infinite divine presence can dwell among finite people.[10]

CASE STUDY 1: THE OT'S PERSONAL AND PERSONIFIED ACCOUNT OF "NATURE"

Chapter 4 already outlined the OT's theology of Yahweh as a nature deity who outdoes all others. In fact, Yahweh is the greatest among ancient Near Eastern deities for combining the roles of nature god (e.g. "Yahweh *of hosts*") with those of national god ("God *of Israel*") and personal god (e.g. "God *of Abraham*"). Precisely because of Yahweh's distinctive omnipotence, however, it has been common to describe the OT's cultural posture as that of *demythologizing* the natural order from deities into merely physical objects that do not possess any spiritual dimension. The following quote illustrates how this can be true even among OT scholars who advocate Christian environmental ethics:

> "The hills are alive with the sound of music," sings Julie Andrews, and, for some of us at least, the mind's eye is transported to a flower-filled alpine meadow, where children sing and play, and where, over the nearby mountain, lies the hope of a better future. *Yet no one believes that the hills are really "alive" in the same way as a human being or a mountain goat or even a tree.* Rather, the song-writer's personification of nature is a figure of speech, testifying to the vibrancy of the children's music-making echoing around the mountains and to the latter's significance in the story that follows.[11]

In actuality, the *vitalism* of believing that hills are alive in the same way as animals comes closer to the biblical perspective than the Western worldview of scientific naturalism.[12] The statement above (with italics added) is the relative newcomer in human history for drawing upon Enlightenment materialism and its distinction between inanimate "things" that are merely physical and

---

10. Jaco Gericke, *The Hebrew Bible and Philosophy of Religion*, SBL Resources for Biblical Study 70 (Atlanta: Society of Biblical Literature, 2012), 254–56; Ronald A. Simkins, *Creator and Creation: Nature in the Worldview of Ancient Israel* (Peabody, MA: Hendrickson, 1994), 150–52.
11. Hilary Marlow, "The Hills Are Alive! The Personification of Nature in the Psalter," in *Leshon Limmudim: Essays on the Language and Literature of the Hebrew Bible in Honour of A. A. Macintosh*, eds. David A. Baer and Robert P. Gordon (London: Bloomsbury, 2014), 189, italics added. Marlow is a leading OT scholar in the Christian environmental movement.
12. Cf. Terence E. Fretheim, *God and World in the Old Testament: A Relational Theology of Creation* (Nashville, TN: Abingdon, 2005), 252–63.

animate "creatures" that also possess a spiritual component. The OT instead holds, in the memorable poetry of Gerard Manley Hopkins, that "the world is charged with the grandeur of God."[13] All of Yahweh's created order pulses with a vibrancy that cuts across the physical and spiritual realms while nonetheless diverging from Eastern pantheism.

The skepticism that mountains could be personal and sentient beings alongside humans can be seen in the cultural clash that occurred in 2015 when Mount Kinabalu in east Malaysia was struck by an earthquake not long after a group of Western tourists engaged in a prank by stripping naked on the mountain. They took joking photographs of themselves despite being warned by a local guide to respect the mountain's spirits.[14] Following an earthquake which led to landslides and several deaths, local explanations about the mountain's anger at being desecrated were mocked by Westerners and eventually downplayed by Malaysians. But such a traditional view of a living natural order is not so different from OT passages that connect earthquakes with the defilement of the earth by human sin (e.g. Ps 60:1–2). In short, the OT's understanding of creation would find greater sympathy from "unscientific" villagers in Malaysia than from "enlightened" moderns who find the notion of a living mountain to be superstition.

Examples of Vitalism in the OT

The worldview of vitalism is reflected in the OT's frequent use of the same Hebrew terminology to describe actions of both humans and the earth. The earth is a narrative character in Israel's history *who* (rather than *which*)[15] can hear God's voice (Jer 22:29; Mic 1:2), rejoice (Ps 96:11; Isa 49:13), cry out (Gen 4:10), mourn (Isa 24:3; Jer 12:4), eat or swallow (Num 16:34), vomit (Lev 18:25, 28), and testify against Israel's sin (Deut 4:26; Isa 1:2) in a manner likened to humans. The sheer number of such verbs predicated of the earth makes it unlikely that such personification is merely a metaphor.[16] In short, the earth plays an important role alongside Scripture as a "second book" by

---

13. To quote the first line of Gerard Manley Hopkins's famous poem "God's Grandeur" (1877).
14. Jennifer Pak, "Malaysia Official Blames Nude Tourists for Deadly Quake," BBC News online, 8 June 2015, https://www.bbc.com/news/world-asia-33058692.
15. Richard Bauckham observes that the biblical theme of creation's worship is usually viewed as "pre-scientific animism or pan-psychism . . . [and] mere poetic fancy" (*Bible and Ecology: Rediscovering the Community of Creation* [Waco, TX: Baylor University Press, 2010], 79).
16. The Earth Bible Team, "The Voice of Earth: More Than Metaphor?," in *The Earth Story in the Psalms and the Prophets*, ed. Norman C. Habel, The Earth Bible 4 (Sheffield: Sheffield Academic Press, 2001), 23–28.

serving as God's address to those who have ears to hear his voice (Ps 19:1–4; Hos 4:1–3).

The fruit and creatures of the earth are also key actors in the history of redemption. The prophecy of Hosea, for example, opens with the accusation that "*the land* commits heinous harlotry in walking away from Yahweh" (1:2).[17] Following this cryptic statement, the creational storyline of chapters 1–3 unfolds with wool, flax, oil, and animals center stage alongside Yahweh and Israel rather than only being the scenery. Since the people of Israel had misattributed these agricultural blessings to the Canaanite fertility god Baal, Yahweh exposes the futility of idolatry by removing these products of the earth from his people. The repentance that follows Israel's chastening leads to reconciliation between Yahweh, his people, and the rest of creation. The interrelationship between them climaxes with Yahweh answering the heavens, who in turn answer the earth, who then answers the earth's agricultural products, who conclude the antiphonal series by answering Israel and confirming the restoration of God's people (2:18–23). Later in Hosea 4–14, other botanical images of judgment and salvation include Yahweh's promise to "rain rightness" if Israel will "sow for yourselves according to righteousness, reap according to faithfulness; till a hard ground for your own sake" (10:12). Renewal from Yahweh is depicted both as the creational resurgence of wool, flax, and oil (2:22) as well as the Creator himself becoming the dew and sacred tree that his people mistakenly sought from Canaanite fertility deities (14:5–8).

Hosea uses numerous images from the animal world to supplement those from agriculture and botany. For example, Yahweh and his prophet mock Israel as a stubborn heifer (4:16; cf. 10:11), silly dove (7:11), and wild donkey (8:9) to sting the idolater's conscience with the reality of their self-degradation. Hosea also portrays Yahweh and Israel's enemies as moth, lion, leopard, and bear who will devour his people (5:12, 14; 13:7–8). These word-pictures often mirror how ancient Near Eastern empires used animal iconography, as noted in the previous chapter. The leonine image in Hosea takes a poignant turn when Yahweh is identified as a tender but roaring lion, like Aslan in C. S. Lewis's *Chronicles of Narnia*, who summons his wayward people home from exile (11:10). Lewis was following the Bible's lead in personifying the animal world in this respect.

---

17. Translations of Hosea verses are taken from Jerry Hwang, *Hosea: God's Reconciliation with His Estranged Household*, Zondervan Exegetical Commentary on the Old Testament (Grand Rapids, MI: Zondervan Academic, 2021).

Much like Hosea, the book of Jeremiah treats creation as a key character with its own roles and voices. This is the case despite nature veneration being a part of the popular religion of Judah (and the northern kingdom of Israel before it during Hosea's time). In Jeremiah 2–4, for example, the covenant that Yahweh first made with his people is described as a fertile plant that grew in the wilderness and enjoyed protection from its enemies (2:2–3). As Judah strayed by pursuing fertility practices (2:27–28), however, its apostasy encountered the reality that such rituals backfired with infertility (2:20–21). These uses of creational images cannot be merely figurative, for creation itself participates in the theological drama when Yahweh enjoins the heavens, "Be appalled, O heavens, at this, be shocked, be utterly desolate, says the LORD" (2:12 NRSV). The heavens are hereby summoned as investigators to confirm that Judah's de-conversion from Yahweh has no precedents in history (cf. 2:9–11). The corroboration of Judah's sin then means that creation will shift its role to enforcer of Yahweh's verdict, as when drought takes hold (2:13) and lions invade Judah's land (2:15).

Yet as Judah continues to defile its land through Canaanite nature religion (3:1–5), Yahweh uses another series of creational images to offer an opportunity for his people to repent:

> Break up your fallow ground,
>> and do not sow among thorns.
> Circumcise yourselves to the LORD,
>> remove the foreskin of your hearts,
> O people of Judah and inhabitants of Jerusalem,
> or else my wrath will go forth like fire,
>> and burn with no one to quench it,
>> because of the evil of your doings. (4:3–4 NRSV)

The final failure of Judah to respond means that creation must become both the victim and the agent of Judah's sins which lead to exile (4:23–26). Notable in this section is the statement that "the earth shall mourn, and the heavens above grow black" (4:28 NRSV), thereby identifying a disintegrating creation as a partner closely related to Judah's destruction. In sum, the testimony of Hosea and Jeremiah indicates that creation is an essential participant in God's purposes, rather than merely the backdrop for salvation history.

Vitalism vs. Pantheism in the OT

The OT displays the vitalism of God's world most powerfully in the Psalms. The creation hymns of the Psalter not only contain some of the OT's most impressive lists of Yahweh's creatures (alongside the speeches in Job 38–41), they also depict his handiwork as personal agents who delight in their Creator just as humans do. In Psalm 104, Yahweh's mighty acts to lay the scaffolding of the sky (vv. 1–4) and the foundations of the earth (vv. 5–9) are an invitation for the rest of his creatures to rejoice in him – birds in their singing (v. 12), people in enjoying food and drink (v. 15), trees who do likewise in drinking their fill (v. 16), the celestial bodies who undertake and "know" (v. 19) their daily routines, the animals who follow these same rhythms and "seek their food from God" (v. 21), and the sea beast Leviathan whom God made to play in the ocean (v. 26). In sum, creation's gladness in Psalm 104 represents a sharing in the Creator's own gladness in what his hands have made (v. 31).[18]

It is noteworthy that both here and in Psalm 148, the summons to praise God includes both "animate" and "inanimate" creatures, with humans playing only a minor role. Terence Fretheim captures the theological importance of this solidarity: "Creation is a seamless web. If this is the case among the creatures, then it is more so between the Creator and creatures; for the oneness of creation and the oneness of the Creator are inextricably connected, or polytheism is very near at hand."[19]

In light of Fretheim's summary, one might ask whether the Psalter's declaration of interconnectedness between the created order and Creator blurs the distinctions between them in the manner of *pantheism* (i.e. God is everything, and everything is God). Hinduism also conceptualizes the universe as a spider web in which the oneness and mutuality of all things are an entwined monad. With reference to Psalm 104, Paul Dion concludes similarly that its description of kinship between deity and natural phenomena indicates that "this psalm is a model of mature Yahwistic *monism*."[20] The move to link the OT's teaching on creational vitalism to the worldview of monistic pantheism reflects Dion's view that an Egyptian precursor stands behind Psalm 104. This is a common perspective on the psalm's composition that we will address below in our discussion of pantheism in the ancient Near East.

---

18. Bauckham, *Bible and Ecology*, 49.
19. Fretheim, *God and World*, 251.
20. Paul E. Dion, "YHWH as Storm-god and Sun-god: The Double Legacy of Egypt and Canaan as Reflected in Psalm 104," *Zeitschrift für die alttestamentliche Wissenschaft* 103 (1991): 69, italics added.

Likewise and on a modern note of pantheism, Hennie Viviers argues that

> the poet of Psalm 104 has long ago succinctly and intuitively
> grasped the essence of what is nowadays called *dark green reli-*
> *gion*. . . . The poet's age-old language of awe and reverence stand-
> ing in the midst of overwhelming nature can also be shared by
> those who opt for the natural life-force instead of naturalism.[21]

Viviers concludes that very little separates Psalm 104's sacral depiction of
creation from the quasi-religious wonder toward nature shown by an environ-
mentalist such as David Attenborough (of *Planet Earth* fame).[22]

Before comparing ancient/modern pantheisms with the vitalism of Psalm
104, it is necessary to understand the background of these statements by Dion
and Viviers. They are responding to the common assertion in Western and/or
Christian thought that the Bible itself stands opposed to Eastern approaches
to reality and their monistic understanding of the cosmos. As articulated in
evangelical circles by OT scholar John Oswalt, the Eastern concept of *conti-*
nuity holds that

> the visible world is only a reflection of the invisible, divine
> world, but as its reflection it is identical with it. A popular term
> for this is pantheism: the divine is everything and everything is
> the divine. *Hinduism is perhaps the most developed expression of*
> *this thought.*[23]

This description of East and West contains true aspects yet also borders on
caricature, highlighting the difficult question of how to draw meaningful
comparisons between the Bible and pantheisms of different kinds. Our discussion below will bring the Old Testament into conversation with Hinduism,
a sprawling belief system that has absorbed opposing elements through the
centuries, such as atheism, theism, pantheism, and polytheism. However, the
principles and categories for undertaking a comparison with South Asian
monism must first be derived from Psalm 104's contextualization within its
own cultural environment.

Closer to Psalm 104's own setting are the ancient Egyptian hymns to the
sun-disk. Their similarities to the biblical psalm have often been noted, most

---

21. Hennie Viviers, "Is Psalm 104 an Expression (Also) of Dark Green Religion?," *Harvard*
Theological Studies 73 (2017): 7.
22. Viviers, "Psalm 104," 7.
23. Oswalt, *Bible among the Myths*, 49, italics added.

notably in *The Great Hymn to the Aten* by Pharaoh Akhenaten (or his royal scribes) from the fourteenth century BC. Akhenaten was a ruler during the New Kingdom period who had replaced Egypt's traditional worship of many deities with devotion to the sun-disk Aten as the sole and unique deity. *The Great Hymn* that participated in this theological revolution exhibits at least six striking parallels to Psalm 104:[24] (1) Yahweh and Aten both designate sundown as the time for lions to leave their dens and go hunting (Ps 104:20–21; Akhenaten lines 27–37); (2) Yahweh and Aten both appoint dawn as the time for lions to return to their dens and for people to work (Ps 104:22–23; Akhenaten lines 38–45); (3) the incomparable creative power of Yahweh and Aten is praised with the similar statements "O [Yahweh], how manifold are your works!" (Ps 104:24 NRSV) and "How manifold it is, what you [Aten] have made! . . . O sole god, like whom there is no other!" (Akhenaten lines 76–82); (4) the sea contains ships and fish frolicking in the presence of Yahweh (Ps 104:25–26) and Aten (Akhenaten lines 53–58); (5) food for all creation as well as the lifespan of all creatures come from the hand of Yahweh (Ps 104:27–28) and Aten (Akhenaten lines 85–86); and (6) the revealing of the deity's face/breath (for Yahweh) or warm rays (for Aten) leads to life, while their disappearance leads to death (Ps 104:29–30; Akhenaten lines 127–28). The fact that *The Great Hymn to the Aten* dates to the Amarna period, well before any proposal for the composition of Psalm 104, has typically led scholars to regard the Israelite composition as a Yahwistic adaptation of the Egyptian poem. The antiquity of *The Great Hymn* is reflected in how conservative OT scholars regard its monotheism as predating that of the books of Moses.[25]

The Great Hymn to the Aten thus represents a cultural breakthrough on several fronts. Yet despite its monotheistic statements which depart sharply from the polytheism and pantheism of ancient Egypt, it still retains pantheism's corollary of *cosmotheism* by identifying Aten as an Egyptian creator-god who created everything from his own being. The relevant section of *The Great Hymn* reads as follows:

> You alone, shining in your form of living Aten,
> Rising, radiant, distant, near.

---

24. John Day, "Psalm 104 and Akhenaten's Hymn to the Sun," in *Jewish and Christian Approaches to the Psalms: Conflict and Convergence*, ed. Susan E. Gillingham (Oxford: Oxford University Press, 2013), 213–20.
25. James K. Hoffmeier, *Akhenaten and the Origins of Monotheism* (Oxford: Oxford University Press, 2015), 238–66.

You made millions of forms from yourself alone,
Towns, villages, fields, the river's course;
All eyes observe you upon them,
For you are the Aten of daytime on high.[26]

Aten is the sole deity ("You alone") who is still intermingled with his creation in inseparable ways ("from yourself alone"). As the eminent Egyptologist Jan Assman explains, the understanding of creation in *The Great Hymn* differs substantially from the biblical tradition:

> The million forms of the visible world such as towns, villages, road and river are explained as transformation of the sun made out of himself (and not out of some material stuff). . . . Akhanyati's [an alternative spelling for Akhenaten] god is pantheistic and cosmotheistic in that he is more of an energy or a principle than of a person.[27]

The holistic vitality of creation in Psalm 104 might appear monistic to scholars like Paul Dion and Viviers,[28] since their starting point for comparison is Western dualism and its penchant for demythologizing the created order into merely physical objects.[29] But when Psalm 104 is set alongside *The Great Hymn* (albeit with a milder form of pantheism than older Egyptian works), the theology of Psalm 104 diverges from the cosmotheism and monism of *The Great Hymn* without falling into the characteristic dualisms of Western thought (e.g. physical vs. spiritual, heavenly vs. earthly, visible vs. invisible).[30]

In short, Psalm 104 sacralizes the spiritual dimensions of creation while maintaining a clear distinction between Creator and creation: "May the glory of the LORD [Yahweh] endure forever; may the LORD [Yahweh] rejoice *in his*

---

26. Miriam Lichtheim, ed., *Ancient Egyptian Literature* (Oakland, CA: University of California Press, 2019), 420.
27. Jan Assmann, "Mono-, Pan-, and Cosmotheism: Thinking the 'One' in Egyptian Theology," *Orient* 33 (1998): 134–35.
28. Though not referring specifically to Psalm 104, Douglas R. Groothuis rightly summarizes: "Rather than a monistic cosmology, the biblical view of creation harmonizes the one (unity of creation) with the many (distinct creations). The biblical view, then, is holistic without being monistic" Douglas R. Groothuis, *Unmasking the New Age* (Downers Grove, IL: InterVarsity Press, 1986), 107.
29. It is commonplace to read in scholarship, for example, of the "OT's View of *Nature*" or of "*natural* theology in the OT" as if little or no divine intervention from God is required for the universe's moral fabric to stay intact.
30. Arthur Walker-Jones finds Psalm 104 to resonate similarly in Oceania ("Psalm 104: A Celebration of the Vanua," in *The Earth Story in the Psalms and the Prophets*, ed. Norman C. Habel, The Earth Bible 4 [Sheffield: Sheffield Academic Press, 2001], 23–28).

works – he who looks at the earth, and it trembles, who touches the mountains, and they smoke" (Ps 104:31–32). Or in the terms used by philosophers of religion, the God-world relationships in *The Great Hymn to the Aten* and the biblical psalm reside at slightly different places in the middle of a spectrum that is framed by Eastern monism and Western dualism. Even as both are creation hymns (to different deities), Psalm 104's praise of Yahweh as distinct from his creatures reflects the biblical doctrine of *creatio ex nihilo* ("creation out of nothing") rather than *creatio ex deo* ("creation out of [a/the] god") and *creatio ex materia* ("[re-]creation out of what exists) as in *The Great Hymn*.[31] The vitalism of creation in the OT instead holds that everything is permeated by Yahweh's electric presence without raising the universe to divine status.

The Vitalism of Creation in Jeremiah and in Hinduism

The OT's interaction with a form of Egyptian pantheism nearer to its context furnishes a useful template for engaging with a South Asian pantheism further afield like Hinduism. Though this is the religio-philosophical system that John Oswalt named earlier as the most prominent of pantheisms, it is problematic to capture the countless regional variations on the Indian subcontinent using a single category of *Hinduism*. The term itself is an oversimplification from the colonial era that sought to bring British India's many subcultures under the rubric of a singular "other." For this and other reasons, the "official" Hinduism of India's cities differs considerably in its manifestations from "village" Hinduism.

Despite these difficulties of definition, it is notable that astrology transcends these categories as a multifaceted part of Hindu self-understanding through the centuries. Not only does the Indian on the street tend to summarize his or her working theology with the dictum "*Astrology* is *karma*,"[32] but the formal astrological discipline of *jyotisha* (Sansk. "light in the sky, luminary") also plays a significant role in several Hindu scriptures, calendrical systems, horoscopes, and rituals.[33] And most relevantly for this study, Hindu astrology developed significantly with the Hellenistic introduction of the same kinds of Mesopotamian astrology which the book of Jeremiah identifies as a temptation

---

31. Cf. Assmann, "Mono-, Pan-, and Cosmotheism," 134.
32. François Chenet, "Karma and Astrology: An Unrecognized Aspect of Indian Anthropology," *Diogenes* 33 (1985): 102, italics original. For more on astrology's role in "everyday Hinduism," see Joyce Burkhalter Flueckiger, *Everyday Hinduism*, Lived Religions 1 (Chichester: Wiley-Blackwell, 2015), 211–18.
33. Michio Yano, "Calendar, Astrology, and Astronomy," in *The Blackwell Companion to Hinduism*, ed. Gavin Flood, Blackwell Companions to Religion 5 (Malden, MA: Blackwell, 2005), 376–92.

for Judah.[34] It is likely that the celestial divination rituals in the Mesopotamian texts of *Enuma Anu Enlil* stand in the backgrounds of both Hindu *jyotisha* and Judah's syncretism with astral religion in the time of Jeremiah.[35] Even without a direct connection between the OT and Egyptian pantheism such as Psalm 104 provides, an indirect connection from the OT to Hindu pantheism remains available via Mesopotamia as a cultural bridge.

In this regard, part of Jeremiah's message as "a prophet to the nations" (1:5, 10) is a critical engagement with the culture of Mesopotamia, particularly its astrology which entails the simultaneous veneration and fear of celestial beings and the divine will supposedly represented by them. Jeremiah warns Yahweh's people that they are being seduced by Mesopotamian astrology's unification of the physical, spiritual, and divine realms: "Do not learn the way of the nations, or be dismayed at the signs of the heavens; for the nations are dismayed at them" (10:2 NRSV; cf. 8:2; 19:13; Ezek 8:16). While this statement clearly prohibits omen interpretations of the kind set forth in *Enuma Anu Enlil*, it is striking that the rest of Jeremiah does not offer the equivalent of a Western, demythologized approach to an impersonal "nature" to replace an Eastern pantheism that views the cosmos as a single, continuous entity. The discussion above has already showed how Jeremiah offers a rich account of a God-ordained, personal, and active creation that exemplifies the ability of the OT to navigate "a middle course between the Gnostic contempt for nature and the pagan adoration of it."[36]

Jeremiah's message that creation is everywhere alive, relational, yet separate from God presents a stark contrast to Hinduism's account of the *Brahman* in the Upanishads as an all-pervading reality which is everywhere alive but tends

---

34. On the parallels between Mesopotamian and Indian rituals, see Toke Lindegaard Knudsen, "House Omens in Mesopotamia and India," in *From the Banks of the Euphrates: Studies in Honor of Alice Louise Slotsky*, ed. Micah Ross (Winona Lake, IN: Eisenbrauns, 2008), 121–33. The commercial and cultural factors that drove the connections between the Near East and India are discussed by Stephan Hillyer Levitt, "The Dating of the Indian Tradition," *Anthropos* 98 (2003): 341–59.

35. David Burnett, *The Spirit of Hinduism: A Christian Perspective on Hindu Thought* (Tunbridge Wells: Monarch, 1992), 115; David E. Pingree, "Mesopotamian Astronomy and Astral Omens in Other Civilizations," in *Mesopotamien und seine Nachbarn: Politische und kulturelle Wechselbeziehungen im alten Vorderasien vom 4. bis 1. Jahrtausend v. Chr.*, eds. Hans Jörg Nissen and Johannes Renger, Rencontre Assyriologique Internationale 25 (Berlin: D. Reimer, 1982), 2:613–31.

36. Northrop Frye, *The Great Code: The Bible and Literature* (London: Routledge & Kegan Paul, 1982), 112–13, quoted in Fretheim, *God and World*, xi.

toward an impersonal cosmic principle.[37] Interestingly, however, South Asian scholars have been prone to overlook Jeremiah's unique response to celestial divination in its cultural context. In the entry on "Astrology" in the *South Asia Bible Commentary*, Jeremiah 10:2 is rightly cited as biblical evidence that "we are not to follow others [i.e. astrologers] or what the stars foretell."[38] But in this same article by an Indian theologian, the statement that "God has already given us all the knowledge we need for the future *through his inspired word*"[39] reflects a more Western penchant for abstract ideas which clashes with Jeremiah's more Eastern penchant for concrete objects. At the same time, the vitalism of Jeremiah does not reflect a monist worldview that ascribes sacral power to the physical world, as in the Rigvedic hymns to the sun-god Savitr or the daily mantra known as the *Gayātri* that Hindus pray to a succession of solar deities.[40]

Yet, Jeremiah assigns the celestial beings the highest honor of testifying to the efficacy of Yahweh's mighty acts in both realms. The "new covenant" oracle of Jeremiah 31 closes with the declaration that the regularity of the sun, moon, and stars supplies proof that God has decreed for his people to remain:

Thus says the LORD,
who gives the sun for light by day
and the fixed order of the moon and the stars for
light by night,
who stirs up the sea so that its waves roar –
the LORD of hosts is his name:
If this fixed order were ever to cease
from my presence, says the LORD,
then also the offspring of Israel would cease
to be a nation before me forever.

Thus says the LORD:
If the heavens above can be measured,

---

37. Frank Whaling, *Understanding Hinduism* (Edinburgh: Dunedin Academic, 2010), 37–38; D. S. Sarma, *Essence of Hinduism* (Bombay: Bharatyia Vidya Bhavan, 1971), 91. Cf. Karan Singh, *Essays on Hinduism*, 3rd ed. (Delhi: Primus Books, 2014), 5.
38. M. T. Cherian, "Astrology," in *South Asia Bible Commentary: A One-Volume Commentary on the Whole Bible*, ed. Brian C. Wintle (Grand Rapids, MI: Zondervan Academic, 2015), 533.
39. Cherian, "Astrology," 533, italics added.
40. Margaret Stutley, *Hinduism: The Eternal Law; An Introduction to the Literature, Cosmology and Cults of the Hindu Religion* (Wellingborough: Aquarian Press, 1985), 20; Whaling, *Understanding Hinduism*, 49.

and the foundations of the earth below can be explored,
then I will reject all the offspring of Israel
because of all they have done,
says the LORD. (Jer 31:35–37)

The stars in the sky thus have a revelatory function in demonstrating the will of God (cf. Gen 15:5; 22:17; Isa 40:25–26), but one that mediates between a Western tendency to demythologize "nature" into impersonal objects on the one hand, and the Eastern tendency on the other to mingle physical things with spiritual beings in a manner that expresses the divine's ability to determine the courses of humanity.

CASE STUDY 2: THE BOOK OF ECCLESIASTES AND HINDU IDEAS OF THE COSMOS

The Old Testament's accent on the regularity of celestial movements sheds new light on an old puzzle. This is the philosophical question of how the Judeo-Christian tradition and its Scriptures conceive the nature of *time* and *space*. With its refrain that "under the sun" lie a multitude of frustrations, the book of Ecclesiastes is typically viewed as the premier statement of existentialism in the Judeo-Christian Scriptures. Such a summary of the book, however, is quintessentially Western for conceiving Ecclesiastes as the *interior* struggles of an *individual*. It neglects the many voices of creation that speak in the book.[41] Before examining the potential of Ecclesiastes to bridge the biblical worldview on creation with Hindu ideas of the cosmos, it is necessary to recount briefly how the Judeo-Christian West tends to conceive its own history as a linear and teleological narrative (focusing on discontinuity with the past and progress into the future). Such a self-understanding is typically set in contrast to views about the shape of the cosmos as cyclical (focusing on continuity and regularity) that are supposedly non-Western. Perhaps the most familiar example is the frequent opinion of Western commentators that Asian people favor indirect communication or talking in circles.[42]

---

41. Katharine Dell, "The Cycle of Life in Ecclesiastes," *Vetus Testamentum* 59 (2009): 181–89.
42. For example, the topic-comment structure of Chinese grammar is often generalized as a cultural trait in terms reminiscent of the "inscrutable Chinaman" stereotype: "There is a fundamental difference in the linguistic objects of Chinese and English. Chinese is designed to obfuscate. The language aims to hide the speaker's exact meaning, to obscure what's in their hearts, and to conceal their thoughts. English's *raison d'être* is to communicate as succinctly, directly, and clearly as possible what you mean, want, feel or think" (Darren Haughn, "A Low-Context Dude in High-Context Places," *The Salty Egg* (blog), 11 March 2018, https://

It has been commonplace to distinguish between Western and non-Western worldviews by focusing on differences in how they ostensibly conceive of *time* as a particular kind of *space*. William Lane Craig, a leading Christian philosopher, asserts that the non-West has a cyclic understanding of time that lacks both coherence and directionality:

> The Judeo-Christian tradition takes time to be linear in its structure, in contrast to views of time as cyclic. Hence, eschatology becomes an important issue for that tradition. Cyclic views of time are dubiously intelligible if tense and temporal becoming are real, since once the cycle has run its course the cycle would seem to begin *a second time*, which presupposes linearity.[43]

Likewise in systematic theology, Robert Herrera asserts that the biblical doctrine of *creatio ex nihilo* "shattered the pagan conception of an eternal universe parceled out in an infinity of cycles. . . . The doctrine of creation entailing linear time opened a vast horizon of novel events that took history beyond the limits of the ancient chroniclers."[44]

The supposed inferiority of cycles or circles to lines in understanding the cosmos has even spilled over into Western scholarship on Ecclesiastes, the OT book which we will examine below. Harold Fisch speaks of creation's cycles in Ecclesiastes 1 as the peak of pointlessness: "Qohelet finds himself in a condition of spiritual claustrophobia. The recognition of circularity involves for him a recognition of how intolerable such a state is and how desperately we need to escape it. . . . Qohelet contemplates the cyclical monotony of such a universe with the deepest pessimism."[45]

The view from Asia has been surprisingly similar to that of the West. Paul Hiebert, an American Christian anthropologist whose time in India as a missionary was foundational for all his work, argues that his two cultures are distinguished by a linear view of time (the American worldview) as opposed to

---

thesaltyegg.net/a-low-context-dude-in-a-high-context-culture/). Interestingly, American guide-books on Germany typically do not make the same point about cultural indirectness even though communication in German frequently hinges on the last grammatical construction in a sentence.

43. William Lane Craig, "Time," in *Global Dictionary of Theology: A Resource for the Worldwide Church*, eds. William A. Dyrness and Veli-Matti Kärkkäinen (Downers Grove, IL: IVP Academic, 2008), 899.

44. Robert A. Herrera, *Reasons for Our Rhymes: An Inquiry into the Philosophy of History* (Grand Rapids, MI: Eerdmans, 2001), 13.

45. Harold Fisch, *Poetry with a Purpose: Biblical Poetics and Interpretation* (Bloomington, IN: Indiana University Press, 1988), 167.

a cyclical one (the Indian worldview).[46] For an Asian theologian like Kosuke Koyama, one finds frequent statements in his pioneering book *Water Buffalo Theology* that the Bible mainly contains a linear and demythologized perspective on history which is qualified at times by the cyclical and mythic orientation of creation.[47] Among theologians, the common identification of Western cultures with the former perspective and Asian cultures with the latter neglects two fundamental questions: (1) What is the biblical view of history? and (2) Are the biblical and Western views of time identical?

Already for decades, OT scholarship has denied the notion that the "biblical" view of time is solely linear and teleological.[48] It was once the consensus, especially in the early and mid-twentieth century, that the OT was unique in its world for holding that Yahweh interrupts the cyclical rhythms of creation by his mighty acts within a linear history.[49] The situation changed radically with the 1967 publication of Bertil Albrektson's *History and the Gods*. This book demonstrated conclusively that other ancient Near Eastern cultures also conceive of their deities as acting in the realm of history.[50] It is not that the Israelite conception of history lacks special traits, but Albrektson exposed the problems with the overdrawn contrast between linear history in the OT and cyclical myth in the ancient Near East which continues to find a home in many other disciplines. Linear and cyclical views of history exist in both Western and non-Western cultures,[51] as well as both perspectives being present in the Bible itself. Marc Zvi Brettler concludes that "those who depict biblical time as linear, with the 'end of time' as a goal or *telos*, are misreading the text."[52] This is true of the book of Ecclesiastes most of all, as we will now explore in comparing biblical and Hindu notions of the cosmos.

---

46. Paul G. Hiebert, *Transforming Worldviews: An Anthropological Understanding of How People Change* (Grand Rapids, MI: Baker Academic, 2008), 338.

47. Koyama, *Water Buffalo Theology*, 20–31.

48. Rolf P. Knierim, *The Task of Old Testament Theology: Substance, Method, and Cases* (Grand Rapids, MI: Eerdmans, 1995), 171–224; Simon J. DeVries, *Yesterday, Today and Tomorrow: Time and History in the Old Testament* (Grand Rapids, MI: Eerdmans, 1975), 343.

49. E.g. G. Ernest Wright, *The Old Testament against Its Environment*, Studies in Biblical Theology 2 (London: SCM, 1950), 20–29.

50. Bertil Albrektson, *History and the Gods: An Essay on the Idea of Historical Events as Divine Manifestations in the Ancient Near East and in Israel*, Coniectanea Biblica: Old Testament Series 1 (Lund: C. W. K. Gleerup, 1967).

51. Jörn Rüsen, ed., *Western Historical Thinking: An Intercultural Debate*, Making Sense of History (New York: Berghahn Books, 2002).

52. Marc Brettler, "Cyclical and Teleological Time in the Hebrew Bible," in *Time and Temporality in the Ancient World*, ed. Ralph M. Rosen (Philadelphia: University of Pennsylvania Museum of Archaeology and Anthropology, 2004), 122.

The Shape of Creation in Ecclesiastes and in Hinduism

The conceptual world of Ecclesiastes finds a welcome reception in Asian contextual theology.[53] The affinity of the book with the "Book of Changes" (*yijing*), a Daoist scripture text, has earned it the label of "The Hebrew Book of Changes,"[54] while its characteristic term *hebel* (Hebrew for "vanity, vapor"; 29x in Ecclesiastes) is often rendered in Asian languages using a Buddhist term for "emptiness" (*sunyata* in the original Pali).[55] For our purposes of examining the shape of reality, how Ecclesiastes and Hinduism each speak of cyclicality is particularly relevant. The most natural connections between these positions might seem to be the *determinism* that apparently characterizes both Ecclesiastes's famous "Catalogue of Times" (3:1–15) and the *fatalism* by which Hindus regard their lot in life as what the universe's causality has bestowed (e.g. Bhagavad-gītā 3.3, 13, 27).[56] Both perspectives employ the notion of cycles in time and space to emphasize one's fate in the face of an unchangeable reality. A Hindu teacher like Jayādvaita Swami finds much in the "Catalogue of Times" that is congenial. In his words, "Qoheleth reasserts that the world offers nothing new but only monotonous repetition, in which the present and the future endlessly redo the past."[57]

However, Jayādvaita Swami's characterization of such a placid universe downplays the irritation of the speaker Qoheleth which opens the book: "What do people gain from all their labors with which they labor under the sun?" (1:3; my translation). Life for Qoheleth, in other words, is exasperating like an unfair trade in which people do *not* receive what is due to them, offering a direct challenge to karmic worldviews and the expected relationship between cause and effect that they espouse (Hinduism among them). For this reason,

---

53. See in Jione Havea and Peter H. W. Lau, eds., *Reading Ecclesiastes from Asia and Pasifika*, International Voices in Biblical Studies 10 (Atlanta: SBL Press, 2020).

54. John Jarick, "The Hebrew Book of Changes: Reflections on *Hakkōl Hebel* and *Lakkōl Zemān* in Ecclesiastes," *Journal for the Study of the Old Testament* 25 (2000): 79–99.

55. In Chinese Bibles, for example, the opening lament that "*xu kong de xu kong, xu kong de xu kong, fan shi dou shi xu kong*" (Eccl 1:2) has distinct overtones of Chinese (Mahayana) Buddhism. 虛空 (*xu kong*) is the Chinese term for *sunyata*. My students from Japan, Korea, Thailand, and Myanmar have confirmed through the years that Ecclesiastes echoes Buddhist themes in their languages as well. For a case study for Thai Buddhism in particular, see Seree Lorgunpai, "The Book of Ecclesiastes and Thai Buddhism," in *Voices from the Margin: Interpreting the Bible in the Third World*, ed. R. S. Sugirtharajah, rev. and expanded 3rd ed. (Maryknoll, NY: Orbis, 2006), 347–54.

56. E.g. Jayādvaita Swami, *Vanity Karma: Ecclesiastes, the Bhagavad-gītā, and the Meaning of Life – A Cross-Cultural Commentary on the Book of Ecclesiastes* (Los Angeles: The Bhaktivedanta Book Trust, 2015), 56–59.

57. Swami, *Vanity Karma*, 73.

creation answers Qoheleth's question with a halting series of regular and irregular movements: "Generations come and generations go, *but* the earth stands forever. The sun rises and the sun sets, *but* hurries back to where it rises" (1:4–5; my translation). Cyclical repetition is certainly present in the passing of generations (1:4a) and the sun's daily routine (1:5a), yet this constancy of movement is interrupted by both the unchanging steadiness of the earth (1:4b) as well as the sun's need to "hurry/pant" directly back to its place (1:5b).[58] The wind and waters behave in similarly restless ways (1:6–7) so that the oscillations of creation themselves come and go. Since the regular irregularity of creation is a microcosm of life itself, Qoheleth concludes that "all things are wearisome, more than one can say" (1:8). Surrendering to the causality of the universe fails to provide solutions for life's mysteries, raising doubts about whether people should perceive it as a closed system in the first place.[59]

As Qoheleth continues his pilgrimage, he eventually discovers the necessity of embracing both cyclicality and linearity. This paradox is necessary to orient one's bearings toward where the book eventually concludes: "Now all has been heard; here is the conclusion of the matter: Fear God and keep his commandments, for this is the duty of all mankind. For God will bring every deed into judgment, including every hidden thing, whether it is good or evil" (12:13–14). The journey toward this destination unfolds in Ecclesiastes through the frequent use of the Hebrew phrase *taḥat haššemeš* ("under the sun"; 29x in Ecclesiastes), emphasizing the watchful eye of the sun in overseeing life's winding pathways.

Both the preposition *taḥat* and the noun *šemeš* in this expression are palindromes. This is a special kind of word whose letters are mirror images of themselves (e.g. "radar, level"). A palindrome initially looks like a random linear sequence of letters like any other word. Its repetition of letters in reverse order only begins to appear after reaching the halfway point. But its cyclical spelling is not fully evident until reaching the end of its chain of letters. In the same way, life "under the sun" is like a palindrome in which seemingly arbitrary sequences do not emerge as patterns in God's purposes until they are viewed with the benefit of hindsight. Such is the uniquely theocentric but

58. Edwin M. Good, "The Unfilled Sea: Style and Meaning in Ecclesiastes 1:2–11," in *Israelite Wisdom: Theological and Literary Essays in Honor of Samuel Terrien*, eds. John G. Gammie et al. (Missoula, MT: Scholars, 1978), 64–65.

59. Cf. Mette Bundvad, *Time in the Book of Ecclesiastes*, Oxford Theology and Religion Monographs (Oxford: Oxford University Press, 2015), 53–56.

indirect way in which Ecclesiastes speaks of "fate" (*miqreh*; 3:19; 9:2–3).[60] The world of Ecclesiastes contains an element of chance that stands in contrast to Hinduism's notion of an impersonal universe in which everything is nonetheless preordained. While the cosmos indeed has some predictability to its timing and rhythms, Qoheleth finds that determining its precise shape is of less importance than to "remember your Creator in the days of your youth" (12:1). In fact, discontinuity in both history and creation will one day overtake continuity – it is true both that "there is nothing new under the sun" (1:9) and that "the sun and the light and the moon and the stars grow dark, and the clouds return after the rain" (12:2).[61]

The hesitant movements of creation between Ecclesiastes 1 and 12 have another significant connection to Hinduism. In chapter 1, it is the natural "wind" (*rûaḥ*) that embodies life's wanderings before "ever returning on its course" (1:6; cf. v. 17). Futility is then named often as "a striving after the wind" (e.g. 2:17; 4:4; 6:9) which parallels the transience of "vapor" (*hebel*) which is blown away. By the end of the book, however, the Hebrew term *rûaḥ* appears in its specific sense of human "spirit/breath": "And the dust returns to the earth which it had been, and the spirit/breath [*rûaḥ*] returns to God who gave it"[62] (12:7; cf. Gen 2:7).[63] The book's repetition of *rûaḥ* identifies the "spirit" of humanity and the futility of "striving after wind" as entwined within an imperfect creation, even as the *rûaḥ* of people has a final destination outside creation which contrasts with the cyclical *rûaḥ* in the rest of creation.[64] These intriguing puns on *rûaḥ* lead one scholar to ask a question that is central to Hinduism: "Did Qohelet believe in reincarnation?"[65]

On this note, the Hindu doctrine of reincarnation extends the notion of cyclicality from the physical to the spiritual realm. But unlike Hinduism's journey of individual consciousness merging with the Supreme Consciousness

---

60. Brittany N. Melton, "*Miqreh* in Retrospect: An Illumination of *Miqreh* in Light of Ecclesiastes 3.1–8 and the Book of Ruth," in *Megilloth Studies: The Shape of Contemporary Scholarship*, ed. Brad Embry, Hebrew Bible Monographs 78 (Sheffield: Sheffield Phoenix Press, 2016), 30–42.

61. Jennifer Barbour, *The Story of Israel in the Book of Qohelet: Ecclesiastes as Cultural Memory*, Oxford Theological Monographs (Oxford: Oxford University Press, 2012), 49–50.

62. Author's translation.

63. C.-L. Seow, *Ecclesiastes: A New Translation with Introduction and Commentary*, The Anchor Bible 18C (New York: Doubleday, 1997), 367–38.

64. T. Anthony Perry, *The Book of Ecclesiastes (Qohelet) and the Path to Joyous Living* (Cambridge: Cambridge University Press, 2015), 76–77.

65. Michael Carasik, "Qohelet's Twists and Turns," *Journal for the Study of the Old Testament* 28 (2003): 195, n. 8.

(*moksha*), Qoheleth states that human knowledge of the past, present, and future is incomplete at best: "No one remembers the former generations, and even those yet to come will not be remembered by those who follow them" (1:11). Qoheleth is frustrated to realize that the shape of creation contains both cycles *and* lines (1:4–9). This leaves humans unable to grasp the elusive dimensions of reality which lie beyond what cycles can reach and bring back to our mental awareness.[66] Reluctantly, Qoheleth concludes that human consciousness is often at odds with both creation and Creator.

Ecclesiastes is therefore not a book of philosophical monism despite its vital interconnections among God, humans, and the earth's other creatures that are sometimes reminiscent of *Brahman* in Hinduism. And since the God-given "spirit/breath" is interwoven with the "wind" of all God's creatures even as distinctions remain between them, Ecclesiastes still draws a firm boundary between creation and Creator. In doing so, however, it diverges from Western forms of dualism (e.g. living vs. nonliving, spiritual vs. physical, immaterial vs. spiritual).

CONCLUSION

E. Stanley Jones was an American Methodist missionary to India in the early twentieth century who maintained a close friendship for decades with Mohandas K. Gandhi, the "Great Soul" (*Mahatma*) of India. In a biography of Jones, Gandhi is quoted as saying that "the Christian missionaries as a body, with honourable exceptions, have actively supported a system which has impoverished, enervated and demoralized a people considered to be among the greatest and most civilized on earth."[67] Jones, however, differed from his missionary colleagues in warning that it would be foolish to caricature India and its culture as dark, primitive, and heathen. The preface to the sixth edition of his pioneering book advocates a posture of respectful engagement so that Indians might become more open to the gospel:

> India is aggrieved, and I think rightly so, that Christian missionaries in order to arouse the West to missionary activity have too often emphasized the dark side of the picture. What they have said has been true, but the picture has not been a true one. This overemphasis on the one side has often created either pity

---

66. Bundvad, *Time in the Book of Ecclesiastes*, 56–58.
67. Paul A. J. Martin, *Missionary of the Indian Road: The Theology of Stanley Jones* (Bangalore: Theological Book Trust, 1996), 7.

or contempt in the minds of the hearers. In modern jargon a superiority has resulted. I do not believe a superiority complex to be the proper spring for missionary activity.[68]

The example of Jones in modeling *The Christ of the Indian Road* (the title of his famous book) allowed him to remain Gandhi's friend through a lifestyle that defied conventional wisdom on why "Christian" empires had come to India.

It is therefore mistaken to assume that Christian missions in India equates to imperialism.[69] Similarly, it would be just as unwise to presume that the Old Testament supports the Western dualisms that have been set against pantheism and thereby supplied humanity with the theological rationale to exploit God's creation through a subject-to-object relationship. The place of humanity *within* the cycles of creation rather than *against* them is often neglected in a harried modern world that lacks restedness and has damaged God's creation in the unending pursuit of "progress."[70] Indian evangelical theology, no less than Western theology, is still feeling its way for how the OT supplies a contextual and contextualizing approach that values the sacredness of creation without losing sight of the transcendent Creator.[71] Yahweh has intentionally fashioned his world with rhythmic voids in both space (i.e. aniconism; see ch. 7) and time (i.e. Sabbath) for his people to cease joyfully from trusting in the work of their own anxious hands.[72]

---

68. E. Stanley Jones, *The Christ of the Indian World*, 6th ed. (New York: Abingdon Press, 1925), 3–4.

69. Ivan Satyavrata, *God Has Not Left Himself without Witness* (Eugene, OR: Wipf and Stock, 2011), 237–40.

70. Fred Bahnson and Norman Wirzba, *Making Peace with the Land: God's Call to Reconcile with Creation* (Downers Grove, IL: InterVarsity Press, 2012).

71. The late Indian evangelical theologian Ken Gnanakan evidently still favored the Western emphasis on salvation history over creation in doing theology for his cultural context: "The Old Testament is the place to start. *Apart from creation*, the one overarching theme that cements the whole sequence of God's dealings with the world is the covenant. This theme provides the all inclusive horizon that will first universalise God's intentions for all peoples and then particularise it to show the purposes of God for humankind" (*Proclaiming Christ in a Pluralistic Context* [Bangalore: Theological Book Trust, 2002], 71, italics added).

72. Abraham J. Heschel, *The Sabbath: Its Meaning for Modern Man* (New York: Farrar, Strauss, and Giroux, 1951), 16–21.

CHAPTER 9

CONCLUSION

This book has sought to explore the crucial but neglected question *What hath contextualization to do with the Old Testament?* Before summarizing my answers, the pun from church history that this wording of the question plays upon deserves a closer look. For it was during the second century AD that the church father Tertullian lodged his celebrated protest *What hath Athens to do with Jerusalem?* In Tertullian's thought, the pagan philosophy of Greek culture symbolized by "Athens" had nothing in common with the purity of biblical faith embodied by "Jerusalem." Tertullian and his anti-Hellenism had passed from the scene, however, by the time the early church drew extensively on Hellenistic philosophy in addressing the mysteries of the Trinity and Jesus Christ's dual natures. The church councils that produced the Nicene Creed (AD 325) and Chalcedonian Creed (AD 451) turned to Greek concepts such as *hypostasis* for the kind of help that would have troubled Tertullian. For this reason and since Tertullian was a North African from Carthage (in modern-day Tunisia), he is often seen as an early champion for non-Western ways of doing Christian theology. In this understanding he also becomes a stark contrast to how other church fathers supposedly "baptized Aristotle in their teaching on the identity and character of God."[1]

Ironically, Tertullian's insistence on a strict separation between faith and culture was written in neither Hebrew nor Greek, the original languages of the Jewish and Christian Scriptures. It was instead in Latin,[2] the language of the Roman Empire which occupied both the territory associated with OT Israel and the diffuse places in which the NT church was then located. Even before the early Christian councils, the diverse experiences of diaspora Jews in the Greco-Roman world (Jesus and his apostles among them) had already imposed the reality of cultural hybridity via their "multiple belonging" to Athens *and* Jerusalem, rather than *or*. In other words, the plea of Tertullian to bifurcate

---

1. To quote the incisive summary of Jürgen Moltmann's view by Allen, "Exodus 3," 180–81. For more on the "Hellenization thesis," see also ch. 1, n. 52.
2. The quote at hand about "Athens" and "Jerusalem" comes from Tertullian's work *De praescriptione haereticorum* ("Prescription against Heretics").

human cultures and biblical faith required the culture and language of the conqueror to make in the first place.[3] And not unlike evangelical missiology in the modern era, Tertullian held to certain dichotomies between cultural impurity ("Athens") and theological orthodoxy ("Jerusalem") which neglected how the Bible does theology by interacting deeply *with* its cultural contexts rather than *against* them. Dean Flemming had already demonstrated this in detail for the New Testament,[4] so the present work has sought to show how theologizing *with* culture is characteristic of the Old Testament as well. This is especially the case when we oscillate "between Asian and Western Perspectives" (the subtitle of this book) with God's truth at the center.

East-West dichotomies and the "Hellenization thesis" are thus rather passé. However, this has not stopped Asian theologians from reusing Tertullian's contrast for their own cultural contexts. It is common in Asian theological circles to encounter appeals to the holism of "Hebraic" thinking which are set against dichotomous "Greek" forms of reasoning, the former equated with Asia and the latter with the West.[5] It is also not atypical to deconstruct Western theology as being too academic and driven by Enlightenment secularism to be useful for Asian contexts.[6] But as hinted earlier, the presence of cultural hybridity both in the Bible and in modern Asia has made such sharp contrasts as idealistic as they are misleading. The ghost of Tertullian still appears often enough to recall the question that Asian theologians sometimes ask their Western counterparts: "What's the difference between Western and Asian ways of doing theology?" Asian theologians are prone to answer without realizing the unintentional humor in saying, "*You* think in dichotomies, but *we* don't!"

I have often witnessed such ironies in my time as a member of OMF International (founded by Hudson Taylor in 1865 as the China Inland Mission), a pioneering missions agency in which Western and Asian colleagues now work shoulder to shoulder. Many missionaries from Western countries serve in the advisory role of encouraging Asian colleagues and local Christians to do Asian contextual theology. Yet the latter group sometimes continues to prefer theology with roots in Europe and North America. This may be because

---

3. In this regard, one thinks also of the Parsi-Indian-American writer Homi Bhabha, who has been a leading exponent of *postcolonialism*. He employs the English language and his Western education in order to criticize Western cultural hegemony.

4. Flemming, *Contextualization in the New Testament*.

5. As in the *yin-yang* approach to Asian theology which is advocated most influentially by C. S. Song, *Third-Eye Theology: Theology in Formation in Asian Settings* (Eugene, OR: Wipf and Stock, 2002).

6. E.g. Hwa, *Mangoes or Bananas?*

an earlier generation of missionaries from these places asserted it was just "theology" (without any qualifiers), or because Asians who go to the West for theological studies are typically afforded extra prestige upon returning home. In any case, my students at Singapore Bible College, who hail from over twenty Asian countries, have told me through the years that they long to do contextual theology but struggle to unlearn colonialism's stubborn legacy in their Christian subcultures that "the West is best." And when Asian evangelicals are unaware of how theology from the West has its own history of development, including the process by which missionaries brought it to non-Western lands, then attempts to do Asian theology become suspect almost by default for deviating from the (usually Western) evangelical "norm."

The world today is thus an interconnected place in which the traditional classifications and categories are inadequate at best. This reality means that the task of doing theology that is authentically Asian, deeply biblical, and fully evangelical cannot be confined to unlearning or discarding the theological habits of the past, as if starting over without the West were possible. It is crucial also to cultivate a greater awareness of self, culture, and history which recognizes how Christianity in modern Asia straddles several horizons that are in constant and vigorous dialogue – East and West, faith and culture, as well as past and future.

On that note, let us revisit the method and rationale for this book's case studies. Each of our chapters has begun with the recognition that the parallel fields of Old Testament studies and missiology both come from the West and must still go through it. This is neither a burden to be unconditionally rejected nor a gift to be uncritically embraced, however. It is simply a historical given which has supplied one half of a series of iterative comparisons with Asian cultures in each chapter. The other waystation for this book's repeated traversals of the "hermeneutical spiral"[7] has been supplied by Western scholarship in OT studies and missiology. The Bible itself has remained our focus throughout this book, not so much as a wall *against* culture, but more as a window into how God's word makes meaning *in* and *with* cultural contexts. For the OT in particular, the ancient Near Eastern environment which furnished the categories for Israel to receive Yahweh's revelation still proves useful for God's people in the modern Far East to do contextual theology.

---

7. To quote the terminology of iteration by Osborne, *Hermeneutical Spiral*, in improving on the older image of a "hermeneutical circle."

WHAT HATH CONTEXTUALIZATION TO DO WITH THE OT?

We are now in a position to revisit our opening question: *What hath contextualization to do with the OT?* This gulf between contextualization and the OT is symptomatic of the problem that has long plagued missiology and the Bible in general. In a 1985 review article of seven books on mission, the eminent scholar David Bosch closed with the lament that his twin passions of missiology and biblical studies remained far apart despite the best efforts of the books' seven authors:

> At the end the church is still left with the nagging question of *whether* its missionary activities today bear any resemblance at all to what biblical scholars call "mission" and also if and how it can appeal to scripture for its missionary service. Perhaps we need a book written by a theologian who is both a missiologist *and* a biblical scholar – if such an animal exists.[8]

In the four decades since, only a few brave souls have heeded Bosch's summons to become such a hybrid creature.[9] Even a polymath like Bosch himself struggled to close the widest gap of all between the disciplines of missiology and the Old Testament. *Transforming Mission,*[10] Bosch's magnum opus, gives only four pages to the OT, whereas he devotes 150 pages to the NT. Similarly from missiology's side of the chasm, a standard evangelical textbook on contextualization by David Hesselgrave and Edward Rommen relegates the OT to nearly a footnote: "In the case of the Old Testament we are hard-pressed to find examples of cross-cultural communication of a specifically religious message."[11] Although the OT figures prominently in several biblical theologies of mission, their discussion tends to center on the OT's narrative of the *missio Dei* more than its missional methods in doing contextual theology.[12] The oc-

---

8. David J. Bosch, "Mission in Biblical Perspective," *International Review of Mission* 74 (1985): 538, italics original.
9. Most notable in this respect is Christopher J. H. Wright, *The Mission of God: Unlocking the Bible's Grand Narrative* (Downers Grove, IL: InterVarsity Press, 2006).
10. David J. Bosch, *Transforming Mission: Paradigm Shifts in Theology of Mission* (Maryknoll, NY: Orbis, 1991).
11. David J. Hesselgrave and Edward Rommen, *Contextualization: Meanings, Methods, and Models* (Pasadena, CA: William Carey Library, 2000), 4.
12. In addition to Wright's major work (n. 9), see also Richard J. Bauckham, *Bible and Mission: Christian Witness in a Postmodern World* (Grand Rapids, MI: Baker Academic, 2003); Michael W. Goheen, *A Light to the Nations: The Missional Church and the Biblical Story* (Grand Rapids, MI: Baker Academic, 2011); James Chukwuma Okoye, *Israel and the Nations: A Mission Theology of the Old Testament,* American Society of Missiology Series 39 (Maryknoll, NY: Orbis, 2006).

casions when the OT's methods do feature have tended to focus on whether the OT envisions Israel's mission as centrifugal or centripetal in orientation.[13]

The inability to find common ground between these fields is largely due to cultural blinders which their shared history in the West has imparted to them. For when *contextualization* is limited to the methods for communicating propositional truth (as recounted and critiqued in chapter 1), efforts to locate contextualization *in the OT* will falter since such a quest is a category fallacy along the lines of "smelling the color nine." Contextualization in this common view is hereby restricted to translating the apostolically revealed message of the NT for new cultural situations. The OT is ruled out as an authoritative sourcebook since contextualization has essentially become a *postbiblical* set of methods, with only the NT's finished revelation of the gospel furnishing a possible starting point.[14] And as a set of culture-specific *methods*, the operating assumption is that the Bible's supracultural message already lies securely within the grasp of (Western) biblical scholarship.

Such a winding history through several disciplines is the reason that (Western) missiologists tend to focus on contextualization as a set of communicative methods which are culture-bound.[15] But in this understanding, they have inadvertently mingled Christendom's cultural values with the gospel in the process of receiving it.[16] In this regard, many social scientists of religion have noted that missiology's signature distinction between contextualization and syncretism (which recalls Tertullian's division between faith and culture) is itself syncretistic in certain ways for deriving from the Enlightenment's impulse to carve out *religion* as a category distinct from *culture*.[17] The consequence of enforcing this artificial separation is that contextualization and syncretism also cease to be neutral descriptors since they already reflect certain polarizing

---

13. Robert Martin-Achard, *A Light to the Nations: A Study of the OT Conception of Israel's Mission to the World* (Edinburgh and London: Oliver & Boyd, 1962); Jiří Moskala, "The Mission of God's People in the Old Testament," *Journal of the Adventist Theological Society* 19, no. 1/2 (2008): 40–60; Walter C. Kaiser, Jr., *Mission in the Old Testament: Israel as a Light to the Nations*, 2nd ed. (Grand Rapids, MI: Baker Academic, 2012).

14. E.g. George W. Peters, *A Biblical Theology of Missions* (Chicago: Moody, 1976), 52; Hesselgrave and Rommen, *Contextualization*, 149.

15. E.g. Donald L. Stults, *Developing an Asian Evangelical Theology* (Manila: OMF Literature, 1989), 138–39.

16. See ch. 1, "The 'Contextualization Debate' in Western Missiology."

17. E.g. H. L. Richard, "Religious Syncretism as a Syncretistic Concept: The Inadequacy of the 'World Religions' Paradigm in Cross-Cultural Encounter," *International Journal of Frontier Missiology* 31 (2014): 209–15.

judgments about right and wrong (which usually remain hidden). As Eugene Heideman observes,

> syncretism and contextualization are most often used as part of a "political" agenda designed in the one case to express disapproval of what someone else is innovating, and in the other case to claim legitimacy for what is being done in the face of potential traditionalist disapproval. To say that these are thus political power words is not to discredit them nor to rule them out, but to give ourselves greater sensitivity to the context in which issues of syncretism and contextualization must be confronted.[18]

The complex relationship between descriptive and prescriptive definitions for syncretism involves many issues which lie outside this book's focus on *Contextualization and the Old Testament*.[19] More pertinent for our discussion, the fact remains that the boundary between "contextualization" and "syncretism" is one that Asian Christians often feel ill-qualified and hesitant to draw. This is owing both to a centuries-long habit of deferring to Western missionaries as their theological authority, as well as the entrenched presuppositions held by Western and Asian evangelicals alike which regard the use of Asian cultural traditions in doing theology as a modification of the gospel itself. In both Testaments, however, the gospel is *both* a set of propositional truths *as well as* an unfolding narrative of redemption that requires time, space, and human cultures to tell. Indeed, Dean Flemming's summary of contextualization in the NT is just as true of the OT with the latter's discerning combination of engagement, sifting, and rejection toward its cultural environment: "Contextualized theology is not just desirable; it is the only way theology can be done."[20]

THE RELATIONSHIP OF CONTEXTUALIZATION AND SYNCRETISM IN THE OT

We can go even further in retracing the shared footsteps of contextualization and the OT in their long journey together. To the extent that contextualization is pitted against syncretism (as in traditional missiology), it becomes

---

18. Eugene S. Heideman, "Syncretism, Contextualization, Orthodoxy, and Heresy," *Missiology: An International Review* 25 (1997): 37–38.
19. For the best overview and critique of various definitions, see André Droogers, "Syncretism: The Problem of Definition, the Definition of the Problem," in *Dialogue and Syncretism: An Interdisciplinary Approach*, eds. Jerald D. Gort et al., Currents of Encounter 1 (Grand Rapids, MI: Eerdmans, 1989), 7–25.
20. Flemming, *Contextualization in the New Testament*, 298.

surprisingly difficult to avoid placing the OT on the side of syncretism more than contextualization. This might be disconcerting for evangelicals like ourselves whose signature belief about the Bible is that it stands above all cultures. There are two reasons, however, that syncretism makes a frequent appearance in the OT. Both of them become obvious and less troubling in retrospect.

The first is that the OT is largely a record of Israel's failures to distinguish itself from the nations rather than its successes in living as a missional people to bless the nations.[21] As explored in chapter 6, for example, Israelite historiography is culturally unique for being state-sponsored media that does not hesitate to shame the state and its main actors rather than to honor them. In fact, this countercultural emphasis on truth-telling at the expense of the powerful is evident in each part of the Hebrew Bible: (1) the Pentateuch begins in Genesis with the halting faith of Israel's patriarchs but ends in Deuteronomy with Israel still outside the promised land; (2) the Former Prophets begin in Joshua with Israel conquering that land but end in 2 Kings with Israel ejected from it to Babylon; (3) the Latter Prophets reflect the tortuous process of attempting to prevent Israel's deportations from the land and the theological catastrophe that resulted after them; and (4) the Writings are a potpourri of the theological diversity that characterizes the OT as a whole. In sum, the OT is too self-critical to supply the confident starting point for theological reflection that conventional approaches to contextualization as communication or application have usually demanded. The issue is not so much that the OT is lacking in contextualization, but that missiology's anxiety to keep contextualization separate from syncretism has led to a sub-biblical understanding of both.

Lest the reader misunderstand, it bears repeating that the OT does not condone the abundance of syncretism described within its pages.[22] Quite the opposite – the painfully honest record of Israel's syncretism found in the OT's pages is a true-to-life picture of how complex are the negotiations between orthodoxy and heterodoxy that occur in reality. Such an ongoing struggle supplies a more relatable method for doing contextual theology than the once-for-all and all-at-once expressions of contextualization which are typically offered to

---

21. Van Rheenen, "Syncretism and Contextualization," 11–12.
22. The opening summary of the Chicago Statement on Biblical Inerrancy explains that the Bible "is to be believed, as God's instruction, *in all that it affirms*" (italics added; online version at https://www.etsjets.org/files/documents/Chicago_Statement.pdf). That is to say, only the *truth claims* of Scripture are true. Awareness of literary genres must thus be joined to humble, Spirit-led interpretation to distinguish properly between descriptive and prescriptive elements in the Bible.

and for Asian Christians by cultural outsiders.[23] In other words, taking the risk of syncretism was an indispensable part of how contextualization in and with the OT accomplished its centuries-long engagement with ancient Near Eastern cultures at every level of human existence, not only the so-called "religious" level.[24] Genuinely biblical transformation for God's people in Asia will demand a similarly rigorous engagement with every sphere of life. This makes the sprawling character of the OT an ideal supplier of source material for building conceptual bridges between the ancient Near East and the modern Far East. On this note, the challenges of doing contextual theology for this immense continent were memorably described in the following way by a group of ecumenical Asian theologians:

> Asia . . .
> We pause in silence
> Before the awesome reality of Asia,
> Her vastness, variety and complexity,
> Her peoples, languages, cultures.
> The richness of her history
> And the present poverty of peoples.[25]

The fact that Asian ecumenism has generally found the Bible inadequate for the task of doing contextual theology reflects how Bible-believing theologians (both Asian and non-Asian) have tended to relegate the OT's complex mix of contextualization and syncretism to the margins of the discussion. The result is that evangelical Christianity in Asia not only has a strongly NT-centric character, but is also typically still viewed in Asia as a Western religion.

The second reason for syncretism in the OT is that its own account of the gospel exhibits a paradoxical blend of contextualization and syncretism. In the gospel of Israel's exodus from Egypt,[26] there is already a "surplus of meaning" (to quote Paul Ricoeur) which transforms the usual dichotomy between

---

23. The classic example is the "Rites Controversy" of the sixteenth century among the Jesuits and Dominicans in China which occurred with minimal input from Chinese Catholics. A contemporary example would be the Insider Movements (IMs) which typically find more enthusiastic support from Western missionaries who are outsiders than from Asian Christians who are insiders (see n. 7 in ch. 1).

24. See ch. 4 for discussion.

25. Quoted by Pui-lan Kwok, *Discovering the Bible in the Non-Biblical World* (Maryknoll, NY: Orbis, 1995), 24.

26. As John Goldingay rightly notes, "the biblical gospel is not a collection of timeless statements such as God is love. It is a narrative about things God has done" (*Old Testament Theology: Israel's Gospel* [Downers Grove, IL: IVP Academic, 2003], 31).

history vs. myth from an *either-or* into a *both-and* proposition. The remarkable ability of the Exodus narrative to blend these ways of making meaning represents what Michael Fishbane, a leading Jewish scholar, has called "the myth-icization of history and the historicization of myth."[27] The historical picture of deliverance from Pharaoh's armies (Exod 14) is juxtaposed with the use of mythical images of cosmic chaos which Yahweh subdues in distinguishing himself among the *Elim* (Exod 15), thus making him the highest of deities within the familiar categories of the Canaanite pantheon and supplanting El as its traditional head.[28] In addition, the familiar descriptions of Yahweh's "strong hand and outstretched arm" (e.g. Exod 6:1, 6; 13:3; Deut 4:34; 5:15) represent the OT's satire toward Egyptian imagery of pharaohs fighting their enemies with cartoonishly large arms (see author's photo).[29]

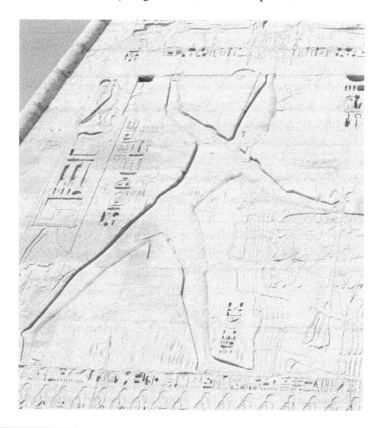

27. Michael Fishbane, *Text and Texture* (New York: Schocken, 1979), 136.
28. See ch. 3.
29. James K. Hoffmeier, "The Arm of God versus the Arm of Pharaoh in the Exodus Narratives," *Biblica* 67 (1986): 378–87.

Ironically, exodus language which modern readers assume to be biblical found its origin in polemical acts of cultural appropriation.[30] The original audience of these passages would have clearly perceived their attack on Egyptian military themes and their reassignment from Pharaoh to Yahweh. The interpretive questions that modern audiences naturally have about contextualization and syncretism would have been less urgent than Yahweh's unmistakable declaration that he is the only powerful deity and Pharaoh is not.[31] And as if this were not provocative enough, many later OT books also recontextualize the figure of the exodus into a prediction of Israel's return from exile as a "new exodus" (e.g. Jer 23:7–8; Hos 11:11), but now with King Cyrus of Persia as the leader of Yahweh's people rather than Moses (Isa 44:28 – 45:1). Incredibly, this saving event has also expanded beyond Israelites to encompass all nations (e.g. Isa 40–55), including empires like Assyria and Egypt from which Israel sought to escape (Isa 19:23–25)! The exodus clearly lies at the heart of OT faith as a dynamic pattern for contextualization and doing theology, rather than a static one.

The exodus was contextualized and recontextualized so successfully, in fact, that it became mangled by Yahweh's people into an excuse for syncretism of the sinful rather than neutral variety. Already in the time of Moses and Joshua, Israel misunderstood Yahweh's *power* to save through the exodus as Yahweh's *promise* to save in any circumstance. It was this near-magical confidence in the God of the exodus which drove the first and second generations of Israel into battles which resulted in several defeats at the hands of their enemies (e.g. Num 14; Josh 7; 1 Sam 4). When the Israelite kingdoms parted ways a few centuries later, Jeroboam I of the northern kingdom conjured up Israel's apostasy with the golden calf (Exod 32) by making not one golden calf but two of them, for his cultic sites at Dan and Bethel to replace Jerusalem in the southern kingdom (1 Kgs 12:28–32). This act evidently accelerated the distortion of Yahweh's intention through the exodus for Israel to "*know* that I am Yahweh" (e.g. Exod 6:7; 7:5). The people of Israel instead gained a sense

---

30. The modern worship song "Thank You Lord" (by Don Moen) has the line "with an outstretched arm/I will bless your name." The "outstretched arm" in the OT is always a military image which occurs in exodus contexts, but the song's author has turned it into a ritual action of lifting one's arms and hands for worship contexts. This would be syncretism, strictly speaking, but since the phrase is of biblical origin and may not be recognized by those singing the song, could it be viewed as an inadvertent act of (re)contextualization instead?

31. The pharaoh in Egyptian royal ideology was conceived as a god, making the exodus from Egypt mainly a battle between Yahweh and Pharaoh (Exod 9:13–17; 12:12) rather than between Moses/Aaron and Pharaoh or Yahweh and (other) gods of Egypt.

of entitlement that "O my god, we – Israel – have *known* you!"[32] (Hos 8:2) even as they continued blissfully in their sins. Amazingly, the book of Hosea confronts such syncretism by recontextualizing the exodus and "knowledge of God" (Hos 6:6), instead of discarding these frequently misunderstood ideas in the manner that one would expect.[33]

Most poignantly of all, the OT dares to use exodus imagery against Yahweh's people rather than for them. The destruction of Israel's first generation in the wilderness is described as the "anti-exodus" when "the LORD's hand was against them until he had completely eliminated them from the camp" (Deut 2:15). Spiritual complacency continued after Israel's conquest, however, so that Yahweh warns that Israel is far from unique among the nations in having an exodus in its history: "'Are not you Israelites the same to me as the Cushites?' declares the LORD. 'Did I not bring Israel up from Egypt, the Philistines from Caphtor and the Arameans from Kir?'" (Amos 9:7). Likewise at the end of biblical Israel's history, Yahweh turns the tables on stubborn Israel by asserting that he is no longer allied with his people: "I myself will fight against you with an outstretched hand and a mighty arm in furious anger and in great wrath" (Jer 21:5). The God of the exodus has now resolved to deploy his "outstretched hand" and "mighty arm" for the exile of his people!

In sum, the OT's many creative uses of the exodus are exemplary for their contextualization. Not only this, they are also syncretism by nearly every definition of the term (whether descriptive or prescriptive). It is telling that what Western scholarship (whether in OT studies or missiology) tends to label *syncretism* has provided a depth of cultural engagement in and with the OT which modern attempts at *contextualization* have not. Shallow contextualization of this sort is itself a form of syncretism which privileges the traditional categories of Western biblical scholarship and missiology.[34] According to the OT itself, however, the exodus is a contextualization of the gospel which is deeply biblical and authentically cultural for both including and transcending syncretism (whatever the definition) in the process of making Israel's counter-cultural faith meaningful. This indicates that attempts to distinguish between

---

32. Author's translation.
33. For details, see Jerry Hwang, "'I Am Yahweh Your God from the Land of Egypt': Hosea's Use of the Exodus Traditions," in *"Did I Not Bring Israel out of Egypt?" Biblical, Archaeological, and Egyptological Perspectives on the Exodus Narratives*, eds. James K. Hoffmeier, Alan R. Millard, and Gary A. Rendsburg, BBR Supplement Series 13 (Winona Lake, IN: Eisenbrauns, 2016), 243–53.
34. Jackson Wu, *One Gospel for All Nations: A Practical Approach to Biblical Contextualization* (Pasadena, CA: William Carey Library, 2015), 17–26.

contextualization and syncretism err in determining the boundaries between them to be identical to the lines drawn between orthodoxy and heterodoxy. By contrast, the OT presents syncretism more as the servant of contextualization and the latter's dynamic theological method than as its equal, opposite, or byproduct.

CONCLUSION

My twist on Tertullian's question has arrived at an unexpected conclusion. What hath contextualization to do with the OT? *Nearly everything*, since it was the OT's sustained cultural engagement, through and beyond the cognitive categories available in the ancient Near East, which enabled Israel to make a distinctive confession of faith in its time, place, and culture. As Moses summarized near the end of his second Deuteronomic speech,

> [Yahweh] your God is God of gods and Lord of lords, the great God, mighty and awesome, who shows no partiality and accepts no bribes. He defends the cause of the fatherless and the widow, and loves the foreigner residing among you, giving them food and clothing. And you are to love those who are foreigners, for you yourselves were foreigners in Egypt. (Deut 10:17–20)

The *transcendence* of this sovereign God is thus set against other "gods" and "lords." At the same time, his status as "great," "mighty," and "awesome" is also the basis for his *immanence* which opposes the corrupt and powerful while caring for the weak and lowly.

Indeed, retracing the steps of contextualization in and with the OT reveals Yahweh to be a unique deity whose incomparability comes precisely from taking over the titles, attributes, and abilities of other deities.[35] In this regard, the deliverance that he effects from all kinds of oppression also surpasses both Western accounts of the exodus as mainly *spiritual* salvation from sin,[36] as much as non-Western accounts of it as *economic*, *social*, or *physical* liberation.[37] He

---

35. See chs. 3–4.
36. E.g. Kenneth J. Turner, "Exodus," in *What the Old Testament Authors Really Cared About: A Survey of Jesus' Bible*, ed. Jason S. DeRouchie (Grand Rapids, MI: Kregel Academic, 2013), 91. In chapter 2, I suggested an Asian recontextualization of this understanding of sin and salvation.
37. E.g. the Minjung theology of Korea, treated most recently in Paul S. Chung, Kyoung-Jae Kim, and Veli-Matti Kärkkäinen, eds., *Asian Contextual Theology for the Third Millennium: A Theology of Minjung in Fourth-Eye Formation*, Princeton Theological Monograph Series 70 (Eugene, OR: Pickwick, 2007).

is thus the consummate Patron whose covenant relationship with his people imparts a countercultural freedom to give rather than receive,[38] as well as new understandings of honor and shame which are able to embrace weakness in addition to power.[39] By contrast, both the "God of the philosophers" (from the West) and the "God of the pantheists" (from the East) remain too small to encompass the uniquely vast *and* (not *but*) accessible God of the OT.[40]

The OT's difficult truth that Yahweh alone is the Sovereign over all realms (Exod 14; cf. 1 Sam 2; Luke 2; Acts 2) may provide another explanation for why OT scholarship and missiology in the West each struggle to see the symbiosis between the OT and contextualization. Both disciplines have traditionally resided in positions of power and privilege vis-à-vis non-Western cultures. But at this particular moment in the twenty-first century, it has become painfully clear that Christendom in the West remains plagued by the problems of exceptionalism and triumphalism toward the "other" (whether in imperialism or in Christian mission). The belated *decolonialization* of the West's relationship to the non-West as told in secular sources is well underway,[41] as seen also in how missions history is being rewritten with Majority-World Christians taking their rightful place at the table alongside the traditional accounts of Western historians and missiologists.[42] In short, the unholy alliances between faith and empire which often characterized Christendom are being turned inside out in

---

38. See ch. 5.

39. See ch. 6.

40. See chs. 7–8. On this note, the famous "Memorial" of Blaise Pascal, the French Christian thinker, records the overwhelming moment when the deity of the Bible became real to him as "the God of Abraham, God of Isaac, God of Jacob, not of philosophers and scholars. . . . The world forgotten, everything except God. . . . I will not neglect your Word. Amen." For the full text of the "Memorial" which Pascal had sewn into his coat lining to remind himself each day, see James M. Houston, ed., *The Mind on Fire: A Faith for the Skeptical and Indifferent, From the Writings of Blaise Pascal* (Portland, OR: Multnomah, 1989), 41–42.

41. For example, witness the soul-searching of *National Geographic* magazine for its long history of simultaneously demeaning and exoticizing non-Western peoples in presenting them as the "other" for white American readers (Susan Goldberg, "For Decades, Our Coverage Was Racist. To Rise above Our Past, We Must Acknowledge It," *National Geographic*, 12 March 2018, https://www.nationalgeographic.com/magazine/article/from-the-editor-race-racism-history). However, the magazine has also encountered major difficulties in following through on its promises (Anna North and Kainaz Amaria, "National Geographic Faced up to Its Racist Past. Did It Actually Get Better?," *Vox*, 6 May 2021, https://www.vox.com/22417191/national-geographic-racial-reckoning).

42. It bears asking why the academic discipline of "*church* history" is often limited to the Reformation and its aftermath in Europe and North America, while "*mission* history" then becomes the task of taking the gospel from the West to the rest. In actuality, the West has had its own history of receiving missionaries, while the Christian church started outside the West. For a more integrative and global approach, see the two-part work of Justo González, *The Story*

a manner resembling the OT's own answer to hegemony (whether political, cultural, economic, or military), especially when this sin was found in Israel itself.[43] The exodus-shaped faith of the OT instead requires an exodus-shaped life in which the sole Savior's people relinquish control and embrace frailty as the peculiarly countercultural way of honoring Yahweh as the Almighty rather than themselves.

This is why it would be mistaken for Asian Christians to "take the mantle of mission" from Western Christians by adopting the latter's missionary paternalism of the past as their own for the present.[44] Doing so would only repeat the reductionism of Tertullian in equating figurative "Jerusalem" with oneself or one's own destination and "Athens" with others who are pagan,[45] while overlooking how actual Jerusalem was sacked in 587/586 BC for attempting to throw off its God-given weakness and imitate the strength of Babylon, Egypt, and other empires. If Asian Christians are mindful of these pitfalls thanks to the help of contextualization in and with the OT, they can produce a deeply biblical, fully evangelical, and authentically Asian theology which overcomes the popular conception of Christianity as a Western religion of power and upward mobility. Few tasks are more difficult and urgent for evangelical Christianity in Asia today, so this book has sought to take modest steps in that direction.

---

of Christianity, Volume 1: The Early Church to the Reformation, rev. and updated ed. (New York: HarperCollins, 2010); and *The Story of Christianity, Volume 2: The Reformation to the Present Day*, rev. and updated ed. (New York: HarperCollins, 2010).

43. This important theme in the OT features in the work of Walter Brueggemann, as explored comprehensively in his *Theology of the Old Testament: Testimony, Dispute, Advocacy* (Minneapolis, MN: Fortress, 2005).

44. Korean missiologists are increasingly noting this pitfall in their own movements which other Asian Christians do well to heed. For one such example, see Joon-Sik Park, "Korean Protestant Christianity: A Missiological Reflection," *International Bulletin of Missionary Research* 36 (Apr. 2012): 59–64.

45. This is a potential weakness of Chinese missions movements which see themselves as playing an unparalleled role in fulfilling the Great Commission. Some elements of the Back to Jerusalem movement and Christian advocates of China's recent "One Belt, One Road" economic initiative, for example, explicitly hold to the exceptionalism that Chinese Christians are set apart by God for the purpose of evangelizing the unreached in the hardest places. Within these movements are also pronounced emphases on physical "Jerusalem" as the final destination of Chinese evangelism efforts and the worldliness of Western Christians which supposedly makes them unavailable to complete the task. For a balanced analysis of the Back to Jerusalem movement in particular, see James Sung-Hwan Park, "Chosen to Fulfill the Great Commission? Biblical and Theological Reflections on the Back to Jerusalem Vision of Chinese Churches," *Missiology: An International Review* 43 (Apr. 2015): 163–74.

Looking ahead and beyond Asia, one might refine Tertullian's question again and ask: *Whither next*, contextualization and the OT? Besides invigorating Asian Christianity, a thoroughly Asian contextual theology of the OT may also prove useful to Western Christianity at a time when it is still frequently compromised by the syncretism of imagining itself to be the center and the non-West to be the periphery.[46] The resulting tendency to read the Bible in one's own cultural image is accelerating the downfall of Christendom and the deepening of the post-Christian age in the West.

This is not to say, of course, that Asian Christians possess an exclusive hold on "Jerusalem" which is superior to the West as "Athens." The OT is divine revelation which makes abundantly clear that all human cultures are fallen. Yet none of them is beyond Yahweh's redemption, whether in the ancient Near East, modern Far East, or any era and locality in the West. The beauty of the "First Testament" thus lies in its unique ability to propound the exclusive truth of salvation by Yahweh alone, even as it has few qualms about "plundering the Egyptians" (Exod 12:36; cf. Hag 2:7) for their cultural treasures to communicate its universal but countercultural message. Indeed, the ability of future generations of Christians to answer wisely the question *Whither next, contextualization and the Old Testament?* will play a major role in God's plan to bring all nations to worship him forever in all their rich diversity (Rev 7:9–10; cf. Pss 87; 96). May the OT continue to be God's instrument in training his people to do contextual theology and live missionally in Asia and beyond. They have the enormous privilege of joining God in his mighty work of writing the last chapter in his great drama of redemption.[47]

---

46. The persistence of a Eurocentric frame of reference is evident in how a venerated missions historian like Philip Jenkins nonetheless speaks of "the coming of global Christianity" as the arrival of "the next Christendom" (to quote the subtitle and title of his influential book *The Next Christendom: The Coming of Global Christianity*, 3rd ed. [Oxford: Oxford University Press, 2011]), as if moving the periphery to the center is logical and inevitable. It is odd to speak of global Christianity's "coming" when it only went "missing" from a Western perspective. As Chinese-American missiologist Allen Yeh notes, it is more accurate to speak of global Christianity as having multiple centers and no periphery (*Polycentric Missiology: 21st-Century Mission from Everyone to Everywhere* [Downers Grove, IL: IVP Academic, 2016]).

47. The God-centered and others-directed character of true Christian living is well explored by Craig G. Bartholomew and Michael W. Goheen, *The Drama of Scripture: Finding Our Place in the Biblical Story*, 2nd ed. (Grand Rapids: Baker Academic, 2014).

BIBLIOGRAPHY

Abd-Allah, Umar F. "Do Christians and Muslims Worship the Same God?"
Christian Century 121 (24 Aug. 2004): 34–36.

Acevedo, Gabriel A. "Islamic Fatalism and the Clash of Civilizations: An Appraisal of a Contentious and Dubious Theory." *Social Forces* 86 (2008): 1711–52.

Albrektson, Bertil. *History and the Gods: An Essay on the Idea of Historical Events as Divine Manifestations in the Ancient Near East and in Israel.* Coniectanea Biblica: Old Testament Series 1. Lund: C. W. K. Gleerup, 1967.

Ali, Ahmed. *Al-Qurʾān: A Contemporary Translation.* Princeton: Princeton University Press, 2001.

Allen, Michael. "Exodus 3 after the Hellenization Thesis." *Journal of Theological Interpretation* 3 (2009): 179–96.

Anderson, Gary A. *Sin: A History.* London: Yale University Press, 2010.

Archer, Jr., Gleason L. "Contextualization: Some Implications from Life and Witness in the Old Testament." In *New Horizons in World Mission: Evangelicals and the Christian Mission in the 1980s – Papers and Responses Prepared for the Consultation on Theology and Mission, Trinity Evangelical Divinity School, School of World Mission and Evangelism, March 19–22, 1979,* edited by David J. Hesselgrave, 199–216. Grand Rapids: Baker, 1979.

Asano-Tamanoi, Mariko. "Shame, Family, and State in Catalonia and Japan." In *Honor and Shame and the Unity of the Mediterranean,* edited by David D. Gilmore, 104–20. Washington DC: American Anthropological Association, 1987.

Assmann, Jan. "Mono-, Pan-, and Cosmotheism: Thinking the 'One' in Egyptian Theology." *Orient* 33 (1998): 130–49.

Athyal, Saphir. "The Old Testament Contextualisations." *World Evangelization Magazine,* October 1997: 8–9.

Bahnson, Fred, and Norman Wirzba. *Making Peace with the Land: God's Call to Reconcile with Creation.* Downers Grove: InterVarsity Press, 2012.

Barbour, Jennifer. *The Story of Israel in the Book of Qohelet: Ecclesiastes as Cultural Memory.* Oxford Theological Monographs. Oxford: Oxford University Press, 2012.

Barkan, Elazar. *The Guilt of Nations: Restitution and Negotiating Historical Injustices.* New York: Norton, 2000.

Barr, James. *The Semantics of Biblical Language.* Oxford: Oxford University Press, 1961.

———. "Theophany and Anthropomorphism in the Old Testament." In *Congress Volume Oxford 1959,* edited by G. W. Anderson, P. A. H. de Boer, G. R.

Castellino, Henri Cazelles, E. Hammershaimb, H. G. May, and W. Zimmerli, 31–38. Supplements to Vetus Testamentum 7. Leiden: Brill, 1960.

Bartholomew, Craig G., and Michael W. Goheen. *The Drama of Scripture: Finding Our Place in the Biblical Story.* 2nd ed. Grand Rapids: Baker Academic, 2014.

Bauckham, Richard. *Bible and Ecology: Rediscovering the Community of Creation.* Waco: Baylor University Press, 2010.

———. *Bible and Mission: Christian Witness in a Postmodern World.* Grand Rapids: Baker Academic, 2003.

Bavinck, Herman. *Reformed Dogmatics.* Edited by John Bolt. Translated by John Vriend. 4 vols. Grand Rapids: Baker Academic, 2003.

Bays, Daniel H., ed. "The Growth of Independent Christianity in China, 1900–1937." In *Christianity in China: From the Eighteenth Century to the Present,* 307–16. Stanford: Stanford University Press, 1996.

Bechtel, Lyn M. "The Perception of Shame within the Divine-Human Relationship in Biblical Israel." In *Uncovering Ancient Stones: Essays in Memory of H. Neil Richardson,* edited by Lewis M. Hopfe, 79–92. Winona Lake: Eisenbrauns, 1994.

Bediako, Kwame. "The Willowbank Consultation Jan 1978: A Personal Reflection." *Themelios* 5 (Jan. 1980): 25–32.

Benedict, Ruth. *The Chrysanthemum and the Sword: Patterns of Japanese Culture.* Boston: Houghton Mifflin, 1946.

Berlin, Adele. *The Dynamics of Biblical Parallelism.* 2nd ed. Grand Rapids: Eerdmans, 2008.

Bevans, Stephen B. *Models of Contextual Theology.* Rev. and expanded ed. Faith and Cultures Series. Maryknoll: Orbis, 2002.

Blenkinsopp, Joseph. "Fragments of Ancient Exegesis in an Isaian Poem (Isaiah 2:6–22)." In *Essays on the Book of Isaiah,* 135–41. Forschungen zum Alten Testament 128. Tübingen: Mohr Siebeck, 2019.

Block, Daniel I. *The Book of Ezekiel, Chapters 1–24.* New International Commentary on the Old Testament. Grand Rapids: Eerdmans, 1997.

———. "The Burden of Leadership: The Mosaic Paradigm on Kingship (Deut 17:14–20)." *Bibliotheca Sacra* 162 (2005): 259–78.

———. "Other Religions in Old Testament Theology." In *Biblical Faith and Other Religions: An Evangelical Assessment,* edited by David W. Baker, 43–78. Grand Rapids: Kregel, 2004.

Bock, Darrell L. *Recovering the Real Lost Gospel: Reclaiming the Gospel as Good News.* Nashville: B&H Academic, 2010.

Boiger, Michael, Derya Güngör, Mayumi Karasawa, and Batja Mesquita. "Defending Honour, Keeping Face: Interpersonal Affordances of Anger and Shame in Turkey and Japan." *Cognition and Emotion* 28 (2014): 1255–69.

Boles, Elson. "Ruth Benedict's Japan: The Benedictions of Imperialism." *Dialectical Anthropology* 1–2 (2006): 27–70.

Bosch, David J. "Mission in Biblical Perspective." *International Review of Mission* 74 (1985): 531–38.

———. *Transforming Mission: Paradigm Shifts in Theology of Mission.* Maryknoll: Orbis, 1991.

Bowe, Barbara E. "Reading the Bible through Filipino Eyes." *Missiology: An International Review* 26 (1998): 345–60.

Bray, Gerald. *Biblical Interpretation: Past and Present.* Downers Grove: IVP Academic, 1996.

Brett, Mark G. *Decolonizing God: The Bible in the Tides of Empire.* Sheffield: Sheffield Phoenix Press, 2009.

Brettler, Marc. "Cyclical and Teleological Time in the Hebrew Bible." In *Time and Temporality in the Ancient World*, edited by Ralph M. Rosen, 111–28. Philadelphia: University of Pennsylvania Museum of Archaeology and Anthropology, 2004.

Brichto, H. C. *The Names of God: Poetic Readings in Biblical Beginnings.* New York: Oxford University Press, 1998.

Broomhall, Marshall. *The Bible in China.* London: China Inland Mission, 1934.

Brown, Rick. "Who Was 'Allah' before Islam? Evidence That the Term 'Allah' Originated with Jewish and Christian Arabs." In *Toward Respectful Understanding and Witness among Muslims: Essays in Honor of J. Dudley Woodberry*, edited by Evelyne A. Reisacher, 147–78. Pasadena: William Carey Library, 2012.

Brown, Robert McAfee. *Theology in a New Key: Responding to Liberation Themes.* 1st ed. Philadelphia: Westminster, 1978.

Brueggemann, Walter. *First and Second Samuel.* Interpretation. Louisville: John Knox, 1990.

———. *Theology of the Old Testament: Testimony, Dispute, Advocacy.* Minneapolis: Fortress, 2005.

Bundvad, Mette. *Time in the Book of Ecclesiastes.* Oxford Theology and Religion Monographs. Oxford: Oxford University Press, 2015.

Burnett, David. *The Spirit of Hinduism: A Christian Perspective on Hindu Thought.* Tunbridge Wells: Monarch, 1992.

Campbell, Ronnie P., and Christopher Gnanakan, eds. *Do Christians, Muslims, and Jews Worship the Same God? Four Views.* Counterpoints. Grand Rapids: Zondervan, 2019.

Carasik, Michael. "Qohelet's Twists and Turns." *Journal for the Study of the Old Testament* 28 (2003): 192–209.

Carroll, Robert P. "The Aniconic God and the Cult of Images." *Studia Theologica: Nordic Journal of Theology* 31 (1977): 51–64.

———. "Synchronic Deconstructions of Jeremiah: Diachrony to the Rescue? Reflections on Some Reading Strategies for Understanding Certain Problems in the Book of Jeremiah." In *Synchronic or Diachronic? A Debate on Method in Old Testament Exegesis*, edited by J. C. de Moor, 39–51. Leiden: Brill, 1995.

Cashin, David. "I Cannot Worship a God Who Does Not Understand Human Suffering." *Evangelical Missions Quarterly* Occasional Bulletin (Special Edition 2016): 8–9.

Catholic News Agency. "'Yahweh' Not to Be Used in Liturgy, Songs and Prayers, Cardinal Arinze Says." 3 September 2008. https://www.catholicnewsagency.com/news/13696/yahweh-not-to-be-used-in-liturgy-songs-and-prayers-cardinal-arinze-says.

Ceresko, Anthony R. "Psalm 121: A Prayer of a Warrior?" *Biblica* 70 (1989): 496–510.

Chai, Sun-Ki, Ming Liu, and Min-Sun Kim. "Cultural Comparisons of Beliefs and Values: Applying the Grid-Group Approach to the World Values Survey." *Beliefs and Values* 1 (2009): 193–208.

Chan, Adrian. "The Sinless Chinese: A Christian Translation Dilemma?" In *Translating Sensitive Texts: Linguistic Aspects*, edited by Karl Simms, 239–43. Approaches to Translation Studies 14. Amsterdam: Rodopi, 1997.

Chan, Simon. *Grassroots Asian Theology: Thinking the Faith from the Ground Up*. Downers Grove: InterVarsity Press, 2014.

Chance, John. "The Anthropology of Honor and Shame: Culture, Values and Practice." *Semeia* 68 (1996): 139–51.

Chang, Lit-Sen. *Asia's Religions: Christianity's Momentous Encounter with Paganism*. San Gabriel: China Horizon, 1999.

Chapman, Stephen B. "Reading the Bible as Witness: Divine Retribution in the Old Testament." *Perspectives in Religious Studies* 31 (2004): 171–90.

Chenet, François. "Karma and Astrology: An Unrecognized Aspect of Indian Anthropology." *Diogenes* 33 (1985): 101–26.

Cherian, M. T. "Astrology." In *South Asia Bible Commentary: A One-Volume Commentary on the Whole Bible*, edited by Brian C. Wintle. Grand Rapids: Zondervan Academic, 2015.

Chin, Clive S. *The Perception of Christianity as a Rational Religion in Singapore: A Missiological Analysis of Christian Conversion*. American Society of Missiology Monograph Series 31. Eugene: Pickwick, 2017.

Chow, Alexander. "The East Asian Rediscovery of Sin." *Studies in World Christianity* 19 (2013): 126–40.

Chung, Paul S., Kyoung-Jae Kim, and Veli-Matti Kärkkäinen, eds. *Asian Contextual Theology for the Third Millennium: A Theology of Minjung in Fourth-Eye Formation*. Princeton Theological Monograph Series 70. Eugene: Pickwick, 2007.

Cohen, Erik. "Christianity and Buddhism in Thailand: The 'Battle of the Axes' and the 'Contest of Power.'" *Social Compass* 38 (1991): 115–40.

Conn, Harvie M. *Eternal Word and Changing Worlds: Theology, Anthropology, and Mission in Trialogue*. Grand Rapids: Zondervan, 1984.

Coogan, Michael D. *A Reader of Ancient Near Eastern Texts: Sources for the Study of the Old Testament*. Oxford: Oxford University Press, 2013.

Cook, Matthew. "Foreword." In *Local Theology for the Global Church: Principles for an Evangelical Approach to Contextualization*, edited by Matthew Cook, Rob Haskell, Ruth Julian, and Natee Tanchanpongs, vii–viii. Pasadena: William Carey Library, 2010.

Corduan, Winfried. *Neighboring Faiths: A Christian Introduction to World Religions*. 2nd ed. Downers Grove: IVP Academic, 2012.

Corwin, Gary. "A Second Look: Telling the Difference." *Evangelical Missions Quarterly* 40 (2004): 282–83.

Covell, Ralph. "Bible Translation in the Asian Setting." *The Bible Translator* 15 (1964): 132–42.

Craig, William Lane. "Time." In *Global Dictionary of Theology: A Resource for the Worldwide Church*, edited by William A. Dyrness and Veli-Matti Kärkkäinen, 899–901. Downers Grove: IVP Academic, 2008.

Creach, Jerome F. D. "Psalm 121." *Interpretation* 50 (1996): 47–51.

Creighton, Millie R. "Revisiting Shame and Guilt Cultures: A Forty-Year Pilgrimage." *Ethos* 18 (Sep. 1990): 279–307.

Crook, Zeba. "Honor, Shame, and Social Status Revisited." *Journal of Biblical Literature* 128 (2009): 591–611.

———. "Reciprocity: Covenantal Exchange as a Test Case." In *Ancient Israel: The Old Testament in Its Social Context*, edited by Philip F. Esler, 78–91. Minneapolis: Fortress, 2006.

Cross, Frank M. *Canaanite Myth and Hebrew Epic: Essays in the History of Religion of Israel*. Cambridge: Harvard University Press, 1973.

———. "Kinship and Covenant in Ancient Israel." In *From Epic to Canon: History and Literature in Ancient Israel*, 3–21. Baltimore: The Johns Hopkins University Press, 1998.

———. "Notes on a Canaanite Psalm in the Old Testament." *Bulletin of the American Schools of Oriental Research* 117 (1950): 19–21.

Crouch, Andy. "The Return of Shame." *Christianity Today*, 10 March 2015. https://www.christianitytoday.com/ct/2015/march/andy-crouch-gospel-in-age-of-public-shame.html.

Cserháti, Márta. "The Insider/Outsider Debate and the Study of the Bible." *Communio Viatorum* 50 (2008): 313–22.

Currid, John D. *Against the Gods: The Polemical Theology of the Old Testament*. Wheaton: Crossway, 2013.

Danielsen, Sabrina. "Fracturing over Creation Care? Shifting Environmental Beliefs among Evangelicals, 1984–2010." *Journal for the Scientific Study of Religion* 52 (2013): 198–215.

Davies, Graham. "Covenant, Oath, and the Composition of the Pentateuch." In *Covenant as Context: Essays in Honour of E. W. Nicholson*, edited by A. D. H. Mayes and R. B. Salters, 71–89. Oxford: Oxford University Press, 2003.

Day, John. "Psalm 104 and Akhenaten's Hymn to the Sun." In *Jewish and Christian Approaches to the Psalms: Conflict and Convergence*, edited by Susan E. Gillingham, 211–28. Oxford: Oxford University Press, 2013.

———. *Yahweh and the Gods and Goddesses of Canaan*. JSOT Supplement Series. Sheffield: Sheffield Academic Press, 2000.

Dell, Katharine. "The Cycle of Life in Ecclesiastes." *Vetus Testamentum* 59 (2009): 181–89.

DeSilva, David A. *Despising Shame: Honor Discourse and Community Maintenance in the Epistle to the Hebrews*. SBL Dissertation Series 152. Atlanta: Scholars Press, 1995.

———. *Honor, Patronage, Kinship and Purity: Unlocking New Testament Culture*. Downers Grove: InterVarsity Press, 2000.

———. *The Hope of Glory: Honor Discourse and New Testament Interpretation*. Eugene: Wipf and Stock, 2009.

DeVries, Simon J. *Yesterday, Today and Tomorrow: Time and History in the Old Testament*. Grand Rapids: Eerdmans, 1975.

Dewan, Parvez. *The Name of Allāh*. New Delhi: Penguin Books India, 2003.

Dick, Michael B. "Prophetic Parodies of Making the Cult Image." In *Born in Heaven, Made on Earth: The Making of the Cult Image in the Ancient Near East*, edited by Michael B. Dick, 1–53. Winona Lake: Eisenbrauns, 1999.

Dijkstra, Meindert. "El, YHWH and Their Asherah: On Continuity and Discontinuity in Canaanite and Ancient Israelite Religion." In *Ugarit – Ein ostmediterranes Kulturzentrum im Alten Orient: Ergebnisse und Perspektiven der Forschung*, edited by Manfried Dietrich and Oswald Loretz, 43–73. Abhandlungen zur Literatur Alt-Syrien-Palästinas 7. Münster: Ugarit-Verlag, 1995.

Dillard, Raymond B. "Reward and Punishment in Chronicles: The Theology of Immediate Retribution." *Westminster Theological Journal* 46 (1984): 164–72.

Dion, Paul E. "YHWH as Storm-god and Sun-god: The Double Legacy of Egypt and Canaan as Reflected in Psalm 104." *Zeitschrift für die alttestamentliche Wissenschaft* 103 (1991): 43–71.

Doi, Takeo. *The Anatomy of Dependence*. Translated by John Bester. New York: Kodansha USA, 2014.

Domeris, W. R. "Shame and Honour in Proverbs: Wise Women and Foolish Men." *Old Testament Essays* 8 (1995): 86–102.

Douglas, Mary. *Natural Symbols: Explorations in Cosmology*. London: Barrie and Jenkins, 1973.

Dower, John W. *Embracing Defeat: Japan in the Wake of World War II*. New York: Norton, 1999.

Droogers, André. "Syncretism: The Problem of Definition, the Definition of the Problem." In *Dialogue and Syncretism: An Interdisciplinary Approach*, edited by Jerald D. Gort, Hendrik M. Vroom, Rein Fernhout, and Anton Wessels, 7–25. Currents of Encounter 1. Grand Rapids: Eerdmans, 1989.

Dyrness, William A. *Insider Jesus: Theological Reflections on New Christian Movements*. Downers Grove: IVP Academic, 2016.

———. *Visual Faith: Art, Theology, and Worship in Dialogue*. Engaging Culture. Grand Rapids: Baker Academic, 2001.

The Earth Bible Team. "The Voice of Earth: More Than Metaphor?" In *The Earth Story in the Psalms and the Prophets*, edited by Norman C. Habel, 23–28. The Earth Bible 4. Sheffield: Sheffield Academic Press, 2001.

Eber, Irene. "The Interminable Term Question." In *The Bible in Modern China: The Literary and Intellectual Impact*, edited by Irene Eber, 135–61. Monumenta Serica Monograph Series 43. Nettetal: Steyler Verlag, 1999.

Eichrodt, Walther. *Theology of the Old Testament*. 2 vols. Old Testament Library. Philadelphia: Westminster Press, 1967.

Ellis, Teresa Ann. "Jeremiah 44: What If 'the Queen of Heaven' Is YHWH?" *Journal for the Study of the Old Testament* 33 (2009): 465–88.

Enriquez, Virgilio G. "Filipino Psychology in the Third World." *Philippine Journal of Psychology* 10 (1977): 3–18.

Farhadian, Charles E. *Introducing World Religions: A Christian Engagement*. Grand Rapids: Baker Academic, 2015.

Fisch, Harold. *Poetry with a Purpose: Biblical Poetics and Interpretation*. Bloomington, IN: Indiana University Press, 1988.

Fishbane, Michael. *Biblical Myth and Rabbinic Mythmaking*. Oxford: Oxford University Press, 2005.

———. *Text and Texture*. New York: Schocken, 1979.

Flanders, Christopher L. "There Is No Such Thing as 'Honor' or 'Honor Cultures.'" In *Devoted to Christ: Missiological Reflections in Honor of Sherwood G. Lingenfelter*, edited by Christopher L. Flanders, 145–66. Eugene: Pickwick, 2019.

Flemming, Dean E. *Contextualization in the New Testament: Patterns for Theology and Mission*. Downers Grove: IVP Academic, 2005.

Flueckiger, Joyce Burkhalter. *Everyday Hinduism*. Lived Religions 1. Chichester: Wiley-Blackwell, 2015.

Freedman, David Noel. "'Who Is Like Thee among the Gods?' The Religion of Early Israel." In *Ancient Israelite Religion: Essays in Honor of Frank Moore Cross*, edited by Patrick D. Miller, 315–55. Philadelphia: Fortress, 1987.

Frege, Gottlob. "Sense and Reference." *The Philosophical Review* 57 (May 1948): 209–30.

Fretheim, Terence E. *God and World in the Old Testament: A Relational Theology of Creation*. Nashville: Abingdon, 2005.

———. "The Repentance of God: A Study of Jeremiah 18:7–10." *Hebrew Annual Review* 11 (1987): 81–92.

———. *The Suffering of God: An Old Testament Perspective*. Overtures to Biblical Theology. Philadelphia: Fortress, 1984.

Friedman, Thomas L. *The World Is Flat: A Brief History of the Twenty-First Century*. Updated and expanded ed. New York: Farrar, Strauss, and Giroux, 2007.

Frye, Northrop. *The Great Code: The Bible and Literature*. London: Routledge & Kegan Paul, 1982.

Fuad, Chelcent. "El, Baal, and Allah: The Translatability of Divine Names in Ancient Israel and Contemporary Indonesia." *International Review of Mission* 108 (June 2019): 178–93.

Furukawa, Emi, June Tangney, and Fumiko Higashibara. "Cross-Cultural Continuities and Discontinuities in Shame, Guilt, and Pride: A Study of Children Residing in Japan, Korea and the USA." *Self and Identity* 11 (2012): 90–113.

Gabler, Johann P. "An Oration on the Proper Distinction between Biblical and Dogmatic Theology and the Specific Objectives of Each." In *Old Testament Theology: Flowering and Future*, edited by Ben C. Ollenburger, translated by John Sandys-Wunsch and Laurence Eldredge, 498–506. Rev. ed. Sources for Biblical and Theological Study 1. Winona Lake: Eisenbrauns, 2004.

Garr, W. Randall. "The Grammar and Interpretation of Exodus 6:3." *Journal of Biblical Literature* 111 (1992): 385–408.

Garside, Charles. *Zwingli and the Arts*. New Haven: Yale University Press, 1966.

Gelman, Samuel. "Disney+ Updates Offensive Content Disclaimer for Aladdin, Peter Pan and More." CBR. https://www.cbr.com/disney-plus-update-disclaimer-aladdin-peter-pan/.

Georges, Jayson. *Ministering in Patronage Cultures: Biblical Models and Missional Implications*. Downers Grove: InterVarsity Press, 2019.

———. *The 3D Gospel: Ministry in Guilt, Shame, and Fear Cultures*. Updated and revised ed. [N.p.]: Timē Press, 2016.

Georges, Jayson, and Mark D. Baker. *Ministering in Honor-Shame Cultures: Biblical Foundations and Practical Essentials*. Downers Grove: IVP Academic, 2016.

Gericke, Jaco. *The Hebrew Bible and Philosophy of Religion*. SBL Resources for Biblical Study 70. Atlanta: Society of Biblical Literature, 2012.

Gilmore, David D., ed. *Honor and Shame and the Unity of the Mediterranean*. Washington DC: American Anthropological Association, 1987.

———. "Introduction." In *Honor and Shame and the Unity of the Mediterranean*, edited by David D. Gilmore, 2–21. Washington DC: American Anthropological Association, 1987.

Girardot, Norman J. *The Victorian Translation of China: James Legge's Oriental Pilgrimage*. Berkeley: University of California Press, 2002.

Glaser, Ida. "The Concept of Relationship as a Key to the Comparative Understanding of Christianity and Islam." *Themelios* 11 (Jan. 1986): 57–60.

Glasser, Arthur F. "Old Testament Contextualization: Revelation and Its Environment." In *The Word among Us: Contextualizing Theology for Mission Today*, edited by Dean S. Gilliland. Eugene: Wipf and Stock, 2002.

Gnanakan, Ken. *Proclaiming Christ in a Pluralistic Context*. Bangalore: Theological Book Trust, 2002.

"God, *n.* and *int.*" OED Online. March 2022. Oxford University Press. https://www.oed.com/view/Entry/79625.

Goheen, Michael W. *A Light to the Nations: The Missional Church and the Biblical Story*. Grand Rapids: Baker Academic, 2011.

Goldberg, Susan. "For Decades, Our Coverage Was Racist. To Rise above Our Past, We Must Acknowledge It." *National Geographic*, 12 March 2018. https://www.nationalgeographic.com/magazine/article/from-the-editor-race-racism-history.

Goldingay, John. *Key Questions about Christian Faith: Old Testament Answers*. Grand Rapids: Baker Academic, 2010.

———. *Old Testament Theology: Israel's Gospel*. Downers Grove: IVP Academic, 2003.

———. *Psalms: Volume 1 (1–41)*. Grand Rapids: Baker Academic, 2006.

González, Justo L. *The Story of Christianity, Volume 1: The Early Church to the Reformation*. Rev. and updated ed. New York: HarperCollins, 2010.

———. *The Story of Christianity, Volume 2: The Reformation to the Present Day*. Rev. and updated ed. New York: HarperCollins, 2010.

Good, Edwin M. *Irony in the Old Testament*. 2nd ed. Bible and Literature Series. Sheffield: Almond Press, 1981.

———. "The Unfilled Sea: Style and Meaning in Ecclesiastes 1:2–11." In *Israelite Wisdom: Theological and Literary Essays in Honor of Samuel Terrien*, edited by John G. Gammie, Walter A. Brueggemann, W. Lee Humphreys, and James M. Ward, 59–73. Missoula: Scholars, 1978.

Gorospe, Vitaliano R. "Christian Renewal of Filipino Values." *Philippine Studies* 14 (1966): 191–227.

Gottwald, Norman K. *The Tribes of Yahweh: A Sociology of the Religion of Liberated Israel, 1250–1050 BCE*. Sheffield: Sheffield Academic Press, 1999.

Green, Gene L. "Relevance Theory and Biblical Interpretation." In *The Linguist as Pedagogue: Trends in the Teaching and Linguistic Analysis of the Greek New Testament*, edited by Stanley E. Porter and Matthew Brook O'Donnell, 217–40. Sheffield: Sheffield Phoenix, 2009.

Greenspahn, Frederick E. "Syncretism and Idolatry in the Bible." *Vetus Testamentum* 44 (2004): 480–94.

Greenstein, Edward L. "The God of Israel and the Gods of Canaan: How Different Were They?" In *Proceedings of the Twelfth World Congress of Jewish Studies*, 47–58. Jerusalem: World Union of Jewish Studies, 1999.

Gregerson, Linda, and Susan Juster, eds. "Introduction." In *Empires of God: Religious Encounters in the Early Modern Atlantic*, 1–15. Philadelphia: University of Pennsylvania Press, 2010.

"Grievous, *adj.*" OED Online. March 2022. Oxford University Press. https://www.oed.com/view/Entry/81409.

Groothuis, Douglas R. *Unmasking the New Age*. Downers Grove: InterVarsity Press, 1986.

Grudem, Wayne A. *Systematic Theology: An Introduction to Biblical Doctrine*. Grand Rapids: Zondervan Academic, 1995.

Gundry, Stanley N. "Evangelical Theology: Where Should We Be Going?" *Journal of the Evangelical Theological Society* 22, no. 1 (March 1979): 3–13.

Gupta, Nijay K. "'They Are Not Gods!' Jewish and Christian Idol Polemic and Greco-Roman Use of Cult Statues." *Catholic Biblical Quarterly* 76 (2014): 704–19.

Hall, Edward T. *Beyond Culture*. New York: Anchor, 1976.

Halpern, Baruch. *David's Secret Demons: Messiah, Murderer, Traitor, King*. Grand Rapids: Eerdmans, 2001.

Harding, Jacob. "Corruption or Guanxi? Differentiating between the Legitimate, Unethical, and Corrupt Activities of Chinese Government Officials." *Pacific Basin Law Journal* 31 (2014): 127–46.

Harnack, Adolf von. *What Is Christianity? Sixteen Lectures Delivered in the University of Berlin 1899–1900*. Repr. ed. San Diego: Book Tree, 2006.

Harrison, Carol. *Beauty and Revelation in the Thought of Saint Augustine*. Oxford Theological Monographs. Oxford: Oxford University Press, 1992.

Haug, Kari Storstein, and Knut Holter. "No Graven Image? Reading the Second Commandment in a Thai Context." *Asia Journal of Theology* 14 (2000): 20–36.

Haughn, Darren. "A Low-Context Dude in High-Context Places." *The Salty Egg* (blog), 11 March 2018. https://thesaltyegg.net/a-low-context-dude-in-a-high-context-culture/.

Havea, Jione, and Peter H. W. Lau, eds. *Reading Ecclesiastes from Asia and Pasifika*. International Voices in Biblical Studies 10. Atlanta: SBL Press, 2020.

Healey, John F. "The Kindly and Merciful God: On Some Semitic Divine Epithets." In *"Und Mose schrieb dieses Lied auf": Studien zum Alten Testament und zum alten Orient: Festschrift für Oswald Loretz zur Vollendung seines 70. Lebensjahres mit Beiträgen von Freunden, Schülern und Kollegen*, edited by Oswald Loretz, Manfried Dietrich, and Ingo Kottsieper, 349–56. Alter Orient und Altes Testament 250. Münster: Ugarit-Verlag, 1998.

Heideman, Eugene S. "Syncretism, Contextualization, Orthodoxy, and Heresy." *Missiology: An International Review* 25 (1997): 37–49.

Heim, Knut M. "Psalm 23 in the Age of the Wolf." *Christianity Today*, February 2016: 60–63.

Heimerdinger, Jean-Marc. "The God of Abraham." *Vox Evangelica* 22 (1992): 41–55.

Heiser, Michael S. "Monotheism, Polytheism, Monolatry, or Henotheism? Toward an Assessment of Divine Plurality in the Hebrew Bible." *Bulletin for Biblical Research* 18 (2008): 1–30.

Herrera, Robert A. *Reasons for Our Rhymes: An Inquiry into the Philosophy of History*. Grand Rapids: Eerdmans, 2001.

Herzfeld, Michael. "Honour and Shame: Problems in the Comparative Analysis of Moral Systems." *Man* 59 (1980): 339–51.

Heschel, Abraham J. *The Prophets*. 2 vols. New York: Harper & Row, 1962.

———. *The Sabbath: Its Meaning for Modern Man*. New York: Farrar, Strauss, and Giroux, 1951.

Hess, Richard S. *Israelite Religions: An Archaeological and Biblical Survey*. Grand Rapids: Baker Academic, 2007.

Hesselgrave, David J. *Paradigms in Conflict: 10 Key Questions in Christian Missions Today*. Grand Rapids: Kregel, 2005.

Hesselgrave, David J., and Edward Rommen. *Contextualization: Meanings, Methods, and Models*. Pasadena: William Carey Library, 2000.

Hickel, Jason. "How Britain Stole $45 Trillion from India: And Lied about It." Al Jazeera, 19 December 2018. https://www.aljazeera.com/opinions/2018/12/19/how-britain-stole-45-trillion-from-india.

Hiebert, Paul G. *Transforming Worldviews: An Anthropological Understanding of How People Change*. Grand Rapids: Baker Academic, 2008.

Hiebert, Paul G., R. Daniel Shaw, and Tite Tiénou. *Understanding Folk Religion: A Christian Response to Popular Beliefs and Practices*. Grand Rapids: Baker, 1999.

Hilderbrand, Kelly Michael, and Sutheera Sritrakool. "Developing a Thai Theological and Biblical Understanding of the World: Rethinking Thai Cosmology in Light of Divine Council Theology." *Transformation: An International Journal of Holistic Mission Studies* 38 (Jan. 2021): 63–77.

Hobbs, T. R. "Reflections on Honor, Shame, and Covenant Relations." *Journal of Biblical Literature* 116 (1997): 501–3.

Hoffmeier, James K. *Akhenaten and the Origins of Monotheism*. Oxford: Oxford University Press, 2015.

———. "The Arm of God versus the Arm of Pharaoh in the Exodus Narratives." *Biblica* 67 (1986): 378–87.

———. *Israel in Egypt: The Evidence for the Authenticity of the Exodus Tradition*. Oxford: Oxford University Press, 1999.

Hollnsteiner, Mary R. "Reciprocity in the Lowland Philippines." *Philippine Studies* 9 (1961): 387–413.

Holter, Knut. "The Current State of Old Testament Scholarship in Africa: Where Are We at the Turn of the Century?" In *Interpreting the Old Testament in Africa: Papers from the International Symposium on Africa and the Old Testament in Nairobi, October 1999*, edited by Knut Holter, Mary N. Getui, and Victor Zinkuratire, 27–39. Nairobi: Acton, 2002.

Hong, Joseph. "Revision of the Chinese Union Version Bible (CUV): Assessing the Challenges from an Historical Perspective." *The Bible Translator* 53 (2002): 238–48.

Hong, Sung-Wook. *Naming God in Korea: The Case of Protestant Christianity*. Global Theological Voices. Oxford: Regnum, 2008.

Houston, James M., ed. *The Mind on Fire: A Faith for the Skeptical and Indifferent, From the Writings of Blaise Pascal*. Portland: Multnomah, 1989.

Howell, Brian M. "Wheaton College, One God, and Muslim-Christian Dialog." *Evangelical Missions Quarterly* Occasional Bulletin (Special Edition 2016): 4–5.

Hsu, Danny. "Contextualising 'Sin' in Chinese Culture: A Historian's Perspective." *Studies in World Christianity* 22 (2016): 105–24.

Hwa Yung. *Mangoes or Bananas? The Quest for an Authentic Asian Christian Theology.* Oxford: Regnum, 1997.

Hwa Yung, and Tan Soo-Inn. *Bribery and Corruption: Biblical Reflections and Case Studies for the Marketplace in Asia.* Singapore: Graceworks, 2010.

Hwang, Jerry. "Are Yahweh and El/Allah the Same God? The OT's Contextualization of Monotheism." *Trinity Journal* 42 (2021): 59–78.

———. "Bible Translation as Contextual Theology: The Case of the Chinese Union Version Bible of 1919." *International Journal of Asian Christianity* 5 (2022): 89–114.

———. "The Book of Jeremiah as Case Study in Asian Contextual Theology." *Asia Journal of Theology* 35 (2021): 25–37.

———. "Contextualization in the Old Testament." *Mission Round Table: The Occasional Bulletin of OMF International Mission Research* 13 (May 2018): 4–9.

———. *Hosea: God's Reconciliation with His Estranged Household.* Zondervan Exegetical Commentary on the Old Testament. Grand Rapids: Zondervan Academic, 2021.

———. "'I Am Yahweh Your God from the Land of Egypt': Hosea's Use of the Exodus Traditions." In *"Did I Not Bring Israel out of Egypt?" Biblical, Archaeological, and Egyptological Perspectives on the Exodus Narratives,* edited by James K. Hoffmeier, Alan R. Millard, and Gary A. Rendsburg, 243–53. BBR Supplement Series 13. Winona Lake: Eisenbrauns, 2016.

———. *The Rhetoric of Remembrance: An Investigation of the "Fathers" in Deuteronomy.* Siphrut: Literature and Theology of the Hebrew Scriptures 8. Winona Lake: Eisenbrauns, 2012.

———. "Syncretism after the Exile and Malachi's Missional Response." *Southern Baptist Journal of Theology* 20 (2016): 49–68.

Ibrahim, Ayman S. "Understanding Insider Movements." The Gospel Coalition, 18 December 2015. https://www.thegospelcoalition.org/reviews/understanding-insider-movements/.

Ingleby, Jonathan C. *Beyond Empire: Postcolonialism and Mission in a Global Context.* Central Milton Keynes: AuthorHouse, 2010.

Jackson, Griffin Paul. "The Top Bible Verses of 2018 Don't Come from Jesus or Paul." *Christianity Today,* 10 December 2018. https://www.christianitytoday.com/news/2018/december/most-popular-bible-verse-2018-youversion-app-bible-gateway.html.

Jacobsen, Thorkild. "The Graven Image." In *Ancient Israelite Religion: Essays in Honor of Frank Moore Cross,* edited by Patrick D. Miller, Paul D. Hanson, and S. Dean McBride, 15–31. Philadelphia: Fortress, 1987.

———. *The Treasures of Darkness: A History of Mesopotamian Religion.* New Haven: Yale University Press, 1976.

Jang, Sehoon. "Is Hezekiah a Success or a Failure? The Literary Function of Isaiah's Prediction at the End of the Royal Narratives in the Book of Isaiah." *Journal for the Study of the Old Testament* 42 (Sep. 2017): 117–35.

Jarick, John. "The Hebrew Book of Changes: Reflections on *Hakkōl Hebel* and *Lakkōl Zemān* in Ecclesiastes." *Journal for the Study of the Old Testament* 25 (2000): 79–99.

Jenkins, Philip. *The Next Christendom: The Coming of Global Christianity*. 3rd ed. Oxford: Oxford University Press, 2011.

Jobes, Karen H. "Relevance Theory and the Translation of Scripture." *Journal of the Evangelical Theological Society* 50 (Dec. 2007): 773–97.

Jones, E. Stanley. *The Christ of the Indian World*. 6th ed. New York: Abingdon Press, 1925.

Jumper, James N. "Honor and Shame in the Deuteronomic Covenant and the Deuteronomistic Presentation of the Davidic Covenant." PhD diss., Harvard University, 2013.

Kadir, Shaik. *Islam Explained*. London: Marshall Cavendish, 2007.

Kaiser, Jr., Walter C. *Mission in the Old Testament: Israel as a Light to the Nations*. 2nd ed. Grand Rapids: Baker Academic, 2012.

Kalluveettil, Paul. *Declaration and Covenant: A Comprehensive Review of Covenant Formulae from the Old Testament and the Ancient Near East*. Analecta Biblica 88. Rome: Biblical Institute, 1982.

Karamustafa, Ahmet T. "Fate." In *Encyclopaedia of the Qur'ān*, edited by Jane Dammen McAuliffe, 2:185–88. Leiden: Brill, 2001.

Kaufman, Whitley R. P. "Karma, Rebirth, and the Problem of Evil." *Philosophy East & West* 55 (Jan. 2005): 15–32.

Keel, Othmar, and Christoph Uehlinger. *Gods, Goddesses, and Images of God in Ancient Israel*. Translated by Thomas H. Trapp. Minneapolis: Fortress, 1998.

Keown, Damien. "Karma, Character, and Consequentialism." *Journal of Religious Ethics* 24 (1996): 329–50.

Khair-Ullah, F. S. "Linguistic Hang-Ups in Communicating with Muslims." *Missiology: An International Review* 4 (1 July 1976): 301–16.

King, Ambrose Yeo-chi. "Guanxi and Network Building: A Sociological Interpretation." In *China's Great Transformation: Selected Essays on Confucianism, Modernization, and Democracy*, 57–81. Hong Kong: Chinese University Press, 2018.

King, Jonathan. *The Beauty of the Lord: Theology as Aesthetics*. Studies in Historical and Systematic Theology. Bellingham, WA: Lexham Press, 2018.

Kitchen, Kenneth A. "Egypt, Qatna, and Covenant." *Ugarit-Forschungen* 11 (1979): 453–64.

Kitchen, Kenneth A., and Paul J. N. Lawrence. *Treaty, Law and Covenant in the Ancient Near East*. 3 vols. Wiesbaden: Harrassowitz, 2012.

Knierim, Rolf P. *The Task of Old Testament Theology: Substance, Method, and Cases*. Grand Rapids: Eerdmans, 1995.

Knoppers, Gary N. "Ancient Near Eastern Royal Grants and the Davidic Covenant: A Parallel?" *Journal of the American Oriental Society* 116 (1996): 670–97.

———. "David's Relation to Moses: The Contexts, Content and Conditions of the Davidic Promises." In *King and Messiah in Israel and the Ancient Near East: Proceedings of the Oxford Old Testament Seminar*, 91–118. JSOT Supplement Series. Sheffield: Sheffield Academic Press, 1998.

Knudsen, Toke Lindegaard. "House Omens in Mesopotamia and India." In *From the Banks of the Euphrates: Studies in Honor of Alice Louise Slotsky*, edited by Micah Ross, 121–33. Winona Lake: Eisenbrauns, 2008.

Koyama, Kosuke. *Water Buffalo Theology*. 25th Anniversary Ed. Maryknoll: Orbis, 1999.

Kutsko, John F. *Between Heaven and Earth: Divine Presence and Absence in the Book of Ezekiel*. Biblical and Judaic Studies 7. Winona Lake: Eisenbrauns, 2000.

Kwok, Pui-lan. *Discovering the Bible in the Non-Biblical World*. Maryknoll: Orbis, 1995.

Labuschagne, C. J. *The Incomparability of Yahweh in the Old Testament*. Pretoria Oriental Studies 5. Leiden: Brill, 1966.

Lakoff, George, and Mark Johnson. *Philosophy in the Flesh: The Embodied Mind and Its Challenge to Western Thought*. New York: Basic, 2010.

Lam, Joseph. *Patterns of Sin in the Hebrew Bible: Metaphor, Culture, and the Making of a Religious Concept*. New York: Oxford University Press, 2016.

Lau, Te-Li. *Defending Shame: Its Formative Power in Paul's Letters*. Grand Rapids: Baker Academic, 2020.

Lebra, Takie Sugiyama. "Shame and Guilt: A Psychocultural View of the Japanese Self." *Ethos* 11 (1983): 192–209.

———. "The Social Mechanism of Guilt and Shame: The Japanese Case." *Anthropological Quarterly* 44 (1971): 241–55.

Lemche, Niels Peter. "Kings and Clients: On Loyalty between the Ruler and the Ruled in Ancient 'Israel.'" In *Biblical Studies and the Failure of History*, 201–11. Changing Perspectives 3. Sheffield: Equinox, 2013.

Lenchak, Timothy A. *Choose Life! A Rhetorical-Critical Investigation of Deuteronomy 28,69 – 30,20*. Analecta Biblica 129. Rome: Pontifical Institute, 1993.

Levinson, Bernard M. "Goethe's Analysis of Exodus 34 and Its Influence on Wellhausen: The *Pfropfung* of the Documentary Hypothesis." *Zeitschrift für die alttestamentliche Wissenschaft* 114 (2002): 212–23.

———. "Reading the Bible in Nazi Germany: Gerhard von Rad's Attempt to Reclaim the Old Testament for the Church." *Interpretation: A Journal of Bible and Theology* 62 (July 2008): 238–54.

Levitt, Stephan Hillyer. "The Dating of the Indian Tradition." *Anthropos* 98 (2003): 341–59.

Levtow, Nathaniel B. *Images of Others: Iconic Politics in Ancient Israel.* Biblical and Judaic Studies from the University of California, San Diego 11. Winona Lake: Eisenbrauns, 2008.

Lewellen, Ted C. *The Anthropology of Globalization: Cultural Anthropology Enters the 21st Century.* Westport: Bergin & Garvey, 2002.

Lewis, Martin W., and Kären Wigen. *The Myth of Continents: A Critique of Metageography.* Berkeley: University of California Press, 1997.

Li, Ling. "Performing Bribery in China: Guanxi-Practice, Corruption with a Human Face." *Journal of Contemporary China* 20 (Jan. 2011): 1–20. https://doi.org/10.1080/10670564.2011.520841.

Lian, Xi. *Redeemed by Fire: The Rise of Popular Christianity in Modern China.* New Haven: Yale University Press, 2010.

Lichtheim, Miriam, ed. *Ancient Egyptian Literature.* Oakland: University of California Press, 2019.

Lie, John. "Ruth Benedict's Legacy of Shame: Orientalism and Occidentalism in the Study of Japan." *Asian Journal of Social Science* 29 (2000): 249–61.

Lin, Liang-Hung. "Cultural and Organizational Antecedents of Guanxi: The Chinese Cases." *Journal of Business Ethics* 99 (Mar. 2011): 441–51.

Lind, Millard C. "Refocusing Theological Education to Mission: The Old Testament and Contextualization." *Missiology: An International Review* 10 (Apr. 1982): 141–60.

Ling, Samuel D. *The "Chinese" Way of Doing Things: Perspectives on American-Born Chinese and the Chinese Church in North America.* San Gabriel: China Horizon, 1999.

Lohfink, Norbert. "Reading Deuteronomy 5 as Narrative." In *A God So Near: Essays on Old Testament Theology in Honor of Patrick D. Miller,* edited by Brent A. Strawn and Nancy R. Bowen, 261–81. Winona Lake: Eisenbrauns, 2003.

Lorenzana, Jozon A. "Ethnic Moralities and Reciprocity: Towards an Ethic of South-South Relations." *Bandung: Journal of the Global South* 2 (5 Feb. 2015): 1–14.

Lorgunpai, Seree. "The Book of Ecclesiastes and Thai Buddhism." In *Voices from the Margin: Interpreting the Bible in the Third World,* edited by R. S. Sugirtharajah, 347–54. Rev. and expanded 3rd ed. Maryknoll: Orbis, 2006.

MacCulloch, Diarmaid. *Thomas Cranmer: A Life.* Rev. ed. New Haven: Yale University Press, 2016.

MacDonald, Nathan. "Aniconism in the Old Testament." In *The God of Israel*, edited by Robert P. Gordon, 20–34. University of Cambridge Oriental Publications 64. Cambridge: Cambridge University Press, 2007.

MacDonald, Scott. "The Divine Nature: Being and Goodness." In *The Cambridge Companion to Augustine*, edited by David Vincent Meconi and Eleonore Stump, 17–36. 2nd ed. Cambridge: Cambridge University Press, 2014.

Maggay, M. Padilla. "Art and Aesthetics." In *Global Dictionary of Theology: A Resource for the Worldwide Church*, edited by William A. Dyrness and Veli-Matti Kärkkäinen, 64–66. Downers Grove: IVP Academic, 2008.

Mak, George Kam Wah. *Protestant Bible Translation and Mandarin as the National Language of China*. Sinica Leidensia 131. Leiden: Brill, 2017.

Maré, Leonard P. "Psalm 121: Yahweh's Protection against Mythological Powers." *Old Testament Essays* 19 (2006): 712–22.

Markl, Dominik. "Divine Mercy in the Ancient Near East and in the Hebrew Bible." In *Raḥma: Muslim and Christian Studies in Mercy*, edited by Valentino Cottini, Felix Körner, and Diego R. Sarrío Cucarella, 39–48. Studi arabo-islamici del PISAI 22. Rome: PISAI, 2018.

Marlow, Hilary. "The Hills Are Alive! The Personification of Nature in the Psalter." In *Leshon Limmudim: Essays on the Language and Literature of the Hebrew Bible in Honour of A. A. Macintosh*, edited by David A. Baer and Robert P. Gordon, 189–203. London: Bloomsbury, 2014.

Martin, Paul A. J. *Missionary of the Indian Road: The Theology of Stanley Jones*. Bangalore: Theological Book Trust, 1996.

Martin-Achard, Robert. *A Light to the Nations: A Study of the OT Conception of Israel's Mission to the World*. Edinburgh and London: Oliver & Boyd, 1962.

Mays, James Luther. *Psalms*. Interpretation. Louisville: John Knox, 1994.

McComiskey, Thomas E. "The Religion of the Patriarchs." In *The Law and the Prophets: Old Testament Studies in Honor of Oswald T. Allis*, edited by John H. Skilton, 195–206. Nutley: Presbyterian & Reformed, 1974.

McConville, J. Gordon. "God's 'Name' and God's 'Glory.'" *Tyndale Bulletin* 30 (1979): 149–63.

———. "Singular Address in the Deuteronomic Law and the Politics of Legal Administration." *Journal for the Study of the Old Testament* 97 (2002): 19–36.

———. "Yahweh and the Gods in the Old Testament." *European Journal of Theology* 2 (1993): 107–17.

McCracken, Brett. "How the Gospel Takes Root in 'Crazy Rich' Singapore." The Gospel Coalition, 24 September 2018. https://www.thegospelcoalition.org/article/gospel-takes-root-crazy-rich-singapore/.

McGrath, Alister E. *In the Beginning: The Story of the King James Bible and How It Changed a Nation, a Language, and a Culture*. New York: Doubleday, 2001.

McKnight, Scot. *The King Jesus Gospel: The Original Good News Revisited.* Grand Rapids: Zondervan, 2011.

Melton, Brittany N. "*Miqreh* in Retrospect: An Illumination of *Miqreh* in Light of Ecclesiastes 3.1–8 and the Book of Ruth." In *Megilloth Studies: The Shape of Contemporary Scholarship,* edited by Brad Embry, 30–42. Hebrew Bible Monographs 78. Sheffield: Sheffield Phoenix Press, 2016.

Mendenhall, George E. *Law and Covenant in Israel and the Ancient Near East.* Pittsburgh: Biblical Colloquium, 1955.

Merrill, Eugene H. *Everlasting Dominion: A Theology of the Old Testament.* Nashville, TN: Broadman & Holman, 2006.

Merz, Johannes. "The Culture Problem: How the Honor/Shame Issue Got the Wrong End of the Anthropological Stick." *Missiology: An International Review* 48 (2020): 127–41.

Mettinger, Tryggve N. D. "The Elusive Essence: YHWH, El and Baal and the Distinctiveness of Israelite Faith." In *Die Hebräische Bibel und ihre zweifache Nachgeschichte: Festschrift für Rolf Rendtorff zum 65. Geburtstag,* edited by Erhard Blum, 393–417. Neukirchen-Vluyn: Neukirchener Verlag, 1990.

———. *No Graven Image? Israelite Aniconism in Its Ancient Near Eastern Context.* Coniectanea Biblica: Old Testament Series 42. Stockholm: Almqvist & Wiksell International, 1995.

Middlemas, Jill. "Exclusively Yahweh: Aniconism and Anthropomorphism in Ezekiel." In *Prophecy and the Prophets in Ancient Israel: Proceedings of the Oxford Old Testament Seminar,* 309–24. Library of Hebrew Bible/Old Testament Studies 531. London: T&T Clark, 2010.

Middleton, J. Richard. *A New Heaven and a New Earth: Reclaiming Biblical Eschatology.* Grand Rapids: Baker Academic, 2014.

Miranda-Feliciano, Evelyn. *Filipino Values and Our Christian Faith.* Metro Manila: OMF Literature, 1990.

Mischke, Werner. *The Global Gospel: Achieving Missional Impact in Our Multicultural World.* Scottsdale, AZ: Mission ONE, 2015.

Moberly, R. W. L. *At the Mountain of God: Story and Theology in Exodus 32–34.* JSOT Supplement Series 22. Sheffield: JSOT Press, 1983.

———. *The Old Testament of the Old Testament.* Overtures to Biblical Theology. Minneapolis: Fortress, 1992.

Modell, Judith. "The Wall of Shame: Ruth Benedict's Accomplishment in *The Chrysanthemum and the Sword.*" *Dialectical Anthropology* 24 (1999): 193–215.

Mohler, Jr., Albert. "What Does God Care What We Call Him?," 22 August 2007. https://albertmohler.com/2007/08/22/what-does-god-care-what-we-call-him.

Mojola, Aloo O. "The Old Testament or Hebrew Bible in Africa: Challenges and Prospects for Interpretation and Translation." *Verbum et Ecclesia* 35 (2014): 1–7.

"Monotheism, *n.*" OED Online. March 2022. Oxford University Press. https://www.oed.com/view/Entry/121673.

Montiel, Cristina Jayme. "Philippine Political Culture: A Conceptual Framework." *Philippine Journal of Psychology* 33 (2000): 112–28.

Moon, Tae-Ju. "The Korean American Dream and the Blessings of Hananim (God)." In *The Global God: Multicultural Evangelical Views of God*, edited by Aída Besançon Spencer and William David Spencer, 231–47. Grand Rapids: Baker, 1998.

Moore, Charles A. "Introduction: The Comprehensive Indian Mind." In *The Indian Mind: Essentials of Indian Philosophy and Culture*, edited by Charles A. Moore, 1–18. An East-West Center Book. Honolulu: University Press of Hawaii, 1978.

Moreau, A. Scott. *Contextualizing the Faith: A Holistic Approach*. Grand Rapids: Baker Academic, 2018.

———. *Contextualization in World Missions: Mapping and Assessing Evangelical Models*. Grand Rapids: Kregel Academic, 2012.

Moskala, Jiří. "The Mission of God's People in the Old Testament." *Journal of the Adventist Theological Society* 19, no. 1/2 (2008): 40–60.

Mowinckel, Sigmund. *Religion and Cult: The Old Testament and the Phenomenology of Religion*. Edited by K. C. Hanson. Translated by John F. X. Sheehan. Eugene, OR: Cascade, 2012.

Müller, Roland. *Honor and Shame: Unlocking the Door*. Philadelphia: Xlibris Corp., 2000.

Muraoka, Takamitsu. *My Via Dolorosa: Along the Trails of the Japanese Imperialism in Asia*. Bloomington: AuthorHouse, 2016.

Musk, Bill A. "Popular Islam: The Hunger of the Heart." In *The Gospel and Islam: A 1978 Compendium*, edited by Don M. McCurry, 208–24. Monrovia: Missions Advanced Research and Communication Center, 1979.

Nakane, Chie. *Japanese Society*. Berkeley: University of California Press, 1970.

Naylor, Mark. "Who Determines if Allah Is God? A Contextual Consideration of the Use of the Term 'Allah' for the God of the Bible." *Evangelical Missions Quarterly* Occasional Bulletin (Special Edition 2016): 20–21.

Nee, Watchman. *Church Affairs*. Anaheim, CA: Living Stream Ministry, 1994.

Nelson, Eric. *The Hebrew Republic: Jewish Sources and the Transformation of European Political Thought*. Cambridge: Harvard University Press, 2011.

Netland, Harold A. "On Worshiping the Same God: What Exactly Is the Question?" *Missiology: An International Review* 45 (2017): 441–56.

Newbigin, Lesslie. *Foolishness to the Greeks: The Gospel and Western Culture.* Grand Rapids: Eerdmans, 1986.

Newell, Marvin J. *Crossing Cultures in Scripture: Biblical Principles for Mission Practice.* Downers Grove: InterVarsity Press, 2016.

Nida, Eugene A. "Translating a Text with a Long and Sensitive Tradition." In *Translating Sensitive Texts: Linguistic Aspects*, edited by Karl Simms, 189–96. Approaches to Translation Studies 14. Amsterdam: Rodopi, 1997.

Niles, D. Premnan. "Example of Contextualization in the Old Testament." *The South East Asia Journal of Theology* 21 (1980): 19–33.

North, Anna, and Kainaz Amaria. "National Geographic Faced up to Its Racist Past. Did It Actually Get Better?" *Vox*, 6 May 2021. https://www.vox.com/22417191/national-geographic-racial-reckoning.

Oak, Sung-Deuk. "Competing Chinese Names for God: The Chinese Term Question and Its Influence upon Korea." *Journal of Korean Religions* 3 (Oct. 2012): 89–115.

Odell, Margaret S. "An Exploratory Study of Shame and Dependence in the Bible and Selected Near Eastern Parallels." In *The Biblical Canon in Comparative Perspective*, edited by K. Lawson Younger, William W. Hallo, and Bernard F. Batto, 217–29. Scripture in Context 4. Lewiston: Edwin Mellen, 1991.

Okoye, James Chukwuma. *Israel and the Nations: A Mission Theology of the Old Testament.* American Society of Missiology Series 39. Maryknoll: Orbis, 2006.

Olson, Roger E. *Questions to All Your Answers: The Journey from Folk Religion to Examined Faith.* Grand Rapids: Zondervan, 2008.

Olyan, Saul M. "Honor, Shame, and Covenant Relations in Ancient Israel and Its Environment." *Journal of Biblical Literature* 115 (1996): 201–18.

Osborne, Grant R. *The Hermeneutical Spiral: A Comprehensive Introduction to Biblical Interpretation.* Rev. and expanded ed. Downers Grove: IVP Academic, 2006.

Oswalt, John N. *The Bible among the Myths: Unique Revelation or Just Ancient Literature?* Grand Rapids: Zondervan, 2009.

Ou, Yingyu. *Ezra.* Tien Dao Bible Commentary. Hong Kong: Tien Dao Publishing, 1998.

Packer, J. I. *Concise Theology.* Wheaton: Crossway, 2020.

Pak, Jennifer. "Malaysia Official Blames Nude Tourists for Deadly Quake." BBC News online, 8 June 2015. https://www.bbc.com/news/world-asia-33058692.

Pardee, Dennis. "On Psalm 29: Structure and Meaning." In *The Book of Psalms: Composition and Reception*, edited by Peter W. Flint, Patrick D. Miller, Aaron Brunell, and Ryan Roberts, 153–81. Supplements to Vetus Testamentum 99. Leiden: Brill, 2005.

Park, James Sung-Hwan. "Chosen to Fulfill the Great Commission? Biblical and Theological Reflections on the Back to Jerusalem Vision of Chinese Churches." *Missiology: An International Review* 43 (Apr. 2015): 163–74.

Park, Joon-Sik. "Korean Protestant Christianity: A Missiological Reflection." *International Bulletin of Missionary Research* 36 (Apr. 2012): 59–64.

Parshall, Phil. *New Paths in Muslim Evangelism: Evangelical Approaches to Contextualization.* Grand Rapids: Baker, 1980.

Parsons, Martin. *Unveiling God: Contextualising Christology for Islamic Culture.* Pasadena, CA: William Carey Library, 2005.

Patnaik, Utsa. "Revisiting the 'Drain,' or Transfer from India to Britain in the Context of Global Diffusion of Capitalism." In *Agrarian and Other Histories: Essays for Binay Bhushan Chaudhuri,* edited by B. B. Chaudhuri, Shubhra Chakrabarti, and Utsa Patnaik, 277–317. 1st ed. New Delhi: Tulika Books, 2017.

Patnaik, Utsa, and Prabhat Patnaik. "The Drain of Wealth: Colonialism before the First World War." *Monthly Review,* 1 February 2021. https://monthlyreview.org/2021/02/01/the-drain-of-wealth/.

Patterson, Colin. "The World of Honor and Shame in the New Testament: Alien or Familiar?" *Biblical Theology Bulletin* 49 (Feb. 2019): 4–14.

Peng, Kuo-Wei. "Cong yi ben shi lun wei lai zhong wen sheng jing yi ben zhi chu yi." *China Evangelical Seminary Journal* 1 (June 2008): 33–49.

———. "Contemplating the Future of Chinese Bible Translation: A Functionalist Approach." *The Bible Translator* 63 (2012): 1–16.

Perdue, Leo G. *The Collapse of History: Reconstructing Old Testament Theology.* Minneapolis: Augsburg Fortress, 1994.

Peristiany, John G., and Julian Alfred Pitt-Rivers. "Introduction." In *Honor and Grace in Anthropology,* edited by John G. Peristiany and Julian Alfred Pitt-Rivers, 1–17. Cambridge Studies in Social and Cultural Anthropology 76. Cambridge: Cambridge University Press, 2005.

Peristiany, John George, ed. *Honour and Shame: The Values of Mediterranean Society.* Chicago: University of Chicago Press, 1974.

Perry, T. Anthony. *The Book of Ecclesiastes (Qohelet) and the Path to Joyous Living.* Cambridge: Cambridge University Press, 2015.

Peters, George W. *A Biblical Theology of Missions.* Chicago: Moody, 1976.

Petersen, Brian K. "A Brief Investigation of Old Testament Precursors to the Pauline Missiological Model of Cultural Adaptation." *International Journal of Frontier Missiology* 23 (Fall 2007): 117–29.

Peterson, Brian Neil. *Ezekiel in Context: Ezekiel's Message Understood in Its Historical Setting of Covenant Curses and Ancient Near Eastern Mythological Motifs.* Princeton Theological Monograph Series 182. Eugene: Pickwick, 2012.

Peterson, Eugene H. *A Long Obedience in the Same Direction: Discipleship in an Instant Society*. 20th anniversary ed. Downers Grove: InterVarsity Press, 2000.

Piers, Gerhart, and Milton Singer. *Shame and Guilt: A Psychoanalytic and a Cultural Study*. Springfield: Thomas, 1953.

Pilch, John J. *The Cultural Life Setting of the Proverbs*. Minneapolis: Fortress, 2016.

Pingree, David E. "Mesopotamian Astronomy and Astral Omens in Other Civilizations." In *Mesopotamien und seine Nachbarn: Politische und kulturelle Wechselbeziehungen im Alten Vorderasien vom 4. bis 1. Jahrtausend v. Chr.*, edited by Hans Jörg Nissen and Johannes Renger, 2:613–31. Rencontre Assyriologique Internationale 25. Berlin: D. Reimer, 1982.

Piper, John. *The Purifying Power of Living by Faith in Future Grace*. Sisters, OR: Multnomah, 1995.

Pitt-Rivers, Julian. "Honour and Social Status." In *Honour and Shame: The Values of Mediterranean Society*, edited by John George Peristiany, 19–77. London: Weidenfeld & Nicolson, 1965.

Plevnik, Joseph. "Honor/Shame." In *Biblical Social Values and Their Meaning: A Handbook*, edited by John J. Pilch and Bruce J. Malina, 95–104. Peabody, MA: Hendrickson, 1993.

Prenger, Jan Hendrik. *Muslim Insider Christ Followers: Their Theological and Missional Frames*. Pasadena: William Carey Library, 2017.

Pury, Albert de. "Le Pentateuque en question: position du problème et brève histoire de la recherche." In *Le Pentateuque en question*, edited by Thomas C. Römer and Albert de Pury, 9–80. 3rd ed. Geneva: Labor et Fides, 2002.

Quisumbing, Lourdes R. "Some Filipino (Cebuano) Social Values and Attitudes Viewed in Relation to Development (A Cebuano Looks at Utang-Na-Loob and Hiyâ)." In *Changing Identities in Modern Southeast Asia*, edited by David J. Banks, 257–68. Berlin: De Gruyter, 1977.

Qureshi, Nabeel. *No God but One: Allah or Jesus? A Former Muslim Investigates the Evidence for Islam and Christianity*. Grand Rapids: Zondervan, 2016.

———. *Seeking Allah, Finding Jesus: A Devout Muslim Encounters Christianity*. Grand Rapids: Zondervan, 2018.

Rad, Gerhard von. "Deuteronomy's 'Name' Theology and the Priestly Document's 'Kabod' Theology." In *Studies in Deuteronomy*, 37–44. Studies in Biblical Theology. London: SCM, 1953.

———. *Old Testament Theology*. Translated by D. M. G. Stalker. 2 vols. Old Testament Library. Louisville: Westminster John Knox, 2001.

Rahmouni, Aicha. *Divine Epithets in the Ugaritic Alphabetic Texts*. Translated by J. N. Ford. Handbook of Oriental Studies, Section 1: The Near and Middle East 93. Leiden: Brill, 2008.

Ramachandra, Vinoth. *Subverting Global Myths: Theology and the Public Issues Shaping Our World.* Downers Grove: IVP Academic, 2008.

Reichenbach, Bruce R. "The Law of Karma and the Principle of Causation." *Philosophy East and West* 38 (1988): 399–410.

Richard, H. L. "Religious Syncretism as a Syncretistic Concept: The Inadequacy of the 'World Religions' Paradigm in Cross-Cultural Encounter." *International Journal of Frontier Missiology* 31 (2014): 209–15.

Richter, Hans-Friedmann. "Von den Bergen kommt keine Hilfe: Zu Psalm 121." *Zeitschrift für die alttestamentliche Wissenschaft* 116 (2004): 406–8.

Ricoeur, Paul. *The Rule of Metaphor: The Creation of Meaning in Language.* Translated by Robert Czerny with Kathleen McLaughlin and John Costello. Routledge Classics. London: Routledge, 2006.

Ringgren, Helmer. "Islamic Fatalism." In *Fatalistic Beliefs in Religion, Folklore, and Literature: Papers Read at the Symposium on Fatalistic Beliefs Held at Abo on the 7th–9th of September, 1964,* edited by Helmer Ringgren, 52–62. Stockholm: Almqvist & Wiksell, 1967.

Ro, Bong Rin. "Communicating the Biblical Concept of God to Koreans." In *The Global God: Multicultural Evangelical Views of God,* edited by Aída Besançon Spencer and William David Spencer, 207–30. Grand Rapids: Baker, 1998.

Robertson, Jennifer, ed. "Introduction: Putting and Keeping Japan in Anthropology." In *A Companion to the Anthropology of Japan,* 3–16. Blackwell Companions to Anthropology 5. Malden: Blackwell, 2005.

Roces, Alfredo R., and Grace Roces. *Culture Shock! Philippines: A Survival Guide to Customs and Etiquette.* Tarrytown, NY: Marshall Cavendish, 2009.

Rogerson, John W. *Myth in Old Testament Interpretation.* Beihefte zur Zeitschrift für die alttestamentliche Wissenschaft 134. Berlin: de Gruyter, 1974.

Routledge, Robin. *Old Testament Theology: A Thematic Approach.* Downers Grove : IVP Academic, 2012.

The Royal Aal Al-Bayt Institute for Islamic Thought. "A Common Word between Us and You." Jordan, January 2009. https://www.acommonword.com/downloads/CW-Booklet-Final-v6_8-1-09.pdf.

Rudolph, Kurt. "Wellhausen as an Arabist." *Semeia* 25 (1982): 111–55.

Rüsen, Jörn, ed. *Western Historical Thinking: An Intercultural Debate.* Making Sense of History. New York: Berghahn Books, 2002.

Rutledge, John. "LifeWay Apologizes to Asian-Americans for Rickshaw Rally." *Baptist Standard,* 8 November 2013. https://www.baptiststandard.com/news/baptists/lifeway-apologizes-to-asian-americans-for-rickshaw-rally/.

Ryang, Sonia. *Japan and National Anthropology: A Critique.* London: Routledge, 2006.

Saint Augustine. *Confessions.* Translated by Henry Chadwick. Oxford World's Classics. Oxford: Oxford University Press, 2008.

Sakuta, Keiichi. "A Reconsideration of the Culture of Shame." Translated by Kimiko Yagi and Meredith McKinney. *Review of Japanese Culture and Society* 1 (1986): 32–39.

Saleh, Fauzan. *Modern Trends in Islamic Theological Discourse in 20th Century Indonesia: A Critical Study.* Social, Economic, and Political Studies of the Middle East and Asia 79. Leiden: Brill, 2001.

Sanders, E. P. "Covenantal Nomism Revisited." *Jewish Studies Quarterly* 16 (2009): 23–55.

Sandmel, Samuel. "Parallelomania." *Journal of Biblical Literature* 81 (1962): 1–13.

Sanneh, Lamin O. *Translating the Message: The Missionary Impact on Culture.* 2nd ed. American Society of Missiology Series 42. Maryknoll: Orbis, 2009.

Santos, Narry F. *Turning Our Shame into Honor: Transformation of the Filipino Hiya in the Light of Mark's Gospel.* Manila: Lifechange Pub., 2003.

Sarma, D. S. *Essence of Hinduism.* Bombay: Bharatyia Vidya Bhavan, 1971.

Satyavrata, Ivan. *God Has Not Left Himself without Witness.* Eugene: Wipf and Stock, 2011.

Schäder, J. "Patronage and Clientage between God, Israel, and the Nations: An Investigation of Psalm 47." *Journal for Semitics* 19 (2010): 235–62.

Schaeffer, Francis A. *Pollution and the Death of Man: The Christian View of Ecology.* London: Hodder & Stoughton, 1970.

Schenker, Adrian. "L'origine de l'idée d'une alliance entre Dieu et Israël dans l'Ancien Testament." *Revue biblique* 92 (1988): 184–94.

Schwartz, Howard. "Does God Have a Body? The Problem of Metaphor and Literal Language in Biblical Interpretation." In *Bodies, Embodiment, and Theology of the Hebrew Bible,* edited by S. Tamar Kamionkowski and Wonil Kim, 201–37. Library of Hebrew Bible/Old Testament Studies 465. New York: T&T Clark, 2010.

Schwartz, Regina M. *The Curse of Cain: The Violent Legacy of Monotheism.* Chicago: University of Chicago Press, 1998.

Schwartz, Seth. *Were the Jews a Mediterranean Society? Reciprocity and Solidarity in Ancient Judaism.* Princeton: Princeton University Press, 2010.

Seow, C.-L. *Ecclesiastes: A New Translation with Introduction and Commentary.* The Anchor Bible 18C. New York: Doubleday, 1997.

Shaw, R. Daniel, Danny DeLoach, Jonathan Grimes, Simon Herrmann, and Stephen Bailey. "Contextualization, Conceptualization, and Communication: The Development of Contextualization at Fuller's Graduate School of World Mission/Intercultural Studies." *Missiology: An International Review* 44 (2016): 95–111.

Shehadeh, Imad N. "Do Christians and Muslims Believe in the Same God?" *Bibliotheca Sacra* 161 (2004): 14–26.

———. Review of *Allah: A Christian Response*, by Miroslav Volf. *Themelios* 36 (2011). https://www.thegospelcoalition.org/themelios/review/allah-a-christian-response/.

Shin, Benjamin C., and Sheryl Takagi Silzer. *Tapestry of Grace: Untangling the Cultural Complexities in Asian American Life and Ministry.* Eugene: Wipf & Stock, 2016.

Silberman, Lou. "Wellhausen and Judaism." *Semeia* 25 (1982): 75–82.

Simkins, Ronald A. *Creator and Creation: Nature in the Worldview of Ancient Israel.* Peabody, MA: Hendrickson, 1994.

———. "Patronage and the Political Economy of Monarchic Israel." *Semeia* 87 (1999): 123–44.

Singh, Karan. *Essays on Hinduism.* 3rd ed. Delhi: Primus Books, 2014.

Siu, Kam-wah (Joseph). "American Missionary Views on Siamese Culture and Their Evangelical and Social Works in Siam between the Mid-19th Century and the Early 20th Century." Paper, Chinese University of Hong Kong, 30 March 2019. https://www.harvard-yenching.org/wp-content/uploads/legacy_files/featurefiles/SIU%20Kam%20Wah_American%20Missionary%20Views%20on%20Siamese%20Culture.pdf.

Smend, Rudolf. "Julius Wellhausen and His Prolegomena to the History of Israel." Translated by A. Graeme Auld. *Semeia* 25 (1982): 1–20.

Smith, Mark S. *God in Translation: Deities in Cross-Cultural Discourse in the Biblical World.* Grand Rapids: Eerdmans, 2010.

Soesilo, Daud. "Translating the Names of God: Recent Experience from Indonesia and Malaysia." *The Bible Translator* 52 (2001): 414–23.

Song, C. S. *Third-Eye Theology: Theology in Formation in Asian Settings.* Eugene: Wipf & Stock, 2002.

Stanley, Brian. *The Bible and the Flag: Protestant Missions and British Imperialism in the Nineteenth and Twentieth Centuries.* Leicester: Apollos, 1990.

Stiebert, Johanna. *The Construction of Shame in the Hebrew Bible: The Prophetic Contribution.* JSOT Supplement Series 346. London: Sheffield Academic, 2002.

Stirrup, A. "'Why Has Yahweh Defeated Us Today before the Philistines?' The Question of the Ark Narrative." *Tyndale Bulletin* 51 (2000): 81–99.

Strand, Mark. "Explaining Sin in a Chinese Context." *Missiology: An International Review* 28 (Oct. 2000): 427–41.

Strawn, Brent A. *The Old Testament Is Dying: A Diagnosis and Recommended Treatment.* Grand Rapids: Baker Academic, 2017.

Stults, Donald L. *Developing an Asian Evangelical Theology*. Manila: OMF Literature, 1989.

Stutley, Margaret. *Hinduism: The Eternal Law; An Introduction to the Literature, Cosmology and Cults of the Hindu Religion*. Wellingborough: Aquarian Press, 1985.

Swami, Jayādvaita. *Vanity Karma: Ecclesiastes, the Bhagavad-gītā, and the Meaning of Life – A Cross-Cultural Commentary on the Book of Ecclesiastes*. Los Angeles: The Bhaktivedanta Book Trust, 2015.

Swearer, Donald K. "Hypostasizing the Buddha: Buddha Image Consecration in Northern Thailand." *History of Religions* 34 (Feb. 1995): 263–80.

Sweeney, Marvin A. *Isaiah 40–66*. The Forms of the Old Testament Literature 19. Grand Rapids: Eerdmans, 2016.

Tanchanpongs, Natee. "Developing a Palate for Authentic Theology." In *Local Theology for the Global Church: Principles for an Evangelical Approach to Contextualization*, edited by Matthew Cook, Rob Haskell, Ruth Julian, and Natee Tanchanpongs, 109–23. Pasadena: William Carey Library, 2010.

Tang, Chongrong. *Zui e yuan tou de tan tao*. Hong Kong: STEMI Ltd, 2012.

Taylor, Steve. "A Prolegomena for the Thai Context: A Starting Point for Thai Theology." *Evangelical Review of Theology* 29 (2005): 32–51.

Terrien, Samuel L. *The Elusive Presence: Toward a New Biblical Theology*. Eugene: Wipf and Stock, 2000.

Thomas, Kenneth J. "Allah in Translations of the Bible." *International Journal of Frontier Missions* 23 (Winter 2006): 171–74.

Thomas, Robert L. *Evangelical Hermeneutics: The New versus the Old*. Grand Rapids: Kregel, 2002.

Tsai, Jingtu. *Sheng jing zai zhong guo: fu zhong wen sheng jin li shi mu lu* [The Bible in China: With a Historical Catalogue of the Chinese Bible]. Hong Kong: Logos and Pneuma Press, 2018.

Tsumura, David Toshio. "Kings and Cults in Ancient Ugarit." In *Priests and Officials in the Ancient Near East: Papers of the Second Colloquium on the Ancient Near East – The City and Its Life, Held at the Middle Eastern Culture Center in Japan (Mitaka, Tokyo)*, edited by Kazuko Watanabe, 215–38. Heidelberg: Universitätsverlag C. Winter, 1999.

Turner, Kenneth J. "Exodus." In *What the Old Testament Authors Really Cared About: A Survey of Jesus' Bible*, edited by Jason S. DeRouchie. Grand Rapids: Kregel Academic, 2013.

Van Rheenen, Gailyn. "Syncretism and Contextualization: The Church on a Journey Defining Itself." In *Contextualization and Syncretism: Navigating Cultural Currents*, edited by Gailyn Van Rheenen, 1–29. Evangelical Missiological Society Series 13. Pasadena: William Carey Library, 2006.

Van Seters, John. "The Religion of the Patriarchs in Genesis." *Biblica* 61 (1980): 220–33.

Vanhoozer, Kevin J. "'One Rule to Rule Them All?' Theological Method in an Era of World Christianity." In *Globalizing Theology: Belief and Practice in an Era of World Christianity*, edited by Craig Ott and Harold A. Netland, 85–126. Grand Rapids: Baker Academic, 2006.

Viviers, Hennie. "Is Psalm 104 an Expression (Also) of Dark Green Religion?" *Harvard Theological Studies* 73 (2017): 1–8.

"Visit, *v.*" OED Online. March 2022. Oxford University Press. https://www.oed.com/view/Entry/223958.

Vogt, Peter T. *Deuteronomic Theology and the Significance of Torah: A Reappraisal.* Winona Lake: Eisenbrauns, 2006.

———. *Interpreting the Pentateuch: An Exegetical Handbook.* Handbooks for Old Testament Exegesis. Grand Rapids: Kregel Academic, 2009.

Volf, Miroslav. *Allah: A Christian Response.* New York: HarperOne, 2012.

Vroom, H. M. *No Other Gods: Christian Belief in Dialogue with Buddhism, Hinduism, and Islam.* Grand Rapids: Eerdmans, 1996.

Wadia, A. R. "Philosophical Implications of the Doctrine of Karma." *Philosophy East and West* 15 (1965): 145–52.

Waghorne, Joanne Punzo. "The Divine Image in Contemporary South India: The Renaissance of a Once Maligned Tradition." In *Born in Heaven, Made on Earth: The Making of the Cult Image in the Ancient Near East*, edited by Michael B. Dick, 211–42. Winona Lake, IN: Eisenbrauns, 1999.

Walker, Christopher, and Michael B. Dick. "The Induction of the Cult Image in Ancient Mesopotamia: The Mesopotamian Mis Pî Ritual." In *Born in Heaven, Made on Earth: The Making of the Cult Image in the Ancient Near East*, edited by Michael B. Dick, 55–121. Winona Lake, IN: Eisenbrauns, 1999.

Walker-Jones, Arthur. "Psalm 104: A Celebration of the Vanua." In *The Earth Story in the Psalms and the Prophets*, edited by Norman C. Habel, 23–28. The Earth Bible 4. Sheffield: Sheffield Academic Press, 2001.

Waltke, Bruce K. "The Phenomenon of Conditionality within Unconditional Covenants." In *Israel's Apostasy and Restoration: Essays in Honor of Roland K. Harrison*, edited by Avraham Gileadi, 123–39. Grand Rapids: Baker, 1988.

Wan, Enoch. "Tao: The Chinese Theology of God-Man." *His Dominion* 11 (1985): 24–27.

Wanfawan, Zakaria. "Qadar in Classical and Modern Islamic Discourses." *International Journal of Islamic Thought* 7 (2016): 39–48.

Watts, James W. *Isaiah 1–33.* 2nd ed. Word Biblical Commentary 24. Nashville: Thomas Nelson, 1985.

Weber, Max. *The Sociology of Religion.* Translated by Johannes Winckelmann. 4th ed. Boston: Beacon Press, 1963.

Weinfeld, Moshe. "The Covenant of Grant in the Old Testament and in the Ancient Near East." *Journal of the American Oriental Society* 90 (1970): 184–203.

———. *The Place of the Law in the Religion of Ancient Israel.* Leiden: Brill, 2004.

Wellhausen, Julius. *Die Composition des Hexateuchs und der historischen Bücher des Alten Testaments.* 4th ed. Berlin: Walter de Gruyter, 1963.

———. *Prolegomena to the History of Israel.* Cleveland: World Publishing Company, 1957.

———. *Sketch of the History of Israel and Judah.* London: Adam & Charles Black, 1891.

Wenham, Gordon J. "The Religion of the Patriarchs." In *Essays on the Patriarchal Narratives,* edited by D. J. Wiseman and Alan R. Millard, 157–88. Downers Grove: InterVarsity Press, 1980.

Westermann, Claus. *Isaiah 40–66: A Commentary.* Translated by David M. G. Stalker. Old Testament Library. London: SCM Press, 1969.

Whaling, Frank. *Understanding Hinduism.* Edinburgh: Dunedin Academic, 2010.

White, Jr., Lynn. "The Historical Roots of Our Ecologic Crisis." *Science* 155 (10 March 1967): 1203–7.

Whybray, R. N. *Isaiah 40–66.* New Century Bible Commentary. London: Marshall, Morgan & Scott, 1975.

———. *The Making of the Pentateuch: A Methodological Study.* JSOT Supplement Series 168. Sheffield: JSOT Press, 1994.

Wikan, Unni. "Shame and Honour: A Contestable Pair." *Man* 19 (1984): 635–52.

Wilkinson, Bruce. *The Prayer of Jabez: Breaking through to the Blessed Life.* Sisters, OR: Multnomah, 2001.

Williamson, H. G. M. *A Critical and Exegetical Commentary on Isaiah 1–5.* International Critical Commentary. London: Bloomsbury, 2006.

Wright, Christopher J. H. *The Mission of God: Unlocking the Bible's Grand Narrative.* Downers Grove: InterVarsity Press, 2006.

Wright, G. Ernest. *The Old Testament against Its Environment.* Studies in Biblical Theology 2. London: SCM, 1950.

Wrogemann, Henning. *Intercultural Theology.* Translated by Karl E. Böhmer. Downers Grove: IVP Academic, 2016.

Wu, Daniel. *Honor, Shame, and Guilt: Social-Scientific Approaches to the Book of Ezekiel.* BBR Supplement Series 14. Winona Lake, IN: Eisenbrauns, 2016.

Wu, Jackson. *One Gospel for All Nations: A Practical Approach to Biblical Contextualization.* Pasadena, CA: William Carey Library, 2015.

Yang, Qing. "Mulan in China and America: From Premodern to Modern." *Comparative Literature: East & West* 2 (2018): 45–59.

Yano, Michio. "Calendar, Astrology, and Astronomy." In *The Blackwell Companion to Hinduism*, edited by Gavin Flood, 376–92. Blackwell Companions to Religion 5. Malden, MA: Blackwell, 2005.

Yapp, Eugene. "The 'Copyright' Controversy of 'Allah': Issues and Challenges of the Malaysian Church (A Case Study)." In *The Church in a Changing World: An Asian Response – Challenges from the Malang Consultation on Globalization*, edited by Bruce Nicholls, Theresa Roco Lua, and Julie Belding, 147–56. Quezon City, Philippines: Asia Theological Association, 2010.

Yariv-Laor, Lihi. "Linguistic Aspects of Translating the Bible into Chinese." In *Bible in Modern China: The Literary and Intellectual Impact*, edited by Irene Eber, 101–21. Monumenta Serica Monograph Series 43. Nettetal: Steyler Verlag, 1999.

Yeh, Allen L. *Polycentric Missiology: 21st-Century Mission from Everyone to Everywhere*. Downers Grove: IVP Academic, 2016.

Yhoshu, Alice. "Healing WWII Wounds after 70 Years: Japan-Naga Reconciliation Summit Underway." *Eastern Mirror Nagaland*. Updated 29 November 2015. https://easternmirrornagaland.com/healing-wwii-wounds-after-70-years-japan-naga-reconciliation-summit-underway/.

Yu, Delin. "Xie zai zi wo mo sheng he gui shun de bian xian shang: he he ben suo cheng zai de yuan sheng shen xue, wen hua xing ji qi shen xue wen fa de (bu) ke neng xing." In *Zi shang di shuo han yu yi lai: he he ben sheng jing jiu shi nian*, edited by Pingran Xie and Qingbao Zeng, 191–209. Hong Kong: CABSA Books, 2010.

Zehner, Edwin. "Thai Protestants and Local Supernaturalism: Changing Configuration." *Journal of Southeast Asian Studies* 27 (1996): 293–319.

Zetzsche, Jost Oliver. *The Bible in China: The History of the Union Version or the Culmination of Protestant Missionary Bible Translation in China*. Monumenta Serica Monograph Series 45. Sankt Augustin: Monumenta Serica Institute, 1999.

Zhou, Lianhua. "Fu bian: zhong wen sheng jing he he ben xiu ding ban zhi yuan qi he guo cheng." In *Zi shang di shuo han yu yi lai: he he ben sheng jing jiu shi nian*, edited by Pingran Xie and Qingbao Zeng, 3–16. Hong Kong: CABSA, 2010.

———. "He he ben yi ben yuan ze he ping gu." In *Zi shang di shuo han yu yi lai: he he ben sheng jing jiu shi nian*, edited by Pingran Xie and Qingbao Zeng, 3–16. Hong Kong: CABSA Books, 2010.

Zhuang, Dongjie. *Kua yue hong gou: zai hua ren wen hua chu jing zhong quan shi zui*. Hong Kong: Taosheng Publishing, 2009.

Zhuang, Rouyu. *Ji du jiao sheng jing zhong wen yi ben: quan wei xian xiang yan jiu.* Hong Kong: International Bible Society, 2000.

Zhuo, Jinping. "Original Sin in the East-West Dialogue: A Chinese View." *Studies in World Christianity* 1 (1995): 80–86.

Zimmerli, Walther. *Old Testament Theology in Outline.* Edinburgh: T&T Clark, 2000.

———. "Sinaibund und Abrahambund: Ein Beitrag zum Verständnis der Priesterschrift." In *Gottes Offenbarung: gesammelte Aufsätze zum Alten Testament*, 205–16. Munich: C. Kaiser, 1963.

Zimmerman-Liu, Teresa. "The Reconfiguration of Guanxi in a Twentieth-Century Indigenous Chinese Protestant Group." *Review of Religion and Chinese Society* 4 (2017): 59–86.

SUBJECT INDEX

A
African evangelicals 5
Allah 58–60, 62, 68
amae 126–27, 130
amphicosmic ontology 157, 159
ancient Near East 73–74, 103–4
aniconism 145, 147–48, 150–53,
    156–57, 161
anthropomorphism 147–50, 153
anti-Semitism 95, 98
Arab Christians 59
Arabic 57, 59
Asia 15–17
Asian Christians 4, 75, 141, 190, 192,
    198
Asian evangelicals 5
Asian theology 187
astrology 174
    Hindu 174
    Mesopotamian 174

B
Baal 53, 64, 74
    Cycle 13, 55, 64
Buddhism 84, 88–89, 91

C
China 123
Chinese 66, 109
    Christianity 110
    Christians 67
    theology 110
Chinese Union Version 24, 27–28, 67
    Easy Wenli 28
    High Wenli 28
    Mandarin 28–32
collectivism 119, 124, 134
colonialism 4
    European 11
conditionality 95, 98–99

contextualization 1–2, 5–7, 13,
    188–92, 195–96
    and syncretism 8–9, 15, 20,
        189–90, 192, 194, 196
    apostolic 7
    biblical 9
"contextualization debate" 6–9, 20
contextualized theology 1, 190
contextual theology 20, 23, 188,
    191–92
    Asian 18–19, 180, 186, 199
    Chinese 31, 47
continuity 171
cosmic justice 84, 91
cosmos 177–78, 182
covenant 94–96, 100–2, 106, 108
    and law 94–95, 99–102, 106
    divine-human 103, 111
    Israelite 103
covenantal nomism 99
creation 170–71, 173, 177, 181,
    183–84
culture 1, 5–6
CUV *See* Chinese Union Version
cyclical 177, 179, 181–82

D
defamiliarization 23–24, 26–27, 31
determinism 180

E
East 16
East Asia 123
Eastern religions 72, 83, 89
egalitarianism 123–24
El 53–54, 63
    and Baal 50
    -compounds 50–52, 55
    -epithets 52
epithets 60–61

231

AUTHOR INDEX

SCRIPTURE INDEX

OLD TESTAMENT

237

Asia Theological Association
54 Scout Madriñan St. Quezon City 1103, Philippines
Email: ataasia@gmail.com Telefax: (632) 410 0312

OUR MISSION
The Asia Theological Association (ATA) is a body of theological institutions, committed to evangelical faith and scholarship, networking together to serve the Church in equipping the people of God for the mission of the Lord Jesus Christ.

OUR COMMITMENT
The ATA is committed to serving its members in the development of evangelical, biblical theology by strengthening interaction, enhancing scholarship, promoting academic excellence, fostering spiritual and ministerial formation and mobilizing resources to fulfill God's global mission within diverse Asian cultures.

OUR TASK
Affirming our mission and commitment, ATA seeks to:

- **Strengthen** interaction through inter-institutional fellowship and programs, regional and continental activities, faculty and student exchange programs.
- **Enhance** scholarship through consultations, workshops, seminars, publications, and research fellowships.
- **Promote** academic excellence through accreditation standards, faculty and curriculum development.
- **Foster** spiritual and ministerial formation by providing mentor models, encouraging the development of ministerial skills and a Christian ethos.
- **Mobilize** resources through library development, information technology and infra-structural development.

To learn more about ATA, visit www.ataasia.com or facebook.com/AsiaTheologicalAssociation

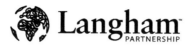

Langham Literature, along with its publishing work, is a ministry of Langham Partnership.

Langham Partnership is a global fellowship working in pursuit of the vision God entrusted to its founder John Stott –

to facilitate the growth of the church in maturity and Christ-likeness through raising the standards of biblical preaching and teaching.

Our vision is to see churches in the Majority World equipped for mission and growing to maturity in Christ through the ministry of pastors and leaders who believe, teach and live by the word of God.

Our mission is to strengthen the ministry of the word of God through:
• nurturing national movements for biblical preaching
• fostering the creation and distribution of evangelical literature
• enhancing evangelical theological education
especially in countries where churches are under-resourced.

Our ministry

Langham Preaching partners with national leaders to nurture indigenous biblical preaching movements for pastors and lay preachers all around the world. With the support of a team of trainers from many countries, a multi-level programme of seminars provides practical training, and is followed by a programme for training local facilitators. Local preachers' groups and national and regional networks ensure continuity and ongoing development, seeking to build vigorous movements committed to Bible exposition.

Langham Literature provides Majority World preachers, scholars and seminary libraries with evangelical books and electronic resources through publishing and distribution, grants and discounts. The programme also fosters the creation of indigenous evangelical books in many languages, through writer's grants, strengthening local evangelical publishing houses, and investment in major regional literature projects, such as one volume Bible commentaries like the *Africa Bible Commentary* and the *South Asia Bible Commentary*.

Langham Scholars provides financial support for evangelical doctoral students from the Majority World so that, when they return home, they may train pastors and other Christian leaders with sound, biblical and theological teaching. This programme equips those who equip others. Langham Scholars also works in partnership with Majority World seminaries in strengthening evangelical theological education. A growing number of Langham Scholars study in high quality doctoral programmes in the Majority World itself. As well as teaching the next generation of pastors, graduated Langham Scholars exercise significant influence through their writing and leadership.

To learn more about Langham Partnership and the work we do visit **langham.org**

Lightning Source UK Ltd.
Milton Keynes UK
UKHW021433140922
408856UK00009B/1887